1. Zacatecas Serra portrait.

Junípero Serra's
LEGACY

By

Martin J. Morgado

First edition, second printing. September 1987.

Printed and bound in the United States of America.

Library of Congress Cataloging-in-Publication Data

Morgado, Martin J., 1956-
  Junípero Serra's legacy.

  Bibliography: p.
     Includes index.
     1. Serra, Junípero, 1713-1784. 2. Explorers—
California—Biography. 3. Explorers—Spain—Biography.
4. Missionaries—California—Biography. 5. San Carlos
Borromeo Basilica (Carmel, Calif.) I. Title.
F864.S44M67 1987 979.4'76 87-12189
ISBN 0-9618339-2-0

Published by Mount Carmel
P.O. Box 51326
Pacific Grove, California 93950

To the memory of

Rev. Maynard J. Geiger, O.F.M., Ph.D.

eternal guardian of Serra's historical legacy

and

Sir Harry J. Downie, K.S.G.

eternal guardian of Serra's material legacy

Contents

$\mathcal{I}$llustrations

Glossary

Foreword

With prophetic insight, John F. Davis wrote in 1913 that the pathetic ruin at Carmel is a "shattered monument above a grave that will become a world's shrine of pilgrimage in honor of one of humanity's heroes."

He went on to say of Fray Junípero Serra that "the memory of the brave heart that was here consumed with love for mankind will live through the ages. And, in a sense, the work of these missions is not dead—their very ruins still preach the lesson of service and sacrifice."

The dedicated missionary who is regarded by all peoples as the spiritual Father of Alta California was a man of outstanding personal qualities. The testimony of his contemporaries and subsequent commentators are unanimous in their praise of the Mallorcan friar.

Serra's apostolic philosophy was stated in a letter he wrote to his superior, shortly after arriving at San Diego. "It will be necessary in the beginning, to suffer many real privations. However, to a lover all things are sweet." Serra expected no Utopia. He presupposed hardships and even embraced them. He took setbacks and disappointments in stride.

The friar was made of tough spiritual fiber. For years he was accustomed to four or five hours of sleep only. He spent long hours in prayer. In the matter of food, he was most abstemious and seemed to care little about its quality. He had prepared himself well for the rigorous apostolate of a cheerless frontier.

Isidore Dockweiler said that "this man whose memory is indissolubly one with the epic of California, was great in humility. He triumphed by his courage, when everything would have appeared bound to discourage him and beat him down. He is one who is worthy of first place among the immortal heroes who created our nation. So his memory will never die, and his name will be blessed from generation to generation."

The literature about Fray Junípero Serra exceeds in quantity of titles and breadth of coverage that of any other personage in western annals. This exquisitely-illustrated and accurately-descriptive book, begun during the bicentennial year of Serra's demise, continued in the rare leisure moments of a legal career and completed for the visit of Pope John Paul II to Carmel, thoroughly delineates the treasures that forever link San Carlos Borromeo to the humble friar who founded the mission in 1770.

It is a volume that confirms the observation made by the distinguished historian, John Tracy Ellis, that Carmel Mission Basilica is the "most attractive ecclesial museum in the United States."

Msgr. Francis J. Weber
Archivist
Archdiocese of Los Angeles

Preface

Junípero Serra's greatest legacy is California itself. As its founding father, every facet of his impact on the state's history and religion has been analyzed. However, one aspect of Serra's legacy has never been thoroughly examined: his personal material legacy. Therefore, the purpose of this book is to begin to identify, document, and describe Serra's "possessions" that are still in existence today. Since his Franciscan vows bound him to "living in obedience, without property, and in chastity,"[1] he literally owned nothing, and "possessions" refer only to what he used, touched, and valued as the "tools" of his missionary ministry.

Apart from a series of Serra's letters at Mission Santa Bárbara, the largest collection of original Serrana is befittingly housed at Serra's California home, headquarters, and burial place: Basilica Mission San Carlos Borromeo del Río Carmelo. This work is a documented historical survey of every extant Mission Carmel artifact that Serra either personally used, or that belonged to the mission during his lifetime. To provide contextual perspective, they are featured within a chronology of Serra's life and Mission Carmel history, drawn mainly from his own writings and those of his biographer Francisco Palóu. The final chapter traces Serra's material legacy from his death in 1784 to the present, with Mission Carmel again as focal point. A glossary is included to define and elaborate terms/topics/persons referred to in the text, which is best utilized in conjunction with the index.

By examining what Serra surrounded himself with, we not only bring his era to life, but ultimately gain further insight into the very nature of the man himself. *Non recedet memoria ejus.*[2]

Carmel
6 May 1987

Martin J. Morgado

Acknowledgments

Junípero Serra represents Mission Carmel at birth; his successor Fermín Francisco de Lasuén its successful maturity. Harry Downie represents Mission Carmel's "re-birth"; his successor Richard-joseph E. Menn its successful "modern" maturity. As Monterey Diocesan Curator and Mission Consultant, Mr. Menn not only follows in illustrious footsteps, but creates his own by guiding Mission Carmel with consummate skill and talent. He also guided this project by providing access to Mission Carmel museum and archives, answering a plethora of questions, arranging introductions to experts in the field, and critiquing the manuscript. Since he has already been lauded in print as a "saint," the best I can offer is simply my deepest gratitude for his unwavering encouragement, patience, and kindness.

To Jeffrey W. Rice, M.D., a great debt of thanks for financing publication. His faith in the merits of a "project" allowed it to become a book.

To William I. Converse of Mount Carmel, credit and thanks for adroitly steering the book through the maze of publication details.

To professional photographer Patrick A. Tregenza, credit and thanks for vividly photographing Serra's possessions, many of which are appearing in print for the first time.

To Reverend Monsignor Francis J. Weber, dean of California mission historians, a debt of thanks for scholarly wisdom and critical insight. He is a true friend along El Camino Real.

For additional scholarly assistance, my thanks to: Norman Neuerburg, Ph.D., Professor Emeritus of Art, California State University, Dominguez Hills; W. Michael Mathes, Ph.D., Professor of History, University of San Francisco; Reverend Mark Ciccone, S.J., Campus Minister, Santa Clara University; Brother Bede McKinnon, O.F.M., Director, Saint Francis Retreat Center, San Juan Bautista; Michael Weller and Edgar Morse, owners, Argentum Antiques, San Francisco; Lydia Hunt, Ph.D., Assistant Professor, Division of Translation and Interpretation, Monterey Institute of International Studies; and Ovidio Casado-Fuente, Ph.D., Head, Program of Hispanic Studies, Monterey Institute of International Studies.

For professional assistance, my thanks to: the research librarians at Monterey Public Library; the research librarians at McHenry Library, University of California, Santa Cruz; Michael Redmon, Librarian, Santa Barbara Historical Society; and a special note of thanks to Katie Ambrosio and the staff of Mission Carmel Gift Shop/Museum for their courteous cooperation and enthusiastic support.

For personal assistance, my thanks to: Jack Keller for the idea to photograph Serra's possessions; my family; Johnny and friends; G. A. N.; and finally to Junípero Serra for his inspirational apothegm: "Do the best you can."[3]

All photographic credit to Patrick A. Tregenza, except:

California State Library, Sacramento: signed plate 85—Owen C. Coy; unsigned plates 74; 77; 81; 88; glossary pages 208 (bottom), 220 (bottom)—Charles W. J. Johnson

Map Library, University of California, Santa Cruz: glossary page 221 (top)

Mission Carmel Archives: signed plates 30—Angeleno Photo Service; 65—special thanks to Richard-joseph Menn for his sketch of Mission Carmel; 69—Carleton E. Watkins; 71, 72—Charles W. J. Johnson; 91, 96, 100—Lewis Josselyn; 102—Lee Blaisdell; 104—Arthur McEwen; 105—John Livingstone; 107—Robert Knudsen; unsigned plates 5; 6; 7; 18; 23; 25; 32; 56; 57; 61; 64; 66; 75; 89; 90; 92; text page 113; glossary pages 177; 179; 180; 184; 186; 189; 190—Karl Obert; 195 (top and bottom); 200; 205; 206; 208 (top)

Monterey, City of: glossary page 220 (middle)

Monterey City Library: unsigned plates 73; 78

Monterey County Library: glossary page 195

Nguyen, Ly: plate 109

Nichols, Donald: plate 108

Pat Hathaway Collection of California Views, Monterey CA: signed plates 68, 76—Charles W. J. Johnson; 82—A.C. Heidrick; 83, 84, 86—Louis S. Slevin; 87—Lewis Josselyn; 95—Joe Hinojos; unsigned plates 79; 80

Santa Bárbara Mission Archive-Library: plate 33

I

Mallorca

1713 - 1749

Always go forward, never turn back

Serra—20 August 1749[1]

1 a.m. Friday 24 November 1713[2]
Feast of Saint John of the Cross—Confessor and Doctor of the Church

Miquel José Serra, third child of five, is born to farmers Antonio Nadal Serra and Margarita Rosa (Ferrer) Serra of #6 Calle Barracar, Petra, Mallorca, Spain.[3] He is baptized on the same day by Rev. Bartolomé Lladó at Petra's San Pedro Church, baptismal entry #85. His godparents are Sebastiana Serra (paternal aunt), and Bartolomé Fiol (maternal relative—status unknown).

Sunday 26 May 1715

Retaining his baptismal name, Serra is confirmed by Most Rev. Atanasio Esterripa y Tranajáuregui, Bishop of Mallorca. His sponsor is the same priest who married his parents on 7 August 1707, Rev. Pere Mestre.

1719—1729

Serra attends Franciscan elementary school at the Convento de San Bernardino, two blocks from home. He excels in Latin.

2. Serra signature with official rubric, which he designed and perfected as a schoolboy (from Serra's Mission Carmel Libro de Confirmaciones*).*

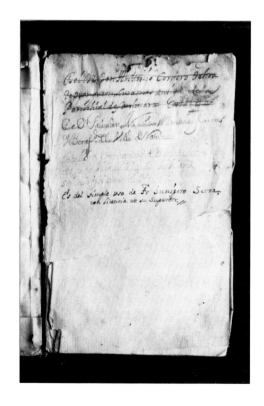

3. Serra signature minus rubric, from frontispiece of Mission Carmel library book. The four inscriptions attest to the book's well-worn past, and reflect the Franciscan concept of using property, but not owning it. Serra's inscription reads: "For the simple use of Fr. Junípero Serra, with permission of his superior" (from Compendio de los cinco tomos del Despertador Christiano *[Compendium of the Five Volumes of the Christian Awakening, Madrid, 1691]).*

September 1729

Serra enrolls as a philosophy student at the Franciscan Convento de San Francisco, Palma.

Thursday 14 September 1730

Serra receives the Franciscan habit at the novitiate Convento de Santa María de los Angeles de Jesús, just outside Palma. He has a facile memory and a strong singing voice, but is excused from turning the large sheepskin choirbook pages, because in his words, "I was almost always ill and so small of stature that I was unable to reach the lectern."[4] Serving as an altar boy instead, he will eventually grow to an adult height of 5 feet, 2 inches, and reach a maximum weight of around 110 pounds.

Saturday 15 September 1731

Serra makes his solemn profession into the Franciscan Order. He assumes the religious name Junípero, after a companion of Saint Francis of Assisi who was simple, sincere, and good-natured. When the original Junípero was chided by others, Saint Francis was to have remarked: "My brothers, my brothers, I wish I had a forest of such junipers."[5] Serra moves to the Convento de San Francisco, Palma, and studies philosophy until June 1734.

Friday 21 December 1731

Administered by Most Rev. Benito Panelles y Escordó, Bishop of Mallorca, Serra receives tonsure and the four minor orders.

Saturday 18 December 1734

Serra is ordained a sub-deacon. He studies theology until June 1737.

Saturday 17 March 1736

Serra is ordained a deacon.

Friday 29 November 1737

Serra successfully competes for the office of Lector in Philosophy at the Convento de San Francisco.

December 1737

Probable month of Serra's ordination to the priesthood, exact date unrecorded.[6]

October 1739—October 1743

Serra teaches the complete course of philosophy at the Convento de San Francisco, and among his students are Francisco Palóu and Juan Crespí, natives of Palma. Just beginning their professional studies, both choose to retain their baptismal names. Serra concludes the three year course by saying:

> I desire nothing more from you than this that when the news of my death shall have reached your ears, I ask that you say for the benefit of my soul "May he rest in peace," and I shall not fail to do the same for you so that all of us will attain that goal for which we have been created. Amen and farewell. . . . I am no longer your professor, but your most humble servant, Fray Junípero Serra of the Order of Friars Minor.[7]

1742

Serra earns a doctorate in Sacred Theology (exact date unrecorded) from the Pontifical, Imperial, Royal and Literary University of Mallorca, commonly known as Llullian University, after Blessed Ramón Llull.

Thursday 13 June 1743

Upon invitation, Doctor Serra delivers the famous annual Feast of Corpus Christi sermon at Palma Cathedral.

Wednesday 16 October 1743

Dr. Serra is appointed *catedrático de prima* of the Duns Scotus Chair of Sacred Theology at Llullian University. He is frequently called upon to preach in Palma and various other Mallorcan cities, and holds the distinguished tenure until his departure for Mexico in 1749.

Saturday 25 January 1749

Dr. Serra is chosen by professors and benefactors to deliver the most prestigious sermon of the year, delivered at San Francisco Church in honor of the feast of Blessed Ramón Llull, patron of Mallorca.

> All who heard him were in admiration. When he finished the sermon, . . . a retired professor who himself was very famous in the professor's chair and in the pulpit, but who was in no way partial to the preacher, [said]: "This sermon is worthy of being printed in letters of gold."[8]

Tuesday 1 April 1749

Serra makes his last *romería* (pilgrimage) to the Petran hilltop shrine of Nuestra Señora de Bon Any. He has decided to become a Mexican missionary, writing that "the dignity of Apostolic preacher, especially when united with the actual duty, is the highest vocation."[9]

Sunday 13 April 1749

In the company of Palóu, who has also decided to become a missionary, Serra sails from Palma to Málaga and Cádiz, the first leg of a 5,000-mile sea journey to Mexico. Serra tells Palóu to "stop using all these titles of respect and superiority in regard to each other; for we are now in every respect equals."[10] En route to Málaga, an anti-clerical skipper threatens to throw the pair overboard, and brandishes a dagger at Serra's throat with "the intention of taking his life."[11] Cádiz Board of Trade officials document all missionaries who pass through, and Serra is recorded as "lector of theology, native of Petra in the Diocese of Mallorca, thirty-five years old, of medium height, swarthy, dark eyes and hair, scant beard."[12] From Cádiz, Serra writes to Petra's parish priest, asking him to deliver a final farewell to his parents. He expresses his "great joy" at becoming a missionary, and is confident that his family will

> always encourage me to go forward, and never to turn back. . . . Let them rejoice that they have a son who is a priest, though an unworthy one and a sinner, . . . in order to become a good religious I have set out on this course. . . . Blessed be God. May His holy will be done.[13]

II

Mexico

1749 ~ 1769

To a willing heart all is sweet

Serra—3 July 1769[1]

Friday 29 August—Saturday 18 October 1749

Serra's transatlantic voyage. When water runs low, his remedy for thirst is "to eat little and talk less in order not to waste the saliva."[2] Arriving at San Juan, Puerto Rico, Serra performs his first work as an apostolic missionary, directing a two-week "mission" of religious services, sermons and Confessions for the local citizenry. He writes:

> The mission . . . proved to be a wonderful spiritual harvest. For days we had to stay in the confessionals, beginning as early as three and four o'clock in the morning, and in the afternoons, too, and we did not finish before midnight.[3]

Saturday 1 November—Saturday 6 December 1749

During Serra's voyage to the Mexican mainland, the ship is temporarily blown off course by a violent storm that threatens shipwreck. He writes:

> For days in that fierce storm we were lost far from our destination. The ship was filling with water, and the mainmast continued in use only by a miracle. We [twenty Franciscan and seven Dominican priests] held a consultation . . . to make some promise to call down on us the Lord's mercy. We decided that each should write, on a piece of paper, the name of his favorite saint. . . . After putting the papers in a bowl, and invoking the Holy Spirit, we recited the prayer of All Saints, to know, by drawing lots, who would be our special patron and protector, . . . in honor of the one elected by lot, we agreed, all would have to assist at a solemn Mass and sermon when safe on land. I wrote down Saint Francis Solano, and Professor Palóu, Saint Michael; but they did not win. Saint Barbara did . . . and it turned out that on her feast day, December 4, at night, the ship sailed back towards port, and we all felt happy and confident.[4]

Sunday 7 December 1749

Serra first steps ashore on continental North America at Vera Cruz, Mexico. He writes to his parents that he was "the only one of all the religious . . . who did not get seasick."[5]

Monday 15 December 1749—Thursday 1 January 1750

With a fellow Spanish Franciscan (either Francisco Patiño or Pedro Pérez), Serra chooses to walk the 275-mile stretch of El Camino Real to the Franciscan Apostolic College of San Fernando in Mexico City. Notwithstanding seemingly supernatural offers of assistance along the way, mosquito or chigger bites infect Serra's left leg, eventual cause of an ulcerated, possibly cancerous growth, and the intermittent, inflammatory swelling of both legs and feet that will affect him for the rest of his life. The pair arrive at Mexico City's Basilica of Our Lady of Guadalupe on 31 December, and remain there overnight. After early Mass on New Year's Day they walk the last five miles to their new San Fernando College home, arriving shortly after 9 a.m.

January—June 1750

Serra asks to repeat his novitiate year as an act of humility during intensive missionary preparation at San Fernando College, and although denied, he performs many humble acts for his fellow Franciscans. He takes little sleep, avoids meat for fish and vegetables, and fasts frequently. He often seems indifferent toward food, prompting some of his confreres to speculate if he lacks a sense of taste. In the context of Europe's eighteenth-century religious Zeitgeist, Serra practices private self-mortification. Under his clothing he wears a coarse "hair shirt" fitted with wire bristles and hooks, and he is known to use his penitential scourge or "discipline" beyond the college's prescribed regulations.

4. Iron and braided-wire "discipline" traditionally assumed to have been used by Serra. 12" x 2-1/2."

Thursday 2 April 1750

After a seven-month journey from Mallorca, Juan Crespí arrives at San Fernando College.

Monday 1 June—Tuesday 16 June 1750

To begin their first missionary fieldwork, Serra and Palóu walk 175 miles north through the rugged Sierra Gorda Mountains to the small town of Jalpan.

Serra works among the Pame Indians in the Sierra Gorda district, and is appointed president of the five-mission chain from May 1751—November 1755. He oversees the construction of five mission churches (all still in use today), and works as a day laborer on Santiago de Jalpan, an ornate churrigueresque-style stone church. He improves agricultural and farming methods by introducing new tools, communal planting/harvesting, and oxen, cows, mules, sheep, goats, and pigs. He learns the Pame Indian language, and composes a native catechism. Applying techniques he will later employ in California, he uses a visual method of teaching religion to attract and Christianize the Indians. Although claiming "he did not know how to sing the scales well enough to be of any help,"[6] Serra is fond of music, using song and hymn to inspire the Indians. He reenacts the events of religious holidays, and choreographs a *Pastores* (Pastoral) Nativity play at Christmas, performed by Indian children.

5. Playwright-actor George Marion portraying Serra in Mission Carmel's 1934 fundraising production, The Apostle of California.

During Lent, Serra carries a cross on his shoulder at outdoor Stations of the Cross processions, "so heavy that I [Palóu], stronger and younger though I was, could not lift it."[7] On Good Friday, Serra washes the feet of twelve elderly Indian men, in imitation of Jesus who washed the feet of his disciples during the Last Supper. That evening, the Deposition Ceremony reenacts Jesus being lowered from the Cross

> by means of a lifelike image which was ordered made with hinges for that purpose. Preaching on this topic with the greatest of devotion and tenderness, he [Serra] placed our Lord in a casket and then the procession of the sacred burial was held. The casket was placed on an altar which had been specially prepared for this purpose.[8]

During sermons Serra occasionally beats his breast with a stone to the point that "his hearers were afraid he would break his chest and fall dead in the pulpit."[9] From the pulpit, he also lashes his back with a chain to urge repentance, or holds lighted candles to his chest to illustrate Hell. To encourage frequent Confession, he silently confesses to Palóu from the sanctuary of the church, in full view of the congregation. While in Jalpan, a mysterious plot against his life is averted.[10]

6. *Imitation of Serra's Deposition Ceremony at Mission Carmel, c. 1938. Simulated thunder and lightning would erupt from the darkened, purple-draped sanctuary following recital of the Twelfth Station of the Cross (Jesus dies on the Cross). The crown of thorns was lowered by means of a concealed ladder, and linen was draped over the cross and under the leather-socketed arms of the original 1791 corpus. The nails were driven from the hands and feet with a hammer, the corpus was slowly lowered in its cloth sling (Thirteenth Station—Jesus is taken down from the Cross), placed on a linen-draped stretcher with its articulated arms placed at its side, carried out the front door of the church, around the courtyard, and back into the mortuary chapel for veneration (Fourteenth Station—Jesus is laid in the Tomb). First revived by Harry Downie in 1932, the three-hour ceremony was performed annually until suspended in 1975.*

7. *Deposition effigy of Jesus at rest in the "sepulcher," c. 1938 (present side-chapel of Our Lady of Bethlehem).*

8. *Mission Carmel confessional traditionally assumed to have been used by Serra, constructed from Mexican cedar packing crates and California redwood. 6'2" tall x 30" x 26."*

Tuesday 5 September 1752

Serra visits Mexico City and takes the oath as Commissary of the Holy Office of the Inquisition for the Sierra Gorda district. He deposits a marble *Cachum* (Mother of the Sun) idol in the San Fernando College archives, relinquished by the Pame Indians upon their Christian conversion.

Tuesday 26 September 1758—Wednesday 15 July 1767

After learning that they have been reassigned to Mission San Sabá de la Santa Cruz (present Menard County, central Texas), Serra and Palóu return to San Fernando College, arriving on 26 September. They are to serve as replacements for two missionaries recently martyred by Comanches at the mission. Serra writes to his nephew in Mallorca: "I am quite conscious of my uselessness . . . for so great an enterprise. However, God is strong enough to accomplish out of nothing works which redound to His great glory."[11] Before they depart, the viceroy declares the volatile area off limits until peace can be restored. The viceroy dies, the assignment is never revived, and Serra spends the next nine years as a home missionary at San Fernando College. He travels as apostolic preacher and confessor throughout the archdiocese of Mexico, as well as the surrounding dioceses of Oaxaca, Morelia, Puebla, Guadalajara, and the region east of the Sierra Gorda. On one such trip, he claims Divine Providence is responsible for the appearance of an aged couple and child offering shelter. On another occasion, he collapses after drinking poisoned wine while offering Mass. Refusing an antidote because he had just received the Eucharist, he nevertheless recovers.[12] Serra continues to serve as Commissary of the Holy Office, and as choir director, master of novices, college counselor, and confessor within San Fernando College. A short book of novenas attributed to Serra is published during this period.[13]

Thursday 16 July 1767

Serra departs for Loreto, Lower California, appointed to the presidency of fifteen peninsular missions just acquired from the expelled Jesuits.

Friday 1 April 1768

Serra arrives in Loreto, having traveled west from Mexico City via El Camino Real to the mainland port of San Blas, and by packet-boat across the Gulf of California. Welcomed by Governor Gaspar de Portolá, they celebrate Easter on Sunday 3 April. After studying his new jurisdiction, Serra assigns his fifteen Franciscans to their new missions.

Tuesday 5 July 1768

José de Gálvez, Inspector General of the Viceroyalty of New Spain, arrives in Lower California. Sent by King Carlos III to oversee several projects involving the entire viceroyalty, his attention is now focused on the geopolitical and economic potential of Mexico's vast northern borderlands. When he informs Serra of the Spanish Crown's forthcoming temporal and spiritual conquest of Upper California, Serra enthusiastically volunteers for the "[Sacred Expedition] . . . to erect the holy standard of the cross in Monterey,"[14] and is appointed president of the future missions. Four separate contingents, two by land and two by sea, will carry the first settlers and supplies to the new territory.

August—December 1768

Serra tours the Lower California missions, recruits volunteers, and collects church/sacristy goods for the future missions of Upper California. He confers with Gálvez, and the two race to see who can wrap and pack goods faster. Gálvez later writes that *he* "was a better sacristan than Father Junípero, for he arranged the vestments and other things . . . quicker than did the servant of God."[15] When Serra asks if one of the new missions will be named after Saint Francis of Assisi, Gálvez replies: "If St. Francis desires a mission in his honor, let him see to it that his port is located, and his name shall be given to it."[16]

✝

The Loreto Silver

The history of Mission Carmel's "Loreto silver" is interwoven with the history of Lower California's Jesuits. In 1572 the Jesuits first arrived in Mexico, and from 1697 to 1767 they established and maintained eighteen missions in Lower California. Oldest and headquarters of the chain, Presidio-Mission Nuestra Señora de Loreto was founded on 25 October 1697. When King Carlos III abruptly expelled the Society of Jesus from Spain and its possessions in June 1767, the Jesuits were forced to leave with only personal essentials, leaving behind a wealth of church goods. Some items had been donated, some purchased through the Pious Fund, and many were already antique, trans- ferred from even older mainland missions, following "the custom that had been practiced by the Jesuit fathers in the founding of missions, . . . so far as they could the old assisted the new that were being founded, as appears in the books of those missions."[17]

Selected as replacements for Lower California's Jesuits, the Franciscans of Serra's San Fernando College were barely settled in their new missions when the "Sacred Expedition" was inaugurated in 1768. Gálvez and Serra gathered supplies from the Jesuit inventory, choosing "superfluous things which would not be missed by the old missions . . . especially as respects vestments, sacred vessels, and utensils of church and sacristy."[18] The sacristy of Presidio-Mission Loreto contributed "six large silver candlesticks two yards [*sic*] [*varas*] high, a silver *palabrero*, with the *lavabo* and the Gospel of St. John [altar cards], of the same material, [and] one silver missal stand."[19] Serra first mentions their use in Upper California on the 14 June 1770 Feast of Corpus Christi, only two weeks after the founding of Monterey's Presidio-Mission San Carlos Borromeo:

> On the altar itself were placed the six big silver candlesticks that came from Loreto, with their altar cards, and a missal stand of the same material. In between we put smaller candle- sticks. . . . They all were lighted throughout the High Mass, the sermon and the procession— and not a breath of air stirred.[20]

All nine items are included in Mission Carmel's 1834 secularization inventory and 1842 post- secularization inventory, and were taken to the Royal Presidio Chapel, Monterey, sometime before the 1852 abandonment of Mission Carmel. Returned during the 1930s' restoration, they now form the nucleus of Mission Carmel's silver collection. Traditionally assumed to be products of Mexico's late seventeenth-century, this is consistent with their complete lack of markings except for the missal stand's Mexican assay office *burilada* (silver test mark in the form of a small zigzag line), since the *cedula real* (royal decree) implementing more elaborate stamping procedures did not take effect until 1733. A simplified system was in effect prior to that date, but was easily circumvented to avoid a twenty percent silver tax. The silver holy water stoup does not appear in any of the detailed original requisition inventories, the only one that does is "a copper pot for holy water." The piece may have been sent later to Mission Carmel, sometime before the Franciscans transferred the Lower California missions to the Dominicans in April 1772. In Mission Carmel's 1774 *Informe*, Serra mentions acquisi- tion of another "holy water pot," but it is "soldered copper." Tradition labels the stoup as a Mission Carmel original. This is substantiated by its decorative Jesuit iconography, which links it to the Lower California missions, and thereby to Serra. It is the oldest documented piece in the collection, bearing the simplified royal hallmark required between 1579-1637.

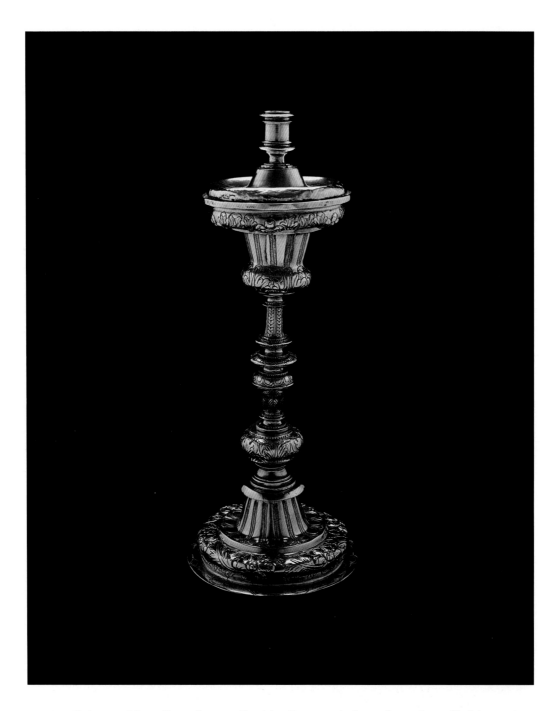

9. *One of six matching silver altar candlesticks. Repoussé sheet silver. Assembled in sections, with cast cup. 74 oz. Troy (includes wood core). 18" tall x 7-3/4" base diameter.*

10. *Silver missal stand. Repoussé decoration on cross, Jesuit IHS emblem, and shell-leaf motif. Cast silver stand. 98 oz. Troy. 13" tall x 13" wide x 13" deep.*

11. *Missal stand profile.*

Ínitium S. Euangelij secundum Joánnem. IN princípio érat Verbum, & Verbum erát ápud Deum, & Deus erát Verbum. Hoc erát in princípio ápud Deum. Omnia per ípsum facta sunt, & sine ipso factum est nihil, quod factum est. Inipso vita erat, & vita erat lux hominum: &lux in tenebris lucet, & tenebræ eam non comprehenderunt. Fuit homo missus á Deo, cui nomen erat Joannes. Hic venit in testimonium, ut testimonium perhiberet de lumine, ut omnes crederent per illum. Non erat ille lux, sed ut testimonium perhiberet de lumine. Erat lux vera, quæ illuminat omnem hominem venientem in hunc mundum. In mundo erat, & mundus per ipsum factus est, & mundus eum non cognovit. In propria venit, & sui eum non receperunt. Quotquot autem receperunt eum, dedit eis potestatem filios Dei fieri, his, qui credunt in nomine ejus: qui non ex sánguinibus, neque ex voluntate carnis, neque ex voluntate viri, sed ex Deo nati sunt. (Hic genuflectitur) Et Verbum caro factum est, & habitavit in nobis: & vidimus gloriam ejus, gloriam quasi unigeniti á patre, plenum gratiæ & veritatis.

12. *Silver altar card inscribed with the Latin* Inítium sancti Evangélii secúndum Joánnem *(The beginning of the Holy Gospel according to John). The prologue of Saint John's Gospel (John i:1-14) is recited by the priest while cleaning the chalice with water at the conclusion of the Mass. Chased lettering and repoussé border. 24 oz. Troy (includes wood backing). 12" tall x 10" wide.*[21]

13. *Altar card profile.*

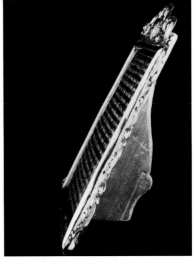

14. *Silver altar card inscribed with the Latin* Lavábo *(I will wash) prayer. Taken from Psalm 26:6-12, it is recited by the priest during the Offertory Rite washing of the fingers. Chased lettering and* repoussé *border. 24 oz. Troy (includes wood backing). 12" tall x 10" wide.*[22]

15. *Silver holy water stoup used during the Asperges ceremony.* Repoussé *strap work design on central section, bulbous base, and spreading foot. Lion-head handle sockets, hollow-cast silver handle. Engraved figures depict Saint Ignatius Loyola with book and Jesuit emblem (rayed IHS monogram and three nails of the Crucifixion); Christ-child with globe; and the Annunciation. Original aspergill lost or destroyed. 88 oz. Troy. 10" tall x 5-1/2" base diameter, 11" top.*

16. *Stoup hallmark. The single, faint interior mark (crowned "M" [Mexico] between Pillars of Hercules) indicates that legal-standard silver was used, taxes were paid, and that the stoup was made sometime between 1579-1637.*

Friday 6 January 1769

Serra blesses the flagship *San Carlos* at La Paz, Lower California. Laden with foodstuffs, supplies, and church goods, it sails for San Diego Bay, joined by the *San Antonio* on 15 February. Expedition leaders are allowed to send personal items, and Serra stows "brandy, wine, a gilt edged chest and various religious ornaments"[23] aboard the *San Antonio*. Gálvez writes that his heart has gone with the expedition even though he could not.

17. One of five original Puebla onyx altar stones shipped to Upper California in 1769. A small hollowed-out, circular sepulchrum (with seal intact), contains the necessary relics for creating a portable consecrated altar when the stone is placed on any table, perfect for use in the missionary field. 16-1/2" x 12" x 1-1/2" thick.

Friday 24 March 1769

Led by Captain Fernando de Rivera y Moncada (second in command to Governor Portolá), the first land contingent of 25 *soldados de cuera*, 3 muleteers, 42 Lower California Christian Indians, and saddle and pack animals set out from the northern peninsular settlement of Velicatá, bound for San Diego. Juan Crespí serves as chaplain and diarist.

Tuesday 28 March 1769

Accompanied by two guards and a Spanish attendant named José Vergerano, Serra begins the 95-day, 750-mile journey north to San Diego, averaging four hours travel per day "at a pack-train pace."[24] Departing from Loreto by mule, the small band will travel alone for the first half of the march, until joining Portolá and the second land contingent still gathering provisions at Mission Santa María de los Angeles. Serra keeps a diary of the entire journey, rating potential mission sites according to availability of water, wood, and Indians.

☦

The Serra Bible

Mission libraries played an integral role in daily life, dispensing not only theological, but practical advice as well, in matters such as history, geography, medicine, agriculture and architecture. California's "first" library at Mission Carmel was gathered from among the handed-down and well-circulated volumes of San Fernando College, its Mexican missions, and the originally Jesuit Lower California missions. By 1778 the library consisted of about thirty volumes, arranged according to size on a new "bookcase with four shelves from larger to smaller, lined with red wood."[25] The library grew to approximately fifty volumes by Serra's death in 1784, and to 302 when it was first cataloged by Lasuén in 1800. At that time each book was numbered at the top of its spine, indicating bookcase number and shelf position. Mission Carmel's 1834 secularization inventory lists 179 titles (404 individual volumes), which were dispersed after the mission's abandonment in 1852. The majority were stored at various locations in Monterey until 1949, when 229 of the original books of the 1770-1842 library were returned to Mission Carmel.

Mission Carmel's "Serra Bible" is not signed by Serra. However, the half-title page is missing, the most likely place for inscriptions. One unclear signature appears on the title page, along with *ex libris* (from the library of), and a partial 1780s' date. There are also several internal Latin inscriptions, although none in Serra's handwriting. The book is not marked "property of San Fernando College," but this was not strictly required until 1809. The base of the spine is marked III2G, but this is merely a 1966 recataloging mark (Lasuén marked the top of the spines). Several Bibles are listed in Mission Carmel's 1834 secularization inventory, but none is described in detail. Therefore, it is not possible to prove that this was indeed Serra's Bible. Nevertheless, local tradition strongly suggests that he personally brought it from Loreto to San Diego in 1769, to Monterey in 1770, and to Mission Carmel in 1771. When Ronald Reagan used this Bible to swear his first-term oath of office as California governor on 2 January 1967, it was described as:

> A Bible brought to California by famed Spanish missionary Father Junipero Serra . . . published in Lyon, France, in 1568 and now . . . housed permanently in the archives of the Carmel Mission. . . . "It is, to my knowledge, the oldest Mission Bible in California," said Harry Downie, curator at the Carmel Mission.[26]

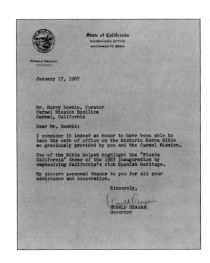

18. Thank you note from California's thirty-third governor after taking his first-term oath of office on Mission Carmel's Serra Bible.

19. The Serra Bible. Vellum (sheepskin) cover. 1,240 pages. 7-1/2" x 5-1/2" x 2-1/2" thick.

20. Title-page translation:

The Holy Bible

Very carefully corrected to accord with the Hebrew and with the testimony of the most reliable manuscripts:
With figures and geographical descriptions in which the structures and various buildings and works, and regions as well, are placed before the eyes of everyone.
There are in addition interpretations of Hebrew, Chaldean, and Greek names, as well as very full indices.

Printed at Lyons by Bartholomaeus Vincentius, 1568

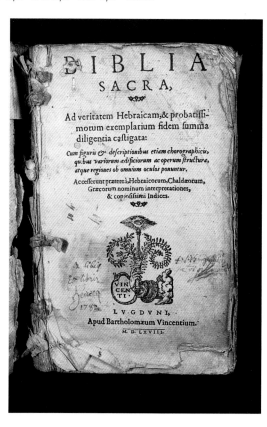

Saturday 1 April 1769

After Serra visits with Palóu (replacement president of the Lower California missions), and selects church goods for the new missions, he leaves Mission San Francisco Xavier. Palóu believes they will never see each other again, wishing Serra goodby "until we meet in eternity."[27] Serra wishes Palóu goodby "until we meet in Monterey."[28]

21. *Altar bell requisitioned by Serra from Mission San Francisco Xavier, listed in the original inventory as "a small bronze bell."[29] Inscription reads "SAN FRAN[co] XAVIEL." 5" tall x 2-1/2" diameter.*

Sunday 9 April 1769

Serra rests at Mission Nuestra Señora de Guadalupe. He visits with Father Juan Sancho, future San Fernando College guardian, who presents Serra with

> a little page, . . . a smart Indian lad, fifteen years old, speaking Castilian and able to serve Mass, read and do any kind of service. He [Sancho] had him all fitted out with change of clothes, leather jacket, boots, etc., and a horseman's complete outfit. He gave him a mule from his own saddle mules. The lad was thrilled; and were his parents proud of him![30]

Tuesday 11 April 1769

The *San Antonio* arrives in San Diego Bay. Local Indians later recount that "there was an eclipse of the sun and an earthquake, all of which, together with the sight of the ship, which appeared to them far too big to be a whale, as they first supposed, was a cause for much amazement."[31]

Sunday 16 April 1769

Serra writes:

> April sixteen . . . the day of the profession of our Father Saint Francis, and also the day our Order celebrates the Feast of Saint Raphael the Archangel, patron of travelers. I observed the day by resting; and made the renewal of my own profession, as do all our religious in the whole world today.[32]

Tuesday 18 April 1769

Continuing to travel north, Serra takes refuge from scorching heat in a cave, and sleeps that evening in an open field.

Saturday 29 April 1769

The *San Carlos* arrives in San Diego Bay.

Monday 1 May 1769

After visiting with Father Fermín Francisco de Lasuén (future second president of the Upper California missions), Serra leaves Mission San Francisco de Borja.

Friday 5 May 1769

Serra joins Portolá and the second land contingent of soldiers, Indians, and supplies at Mission Santa María de los Angeles He writes: "We were as happy as possible to see each other, all eager to start on our new venture across the desert . . . peopled by pagans in great numbers."[33]

Sunday 7 May 1769

Serra passes "a convenient watering place," where a "pretty antelope" is caught. He names the place "Antelope Well."

Thursday 11 May 1769

Serra discovers an oasis, "a site to see—palm trees, grass and water in abundance, and stretches of land suitable for irrigation, orchards and grain."[34]

Friday 12 May 1769

Serra has still not seen any "pagan" Indians, and writes:

We saw various little *rancherías* of pagan Indians and recent footsteps; but none of them, neither young nor old, did we see; and so I had to give up any thought of speaking to them and winning their good graces.[35]

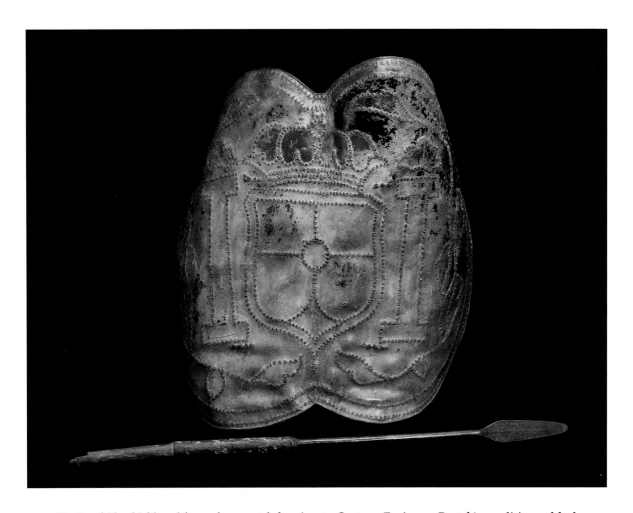

22. Rawhide shield and lance fragment belonging to Caetano Espinosa, Portolá expedition soldado de cuera. *The shield bears the Spanish Royal Coat of Arms of Carlos III, consisting of a heraldic "shield" surmounted by a crown and flanked by the "Pillars of Hercules," symbolizing the Strait of Gibraltar. The quartered-heraldic shield was painted with the coat of arms of Castile-León, two yellow castles on red background, opposed by two red lions rampant wearing gold crowns, on white (Aragon and Navarre, Spain's other two historic kingdoms, were not represented in its New World heraldry because when Pope Alexander VI drew the Line of Demarcation between Spanish and Portuguese zones of exploration in 1493, he conceded the Americas not to the newly united Spain, but to the Crown of Castile). The center circle contained three gold fleurs-de-lis on blue, a popular French royal symbol added to the coat after Bourbon accession to the Spanish throne in 1700. The diamond-shaped base displayed the royal "Apple of Granada," a pomegranate with skin split and seeds showing (symbolic of wealth), on white. Granada was included due to its special significance as the last Spanish kingdom to be wrested from the Moors (in 1492). 18" tall x 17" wide x 1" thick. Lance 24" long.*

Sunday 14 May 1769

After Serra says Mass on Pentecost Sunday at the frontier outpost of San Fernando de Velicatá, he erects and blesses a cross to establish his first Indian mission "with all the surroundings of holy poverty."[36] He records:

> Repeated discharges of firearms by the soldiers added to the solemnity: and for once the smoke of powder took the place of burning incense, which we could not use because we had none with us. . . . The congregation was made up of ourselves [Serra and Father Miguel de la Campa, who had accompanied Portolá from Mission San Ignacio], the soldiers and the Indian neophytes who came with us, while no gentile dared come near, frightened perhaps by so much shooting.[37]

On this same day, Rivera y Moncada and the first land contingent arrive at San Diego.

Monday 15 May 1769

While still at Velicatá, Serra writes:

> It was for me a day of great joy, because just after the Masses, while I was praying, retired inside of the little brush hut, they came to tell me that Indians were coming and were close by. I gave praise to the Lord, kissing the ground, and thanking His Majesty for the fact that, after so many years of looking forward to it, He now permitted me to be among the pagans in their own country. I came out at once, and found myself in front of twelve of them, all men and grown up, except two who were boys, one about ten years old and the other fifteen. I saw something I could not believe when I had read of it, or had been told about it. It was this: they were entirely naked, as Adam in the garden, before Sin. So they go, and so they presented themselves to us. We spoke a long time with them, and not for one moment, while they saw us clothed, could you notice the least sign of shame in them for their own lack of dress. One after the other, I put my hands upon the head of each one of them, in sign of affection. I filled both their hands with dried figs, which they immediately began to eat. We received with show of much appreciation the presents they offered us, *viz:* a net of roasted *mescales* [cactuses], and four fishes of more than medium size. . . . Meanwhile, with the help of the interpreter, I gave them to understand that now, in that very spot, a Father [de la Campa] would stay with them; . . . that they should come to him, they and their friends, and visit him; that they should tell the others not to have any fear or timidity; that the Father would be their best friend . . . they seemed to understand fairly well. . . . I was convinced that, before long, they would be caught in the apostolic and evangelical net.[38]

Thursday 18 May 1769

Serra writes, "I had much trouble in standing on my feet, because the left one was much inflamed. . . . The swelling has reached halfway up my leg, which is covered with sores."[39] Portolá tries to deter him from going further, but Serra replies: "I trust that God will give me the strength to arrive at San Diego. . . . But even though I die on the road, I will not turn back. Although I be buried there, I shall gladly remain among the pagans, if it be the Will of God."[40] As final alternative to being carried on a stretcher, Serra asks the muleteer to prepare a hot tallow and herb poultice for his leg. The muleteer is hesitant, but Serra says: "Just imagine me to be an animal. . . . Make me the same remedy which you would apply to an animal."[41] The next day he comments: "I felt much improved and said Mass."[42] Serra is also consoled by a letter from Father de la Campa at Mission San Fernando de Velicatá, in which he learns:

> The same Indian[s] whom I saw and treated kindly [at Velicatá], . . . called again with a larger number of men, women, boys and girls, all together forty-four; and . . . they all

wanted to receive holy Baptism; and the same day . . . [began] their instruction. That was an immense joy to me, and I sent congratulations, a thousandfold.[43]

Sunday 21 May 1769

An old Indian man approaches camp, and Serra writes:

> We treated him kindly and gave him to eat. . . . He cared not a whit about anybody or anything. . . . While he was in conversation with us, right in the middle of the crowd he squatted down, and not having any clothes to bother about, right then and there attended to nature while continuing to speak to us; and he remained just as calm as he was so relieved. The interpreters asked him if he wanted to become a Christian. He said he did, . . . that it should take place immediately. They told him that first he must be taught the law of God. . . . The interpreter began to explain to him the first lessons of the catechism, I do not know what outcome it all had; all I know is that the good old man felt happy, and would not fail to tell his people of the kindly treatment at our hands.[44]

Wednesday 24 May 1769

Under a "blazing sun," Serra passes through "ugly steep hills" and "a dry river." A "roaring [mountain] lion" keeps him awake that night.

Thursday 25 May 1769

Serra discovers another oasis, and

> a very tall tree . . . all covered with greenery such as we had not seen outside the missions. Coming close up I saw it was a cottonwood [*sic*] [poplar]. It caused considerable comment so we called that spot El Álamo Solo [The Single Poplar]. Thereafter the country became more pleasant and agreeable than before, with a variety of tall and leafy trees . . . and all kinds of flowers besides.[45]

Friday 26 May 1769

Serra meets an Indian with "a big shock of hair tied back with a blue ribbon of fine workmanship," claiming that many other Indians are "assembled for the attack—lying in ambush behind the rocks." Serra pardons his "murderous intentions, and loading him down with presents . . . let[s] him go in order that he might tell his people how well we treated him."[46]

Sunday 28 May 1769

Serra encounters pipe smoking Indians who,

> according to our interpreters, . . . [said] we should not go farther but go back and that they wanted to fight. We spent much time patiently trying to send them away in a friendly way. It was all in vain, no use whatever, and we feared bloodshed. By order of the Governor, four soldiers, mounted on horses, forming a line, forced them to retreat. But they again refused to go. At first one, then, a little later, a second shot was fired into the air by a soldier. On hear-

ing it they fled. . . . But as if to relieve us from the displeasure which they had caused us, Our Lord God sent us other Indians of a more pleasing character: and so one league before arriving at our camping grounds, twelve new gentiles came to us; very politely they said they would show us the way and the place, which they did. And with remarkable courtesy, at our arrival, while we were busy with unloading, so as to avoid embarrassing us, they retired to a nearby hillside and remained sitting there motionless. When we were free, I sent them my page, and an Indian interpreter, carrying presents of figs and meat, with an invitation to come and meet us without fear, since we were their friends. They replied, showing they were highly delighted, but that they could not come and see us until the present they wanted to offer us had arrived, and that they had sent for it to their *ranchería* nearby. And so it happened that after we had taken our meal and some rest, they came with their nets [full] of cooked *mescal* [cactus], and all their weapons, which they laid on the ground. They started in to explain their use in battle, one after the other. They played all the parts both of the attacker and of the attacked in such a vivid way, and with such address, that it was a pleasant moment of relaxation for us. As to what they wished to convey to us on the matter, there was no need of interpreters at all. So far we had not seen any women among them, and, till now, I was anxious not to see them, because I feared that they went as naked as the men. But when, in the midst of all this entertainment, two women appeared, talking as rapidly and efficiently as that sex is accustomed to do, and when I saw them so decently covered that we would feel happy if no greater display of indecency were ever seen among the Christian women of the missions, I no longer regretted their arrival. The younger of the two, who was, they said, the wife of the Chief, who also was there, carried upon her head the present, the like of which I had never seen—a great pancake of a thing like dough, but full of thick fibers. I went to lay my hands upon her head, and she left the cake in my hands. She and her husband immediately began to explain to me how it was eaten. The older woman spoke also, yelling louder than all the rest. The Chief continued his explanations, and those with him too, and all were so engrossed in it that we did not notice when the women went away. And so a little later asking for them, to give them a present, we found that they had gone. May God bless them. To the Chief we gave a present for his wife, and a gift was given to each of the others. We bade them farewell and they left, satisfied and content, but saying that they wanted to go farther with us, and follow us as friends.[47]

Tuesday 30 May 1769

Serra rests at a spot he names San Fernando [Lower California] in honor of

the Feast of our Patron San Fernando, King of Spain . . . [and because] it is the king of sites in California. There is no mission, of all I have seen, which, even after all improvements have been made, can present so fair a view as this spot; and all its attractions have been given it by the Lord, the Author of Nature. Groves of cottonwood [*sic*] [poplar] and other trees more than in any mission; level land, green pasture, water running on the surface, and some pieces of land bathed in it; what has all the appearances of wheat fields with high green stalks; again what appears to be green bean fields; in short, unless you knew it, looking at the panorama from a distance, you would take it for a mission made prosperous by many years of labor.[48]

Friday 2 June 1769

Serra writes:

It seems that the thorns and rocks of [Lower] California have disappeared, . . . there are flowers in abundance and . . . when we came to our stopping place, we met the queen of flowers—the Rose of Castile. While I write this, I have in front of me a cutting from a rose-tree with three roses in full bloom, others opening out, and more than six unpetaled: blessed be He who created them![49]

Saturday 3 June 1769

Serra finds so many rose bushes that "a purveyor of perfume could easily make a fortune." He names the nearby stream "River of Roses."[50]

Tuesday 6 June 1769

Serra writes:

> Coyotes, deer, and more elk—and here in great numbers—were to be seen. But our huntsmen were put to shame. Not a shot found its mark. The game went quietly on their way and as for fresh meat we remained only with the desire for it.[51]

Saturday 10 June 1769

An Indian enters Serra's camp, explaining that he is "the dancer of that country, . . . not allowed to eat anything without first dancing around it." Food is offered, and he begins his ceremonial dance,

> whooping and cavorting around the offerings. Just then a soldier happened along with a piece of *tortilla* or biscuit, or meat, or something; and wanted to put it in his mouth; he [the Indian] would have nothing of it, making signs that they should put it on the pile for him to dance over. And every time anything new was added to the pile he changed his song. But the size of the pile seemed to him all too small, and after having first asked our permission, he began to dance all around our provisions, and so it looked as if he would finish up by eating all our provisions. With that he seemed quite pleased and declared now all fear had left him; and he began to eat and chat quite freely.[52]

The Indian offers to act as guide if he can "dance all the way," but soon after he "went straight for the hills running like a deer, taking with him none of the things given him, except only his timbrel [tambourine-like instrument] and stick just as he came."[53]

Wednesday 14 June 1769

Serra notes that

> after midday, and after eating their dinner, at one fell swoop nine Indians who belonged to our company deserted: six of them from San Borja Mission, and three others from Santa María de los Angeles Mission. . . . They had always given the impression of being well satisifed. . . . May Our Lord God bless them for the services they have rendered us.[54]

Thursday 15 June 1769

Finding another suitable mission site, Serra names it San Antonio, Lower California. He writes: "If San Diego is close by, as we imagine, he will have in San Antonio a fine neighbor."[55]

Friday 16 June 1769

Exploratory scouts sight the Pacific Ocean.

Tuesday 20 June 1769

Calling it the "West Coast Sea," Serra camps near the ocean at Ensenada Bay.

Thursday 22 June 1769

Expedition members spend the day "fishing and hunting for relaxation. But the fishermen did not hook a single fish, nor did the huntsmen—and rabbits and hares frisk playfully and plentifully around."[56]

Friday 23 June 1769

Passing through several Indian *rancherías,* the party now travels with a large, curious escort of coastal Indians. Serra writes:

> Their fine stature, deportment, conversation and gaiety won the hearts of all of us. They loaded us down with fish and abalones; they went out in their little canoes to fish especially for us; they put on their dances for our benefit . . . all the gentiles have pleased me, but these in particular have won my heart. . . . The women are very decently dressed, but the men are naked like the rest of them. They carry on their shoulders a quiver as you see in pictures. On their heads they wear a kind of circlet made of otter or other fine fur. Their hair is cut just like a wig and plastered with white clay, all done very neatly. May God make their souls attractive, too! Amen.[57]

Saturday 24 June 1769

Serra writes:

> After Mass there was an exchange of trinkets between the soldiers and gentiles, bartering pieces of white cloth—to which they are very partial—for basketfuls of fresh fish. In this they showed themselves to be real businessmen: if the piece of cloth was small, the amount of fish in exchange was less—with no arguing allowed. But when the piece was larger, they doubled the quantity of fish. . . . [That night] we slept under the stout branches of a monster live oak; but here we did not enjoy the California privilege of being free from fleas, because we were covered with them and with ticks, too.[58]

Monday 26 June 1769

Serra names a well-populated site San Francisco Solano, in honor of his "favorite" saint. A crowd of Indians sit in a circle around him, and "one of them thought it would be amusing to give me her baby—a nursing child—to hold for a while. And so I held it sincerely wishing to baptize it before giving it back to her."[59] The well-fed Indians refuse gifts of food, but to get hold of gaudily colored cloth or any kind of rags, they will jump out of their skins—as the saying goes—or take any risk. . . . [They] want my habit which they tug at by the sleeve. If I had given the habit to all who wanted it, there would be by this time a pretty large community of gentile friars. What I would like to imprint deep in their hearts is this: *Induimini Dominum Jesum Christum* [Put on the Lord Jesus Christ].[60]

Tuesday 27 June 1769

Friendly Indians mimic the movements of expedition members, laugh at everything that is said, and continue to covet their possessions. Serra lets an Indian look at his eyeglasses, and "God alone knows what it cost me to recover them once more, because he ran away with them. At last, after no end of trouble, I got them back after they had gone through the hands of the women and of everyone who wanted them."[61] The Indians give Serra a

> great piece of cooked fish . . . [and a] powder. . . . The smell was so agreeable and afterwards the taste that we concluded it must be a mixture of fine ground spices. So it was, and we sprinkled some of the powder on the roasted fish. It tasted as if we were eating it with cloves and pepper.[62]

Wednesday 28 June 1769

Expedition scout Sergeant José Ortega arrives with ten soldiers from the Rivera y Moncada camp, to escort Serra and the Portolá contingent on its final two-day march to San Diego. Serra sums up the long journey:

> We met with no hostile demonstrations, in fact just the reverse. On many occasions we were regaled by the gentiles—reversing the proverb, "The stingy man gives more than the naked man," because these naked Indians gave us more than any stingy men would have given us.[63]

III

California

1769 - 1784

San Francisco de Asís

San José

Santa Clara de Asís

Monterey

San Carlos Borromeo del Río Carmelo

San Antonio de Padua

San Luís Obispo de Tolosa

Santa Bárbara

San Buenaventura

Los Angeles

San Gabriel Arcángel

San Juan Capistrano

MISSION ●
PRESIDIO ■
PUEBLO ▲

San Diego de Acalá

Let what we are doing be done well

Serra—18 June 1784[1]

Saturday 1 July 1769

"Filled with joy," Serra arrives "at the famous and wished for Port of San Diego,"[2] in "a good country)—distinctly better than Old [Lower] California."[3] His left "foot is as completely well as the other; but from the ankle half way up the leg, it is like the foot was before—one large wound, but without swelling or pain. . . . Anyway it is a matter of little moment."[4] He learns that scurvy has killed many crewmen of both ships, reducing their ranks from 45 to 12, and of 86 Christian Indians traveling with both land expeditions, 55 have deserted and 5 died before reaching San Diego.

Sunday 9 July 1769

The *San Antonio* sails for San Blas to obtain more seamen and supplies. Serra notes the "gifted" numerous "west coast Indians," the "roses of Castile and trees in abundance," and "so many vines grown by nature and without human help that it would mean little expense to follow the example of our good father Noe [Noah]."[5]

Sunday 16 July 1769

Two days after Portolá's northern departure by land to search for Monterey Harbor, Serra establishes the military presidio and Indian mission of San Diego de Alcalá, California's first (**Note**: Use of the name California will hereinafter refer solely to the present U.S. State of California. Lower or "Baja" California will continue to be distinguished). A few weeks later, Serra's first California Baptism is thwarted as he begins to pour the water over an Indian baby's head, and the parents suddenly snatch the infant and run away.

Tuesday 15 August 1769

A daytime "pagan" Indian attack at San Diego endangers Serra's life. Holding a crucifix in one hand and an image of the Blessed Virgin Mary in the other, he later recounts: "My thoughts were, that with such defenses either I would not have to die, or that I would die well, great sinner that I am."[6] José Vergerano, who had accompanied Serra from Loreto, dies at his side, killed by an Indian arrow. Three others are wounded, and several attacking Indians are killed.

Wednesday 24 January 1770

Having marched over 1,200 miles in six months, and "smelling frightfully of mules" that were eaten for survival, the sixty-two member Portolá party returns to San Diego with accounts of future mission sites, Indians met, earthquakes, oil, redwood trees and Castilian roses. Having used the Vizcaíno expedition's overly enthusiastic 1602 description as a guide, the explorers failed to recognize Monterey's unassuming harbor within crescent-shaped Monterey Bay. Diarist Crespí conjectured that it had filled up with sand! Passing by its very shore, they marched north and accidentally discovered present San Francisco Bay. On their return trip they marked Monterey and Carmel Bays with two large crosses to alert any passing supply ships, still uncertain as to their exact location. Serra is incredulous, telling Portolá: "You come from Rome without having seen the Pope."[7]

23. Dedication and blessing of Portolá cross replica at the mouth of Carmel River on 10 December 1944, 175 years after the original. Rev. Michael O'Connell, Mission Carmel Pastor, officiating. Hewn by Harry Downie, the redwood cross was placed in approximately the same location as the original, immediately south of the river (as described by Palóu),

> on a hill on the edge of the beach of the little bay which lies to the south of the Point of Pines, . . . where an estuary of salt water enters the land. It receives the waters of a small but copious little river which comes down from the mountains through a valley. . . . On it [the cross] were inscribed these words: "Dig at the foot and you will find a letter," so that if any of the packets [supply ships] should arrive in this vicinity it would get news of the land expedition, and in accordance with it, would decide to return to San Diego.[8]

Sunday 11 March 1770

The *San Antonio* has not returned from San Blas, and a severe lack of supplies forces the decision to abandon San Diego on 20 March. Serra writes "we are not dead yet, thank God," and that he and Crespí will remain even if the settlement is abandoned, "relying on God's Providence."[9] Serra and the men begin a nine-day novena of prayer to Saint Joseph, patron of the expedition.

Monday 19 March 1770

On the Feast of Saint Joseph, at 3 p.m., the *San Antonio* appears on the southern horizon. For the rest of his life, Serra celebrates a High Mass of Thanksgiving on the nineteenth of each month.

Monday 16 April 1770

Serra sails north from San Diego on the *San Antonio*, convinced that the "really and truly . . . famous port"[10] of Monterey will be found. Portolá also heads north with another land party.

Thursday 24 May 1770

Portolá once again arrives at Monterey Bay, "the object of so many controversies. We now recognized it [Monterey Harbor] without any question, . . . both as to its underlying reality and its superficial landmarks,"[11] most notably "quite near, the ravine of the little pools, the live oaks, especially the large one, whose branches bathe in the waters of the sea at high tide, under which Mass was said . . . [by] Sebastián Vizcaíno."[12] He is surprised to see the previously erected crosses festooned with "strings of sardines and pieces of deer meat, and at the foot of the cross [the Indians] had shot many broken arrows."[13]

Thursday 31 May 1770

A sail is spotted off Point Piños, and three shoreline fires are lighted, prearranged signals to indicate the land expedition's presence. The *San Antonio* answers with a volley of cannonfire as it enters Monterey Bay.

Friday 1 June 1770

From their camp at Carmel Bay, Portolá and Crespí ride over Carmel Hill to the Monterey shore. A launch takes them out to the *San Antonio*, where they joyously celebrate and plan the founding of Presidio-Mission San Carlos Borromeo.

Pentecost Sunday 3 June 1770

At a "little chapel [an *enramada*] and altar . . . erected in that little valley, and under the same live-oak, close to the beach,"[14] where Vizcaíno's Carmelites had said Mass 167-1/2 years before, Serra establishes Presidio-Mission San Carlos Borromeo, California's second. In his words:

> Our arrival was greeted by the joyful sound of the bells suspended from the branches of the oak tree. Everything being in readiness, and having put on alb and stole, and kneeling down with all the men before the altar, I intoned the hymn *Veni, Creator Spiritus* at the conclusion of which, after invoking the help of the Holy Spirit on everything we were about to perform, I blessed the salt and the water. Then we all made our way to a gigantic cross which was all in readiness and lying on the ground. With everyone lending a hand we set it in an upright position. I sang the prayers for its blessing. We set it in the ground and then, with all the tenderness of our hearts, we venerated it. I sprinkled with holy water all the fields around. And thus, after raising aloft the standard of the King of Heaven, we unfurled the flag of our Catholic Monarch likewise. As we raised each one of them, we shouted at the top of our

voices: "Long live the Faith! Long live the King!" All the time the bells were ringing, and our rifles were being fired, and from the boat came the thunder of the big guns. Then we buried at the foot of the cross a dead sailor, a caulker, the only one to die during this second expedition.[15] With that ceremony over, I began the High Mass, with a sermon after the Gospel; and, as long as the Mass lasted, it was accompanied with many salvos of cannon. After taking off my chasuble after Mass, all together we sang in Spanish the *Salve Regina* in harmony, in front of the wonderful painting [*sic*] [statue][16] of Our Lady, which was on the altar. The Most Illustrious Inspector General had given us the picture [*sic*] for this celebration, but with the obligation of returning it to him afterwards, as I will do when the boat sails. At the conclusion to the liturgical celebration, standing up I intoned the *Te Deum laudámus;* we sang it slowly, and solemnly, right to the end, with the responses and prayers to the Most Holy Trinity, to Our Lady, to the Most Holy Saint Joseph, patron of the expedition, to San Carlos, patron of this port, presidio and mission, and finally the prayer of thanksgiving. May God be thanked for all things! Meantime, having put off my vestments, and while I was making my thanksgiving after the Mass of the day, the officers proceeded to the act of taking formal possession of that country in the name of His Catholic Majesty, unfurling and waving once more the royal flag, pulling grass, moving stones and other formalities according to law—all accompanied with cheers, ringing of bells, cannonades, etc. In addition there was a banquet

24. Monterey—Father Serra's Landing Place, *fanciful oil on canvas depiction by French vagabond landscapist Leon Trousset, 1877. 6' x 4'5."*

served afterwards to all of us gathered together on the beach; later a walk at sunset along the ocean concluded the celebration, when the men of the land expedition returned to their Carmel, and we to the boat.[17]

25. *Monterey's founding reenacted in Perry Newberry's 1915 production* Junípero Serra, *also performed that year at San Francisco's Panama-Pacific International Exposition. Note two silver Loreto candlesticks and missal stand on altar, and holy water stoup on platform to right of organ.*

Monday 4 June 1770

A site for Monterey's presidio-mission is chosen. Serra describes it as a "pretty plain about a rifle shot from the beach,"[18] and later writes to his nephew:

> Just get out a map of America and look at it. . . . Follow the coast to the north, . . . you will find on some maps the name: Port of Monterey. Well, it is there . . . that your uncle is living.[19]

Serra also writes to the San Fernando College guardian, outlining California missionary-life prerequisites:

> I must insist that they not be men who put on a glum face whenever there is work to be done, and are scarcely here before they become dissatisfied and anxious to return to the College. Hardships they will . . . face—these men who come to sacrifice themselves in so holy an enterprise—as everyone knows. . . . Where distances are so great, . . . they are felt all the more keenly by one who is unwilling to be deprived of anything. However, I do not like to think that any of those who are coming are made of such poor clay.[20]

14 June 1770

In their first *jacal* style church, the Monterey community of approximately forty persons (Serra, Crespí, Fages, surgeon, soldiers, Lower California Indians) celebrate the Feast of Corpus Christi "with such splendor that it might have been gazed upon with delight even in Mexico."[21]

Tuesday 3 July 1770

Serra celebrates a farewell Mass in honor of Our Lady of Bethlehem, and the borrowed statue sails on the departing *San Antonio* to be returned to Inspector General Gálvez.

✝

Our Lady of Bethlehem

Devotion to Our Lady of Bethlehem originated in fifteenth-century Portugal. Prince Henry the Navigator built a small chapel at Restelo, on the banks of the Tagus River as it enters Lisbon, so that sailors might invoke the Blessed Virgin Mary's intercession. Vasco da Gama is said to have paid his respects there before and after his 1497-99 voyage that opened a sea route to India. Prompted by the expedition's success, King Manuel I transformed the chapel into the magnificent Church of Santa María, and added the title Nossa Senhora de Belém (Nuestra Señora de Belén in Spanish, Our Lady of Bethlehem in English) to the statue of Mary. Mariner devotion grew and spread to Spain during the 1580-1640 dual monarchy, and migrated to the New World via explorers and missionaries.

Mission Carmel's statue was originally owned by Most Rev. Francisco Antonio Lorenzana y Butrón, Archbishop of Mexico City from 1766 to 1771. He gave the statue to Inspector General Gálvez, who "destined it for the first maritime expedition [to Upper California], so that it might go with the title of *Conquistadora*" [22] (Our Lady of the Conquest).

Our Lady Of Bethlehem Chronology

15 February 1769

Departing from La Paz, Lower California, the statue sails on board the *San Antonio* for San Diego Bay.

16 July 1769

The statue is present at Presidio-Mission San Diego's founding, and afterward "for almost a year it . . . [was on] the altar. . . . It was there during all Masses, high or low, that were celebrated there; also during the daily prayers, both morning and evening."[23]

16 April 1770

Departing from San Diego with Serra, the statue sails on board the *San Antonio* for Monterey.

3 June 1770

Serra mentions the statue at the founding of Presidio-Mission San Carlos Borromeo on 3 June 1770.

14 June 1770

The Feast of Corpus Christi celebration. Serra writes to Gálvez:

> The . . . beautiful statue of Mary, Most Holy (belonging to Your Most Illustrious Lordship), occupied the middle space directly above the monstrance of her Most Holy Son. And there Our Lady stood on guard over the church.[24]

24 June 1770

Serra performs a High Mass of Thanksgiving in fulfillment of a promise made by *San Antonio* Captain Juan Pérez for safe passage to Monterey. Three unaccounted-for paintings had just been discovered by the ship's steward, and before Mass Serra says:

> My delight knew no bounds. We took my saints [San Carlos, San Buenaventura and San Diego] on shore to remain there. We put them on the altar, and there was the Blessed Virgin surrounded by Cardinals and her lay sacristan, seemingly as pleased as could be. The altar looked just marvelous.[25]

29 June 1770

Serra notes: "On the Feast of Saint Peter, at my suggestion, we also sang a Mass in honor of Our Lady."[26]

3 July 1770

Farewell Mass and departure of the borrowed statue. Serra writes to Gálvez:

> Now it returns by boat, after it has been formally handed over to Captain Don Juan Pérez, to be delivered into the hands of Your Most Illustrious Lordship. And, in doing this, I am carrying out the promise I made to Your Illustrious Lordship so to do, while I was at the Port of La Paz. . . . Don Juan Pérez promised that he would take the Blessed Virgin's . . . [statue] from the boat with solemnity at San Blas, and that he and Don Miguel Pino would pay all expenses for the celebration there with a festive High Mass and sermon in thanksgiving. I congratulated them on the splendid idea especially as they gave me their word that the festivities would not include any dancing. Thanks be to God, they promised not to allow that.[27]

Gálvez will eventually return the statue to Serra at Mission Carmel, exact date of re-shipment and arrival unknown.

23 May 1774

The maiden voage of the *Santiago* ends safely, bringing Serra from San Blas, and desperately needed supplies to Monterey. Serra says a "Mass of Thanksgiving in honor of Our Lady Of Monterey; it was a promise made by the sailors in their time of peril."[28] Not known if the statue has already been returned.

10 June 1774

The *Santiago* is about to leave for the first Spanish scientific expedition of the Pacific northwest coast, and at the request of Captain Juan Pérez, Serra sings a High Mass at

> the very same spot where Mass was celebrated of old by Vizcaíno's expedition . . . and under the oak tree where, four years and six days before, [I] had sung the first Mass, when the royal standards were unfurled. . . . The little chapel was prepared with banners and lanterns from the boat. . . . The mission's richest vestments and everything else of the best [were used. I] sang a solemn Mass . . . in honor of Our Lady of the Coast . . . and preached during it. Many religious, who formed the choir, assisted at the Mass, there being ten of them at the mission [new arrivals destined for other missions]. There were present, too, all the officers of the two ships, the army officers, the sailors, the soldiers and the Indians, both Christian and gentile. The Mass was offered up for the success of the new expedition—that it should meet with the same happy results as, to the joy of all hearts, had been the good fortune of the expedition which had opened up all of this country. . . . Later we had a banquet, at the same place, for all, gathered together in a body. In the afternoon we parted, those on land from those on sea. The former went aboard ship; we returned home. The next day the frigate set sail with a favorable wind. . . . God bless it. Amen![29]

Not known if the statue has already been returned.

15 October 1775

The *Santiago,* under the command of Bruno de Hezeta, and the *Sonora,* under Juan Francisco de la Bodéga y Quadra, have just arrived in Monterey after a second Pacific coastal exploratory voyage.

> They [the crews] wished to render thanks, fulfilling the promises that they made . . . that if they should return safely to Monterey a solemn Mass would be sung to Nuestra Señora de Belén, who is venerated in the church of San Carlos on Río Carmelo. . . . The illustrious visitor-general, Don José de Gálvez, . . . *again shipped it* [italics mine] so that it might be placed in the church of that mission, as was done. . . . All the people . . . went to the Mission on the Carmelo River to fulfill the promise, and a solemn Mass was sung by the ministers in which all those of the expedition, from the captains and pilot to the last cabin boy, took communion, to the edification of all, who gave thanks to the Lord and His Most Holy Mother.[30]

The statue had clearly been returned by this date.

26 July 1779

The *Santiago* sails from San Francisco Bay to Monterey, and

> it was in evident danger of being wrecked, not only at the start, when it struck the steep cliff of the opposite coast with the point of the bowsprit, but also in the little bay outside of the harbor, in which it dropped anchor, for, the stream cable having clipped under the keep, it was about to turn the ship over. They attributed the escape from both perils to a miracle of Nuestra Señora. It got into a third danger at Point Año Nuevo, for while they were anchored the rudder struck heavily on the rocks several times. But, freed from all these dangers they arrived safely at Monterey, giving thanks to God and His Immaculate Mother with a High Mass in the mission of San Carlos de Monterey.[31]

13 September 1784

Shortly after Serra's death, Palóu writes to the San Fernando College guardian, asking that Serra be memorialized in a painting, "kneeling and before the altar of Our Lady."

December 1802

In fulfillment of a personal vow, the statue receives a silver crown (parcel [partially] gilt with *repoussé* decoration, hand stamped lettering, 12" tall x 10" diameter) from Mexico, inscribed:

> A devocion del Teniente de Navio D,^{n} Juan Bau,^{ta} Matute, Com,^{te} de la Fra,^{ta} de la Puri,^{ma} Comp,^{on} consiguio alibiarse de dicando ecta Corona Oag^{re} de 1798
>
> [Out of the devotion of Naval Lieutenant Don Juan Bautista Matute, Commander of the frigate the *Most Pure Conception*. He obtained relief, dedicating this crown October of 1798]

June 1842

The statue is not listed in Mission Carmel's final post-secularization "auction" inventory. For safekeeping, it has already been removed from its central niche in the church's *reredos*, and taken to the mission orchard *adobe* by the Cantua family, last Mission Carmel resident Indians. The baby and crown are eventually taken to the Royal Presido Chapel in Monterey.

1876

Cantua daughter María Ignacia Dutra moves to Monterey, taking the statue with her. Many people pay devotional visits to her home, where the statue is displayed wearing Mrs. Dutra's wedding dress.

1925

The statue is inherited by Gertrude Ambrosio, descendant of Monterey's pioneer Boronda family.

December 1945

Mrs. Ambrosio returns the statue to Mission Carmel. Maintaining the original 5 feet, 2 inch overall height, curator Harry Downie carves a new wooden lower torso to replace the termite-destroyed original. He dresses the statue in a Mexican silk and silver embroidered gown, silk and gold brocade cope, and reunites it with the original crown and baby, which had been stored in Monterey. Our Lady of Bethlehem is placed above the Gospel side of the altar and blessed just before Christmas Eve midnight Mass, where it remains until final placement over a specially designed side-altar in the church's former mortuary chapel.

9 May 1954

As culmination of the year-long Franciscan National Marian Congress commemorating the centennial of the proclamation of the Catholic Dogma of Immaculate Conception, a Solemn Pontifical Mass is offered at Mission Carmel by Most Rev. Aloysius Willinger, C.Ss.R., D.D., Bishop of Monterey-Fresno. Afterward, more than 4,000 people attend a special Mother's Day celebration in honor of

> the statue of Our Lady of Belen, the first statue of Mary to be brought into the state. . . . It was placed under a canopy in the quadrangle during the nationality tributes, the focal point

27. *Never retouched, Our Lady of Bethlehem's wooden face and hands show original* encarnación *mat finish. Glass eyes and traces of real eyelashes still remain, real hair added by curator Downie, as in original. Nineteenth-century acorn earrings gift of Mrs. Gertrude Ambrosio.*

of the honors. . . . The Mexicans, Filipino, Spanish, Irish, Portuguese and others sang and danced gaily before Our Lady, dressed in bright costume. The New Zealanders, Chinese, Germans, Ukranians and others sang native hymns and offered prayers.[32]

During an evening candlelight ceremony, the Blessed Virgin Mary is declared "the ideal of consecrated motherhood . . . symbolized by the statue," and crowned "Madonna of the Sacred Expedition of 1769" with the Matute crown and a garland of flowers.

14 December 1967

Rome's Sacred Congregation of Rites decrees that Our Lady of Bethlehem and Saint Joseph are to be principal patrons of the newly "re-created" Diocese of Monterey in California, comprising the counties of Monterey, San Benito, San Luis Obispo and Santa Cruz.

◄ *26. Our Lady of Bethlehem with original Infant Jesus and Matute crown. Mexico. Mid-eighteenth century.*

Wednesday 1 August 1770

The "delightful news of the occupation of Monterey"[33] reaches Mexico City. Viceroy Carlos Francisco de Croix orders "a general ringing of bells at the cathedral and all the other churches in the capital of Mexico, proclaiming with this glad peal the joy that he felt in his heart."[34] A proclamation bearing the "good tidings" is printed and distributed throughout "the whole of New Spain," and a Mass of Thanksgiving is offered at the cathedral, attended by the viceroy, Inspector General Gálvez, and "all the tribunals."[35]

Wednesday 26 December 1770

Serra performs his first California Baptism, Bernardino de Jesús. The five-year old local Carmel Indian boy wears the "Brittany cloth [linen] baptismal cap with lace and colored ribbons . . . [used] for Baptisms of small children."[36] Monterey Presidio Military Commandant Pedro Fages serves as Bernardino's baptismal sponsor.

Tuesday 21 May 1771

The *San Antonio* returns with ten new missionaries and Serra's first news in two years from "Christian lands," ending a "second novitiate" as a "hermit cut off from all human society."[37] He also receives "several cases containing the furnishings and everything else relative to the supplies for said missionaries and missions"[38] donated by Viceroy Croix.

✝

Cloth of Gold Vestments

Describing Serra as "that exemplary and zealous missionary,"[39] Viceroy Carlos Francisco de Croix was "jubilant" when he learned that Monterey had finally been established. As a gift, and in response to Serra's 1770 request for "vestments of all sorts, sacred vessels for the churches, utensils for the houses, and implements for the field,"[40] he donated several cases of church goods to the new enterprise, including a silk "cloth of gold" liturgical dalmatic, humeral veil, and stole. In thanking the viceroy, Serra wrote:

> I received the complete vestments—especially chosen and the finest of all that came—by the generosity of Your Excellency as a gift to this your favorite Mission of San Carlos de Monterey. I soon had an opportunity of showing it all off to advantage on the Solemnity of Corpus Christi that was not far off. We made a great event of it this year, with additional splendor, because of the participation of a group of twelve Franciscan priests and the arrival of the boat with all its crew in good health. There were, too, other circumstances which helped, among them particularly the presence of quite a number of convert Christian boys from here who played the part of acolytes and choristers during the procession. For your magnificent gift, I wish to return to Your Excellency all proper thanks—hoping that the Divine Majesty will reward you most abundantly for the help you have rendered to His Divine service.[41]

28. *Eighteenth-century "cloth of gold" liturgical dalmatic, stole, and humeral veil (this is rather small for a humeral veil, and may simply be an ornamental collar). 43" tall x 66" wide, 32" wide bottom. Stole 101" x 3" wide.* ➤

29. *Detail of dalmatic's ivory satin background, multi-colored brocade, and gold metallic border. Made from Chinese silk exported to Mexico via the Philippines.* ➤

Friday 21 June 1771

Serra writes to Palóu, confiding how disagreeable Monterey's Military Commandant Pedro Fages has become. He mentions how "docile" the Indians are, and that four baptized "big boys" can already say their prayers, understand Castilian, and two of them, "Buenaventura and Fernando, one about eight, the other about ten years old, will go with the boat [supply ship], so attached to it have they become. . . . The whole idea is that by the time they return [from San Blas] they will both speak Spanish like natives."[42] Clearing the record on a personal note, he mentions the case of snuff he had called *pura tierra* (pure dirt) in an earlier letter. Upon closer examination he says, "we found it so good."[43]

Sunday 14 July 1771

In the Valley of the Oaks in the Sierra de Santa Lucía Mountains, Serra establishes Mission San Antonio de Padua, California's third. Ringing the bells and shouting "Come you pagans; come, come to the Holy Church; come, come to receive the Faith of Jesus Christ," Serra is reminded by Father Miguel Pieras (first co-resident San Antonio missionary along with Father Buenaventura Sitjar) that not even one Indian is present. He replies: "Allow my overflowing heart to express itself. Would that this bell were heard throughout the world, as the Venerable Mother, Sister Mary of Agreda, desired it, or at least, that it were heard by every pagan who inhabits this sierra."[44] Encountering some Salinas Valley Indians on the way back to Monterey, Serra asks one her name. She seems to say "Soledad" (Solitude), which greatly impresses Serra, and he names the area "La Soledad," after Our Lady of Sorrows. These Indians never forget him, and after learning a bit of Spanish, they often send regards to "Padre Viejo" (Old Father). Serra later writes:

> And if they tell the truth, that I am old, what am I to do about it. . . . I have passed through their territory, and have seen the large numbers of all ages who live there, besides many *rancherías* all around. All are as friendly as can be—so much so that they ordinarily accompany me for quite a stretch of the road—young and old crying out: *Amar a Dios, Padre! Viva Jesús!* [Love God, Father! Hail Jesus!]. Since they were told to use that expression, they have taken to it with much enthusiasm—either because they know that they please us by doing so, or because, without knowing why, that greeting falls like sweet music on their ears—in any case, it is the first thing one hears from them, when we meet them.[45]

Monday 5 August 1771

To provide a less confining and distractive environment for the Indians, and for "some peace of mind," Serra decides to sever Mission San Carlos Borromeo from the Monterey presidio. With the viceroy's permission, he directs preliminary clearing and construction at a new site he has selected, about five miles south of Monterey, "on the banks of the Carmel River and in view of the sea at the distance of about a cannon shot [from] where it forms the little bay south of Point Piños,"[46] "a truly delightful spot, which, thanks to its plentiful supply both of land and water, gives promise of abundant harvests."[47]

Saturday 24 August 1771

A "holy cross [is] set up"[48] at the new site, and after blessing it Serra says Mass under an *enramada* shelter of branches and brush, Mission Carmel's first temporary church. He remains through Christmas Eve to assist the twelve soldier/sailor/Indian workers.

30. *Replica of Serra's Mission Carmel founding cross at its original location within the present quadrangle. Harry Downie discovered the exact spot on 14 December 1939 "while digging to put in a pepper tree." He came across*

> *several water-washed stones. . . . He soon discovered that they weren't the remnants of an old foundation because they were only in one spot, perhaps four feet in diameter. In the center of the pile he found a hole such as might have received a post, and mixed with the earth were small and dusty fragments of wood. . . . [He] knew that at last he had discovered the remnants of the first cross that Padre Junipero Serra had put up in the center of the little flat where he proposed to erect his Mission and its buildings. . . . Downey [sic] [Downie] built a new cross out of 10" x 10" square hewn timbers from the Mission itself. . . it rises nearly fifteen feet. . . . Design of the cross, with its peculiar cap-piece, was copied from the engraving made by Sykes [of the 1792 Vancouver expedition].*[49]

Most Rev. Robert Armstrong, D.D., Bishop of Sacramento, blessed and dedicated the cross on 14 July 1940, in conjunction with Mission Carmel's celebration commemorating the centennial of the establishment of California's Catholic heirarchy in 1840.

31. *Fragments of original 1771 cross.*

Sunday 8 September 1771

Serra is not present for the founding of California's fourth mission, San Gabriel Arcángel. The Gabrielino Indians are pacified by "a most beautiful likeness" of Our Lady of Sorrows, but skirmishes soon lead to the death of a local Indian chief.

Tuesday 24 December 1771

Despite complaints of the "ugly climate," Crespí moves from the Monterey Presidio to join Serra at Mission Carmel, where the second temporary church is complete for Christmas Eve Mass. The church consists of

> one . . . whitewashed . . . cell . . . in the principal building . . . [which is] divided into six rooms, all with their doors and locks . . . fifteen yards [*sic*] [*varas*] wide and fifty and a half long . . . the walls are made of stout limbs of pine trees, stripped off and well trimmed, the spaces inbetween filled with stones, rubble or branches and stuccoed all over both inside and out. The roof is made of thick beams of both pine and cypress well trimmed, and covered with poles and straw protected by plastered clay and mud. . . . Some of [the] doors are made . . . of a red wood whose name we do not know, but which is from a fine and noble tree [California coast redwood].[50]

Known as a *jacal*, this building also serves as Serra's home and headquarters. He writes: "In short we have a place to live in, and can put under lock and key what is sent us. . . . But because it is not firmly nailed together—we did not possess any nails—an entrance can easily be effected by knocking down or pushing aside some of the poles. . . . May God look to it!"[51] The mission begins operation with "nine cows, one bull, two heifers and six small calves,"[52] a "miserable garden," and "no sowing" because

> before definitely establishing [the mission] here, the first concern was to have the men familiar with farming see and state whether it would be easy or difficult to take water from the river for irrigating these lands. All agreed that it would be [easy]. Now when we tried to carry it out, they all reversed themselves and declared it impossible. . . . We determined to dry farm [instead].[53]

May 1772

A delayed supply ship prompts Military Commandant Fages to lead most of Monterey's soldiers on a hunting expedition to the San Luis Obispo area. Some of the men "had to eat grass" and sell their clothes "to the gentiles for food,"[54] but they finally return after three months with a supply of bear meat. The local Indians later express their gratitude for the decline in bear population.

Tuesday 18 August 1772

Serra notes that Mission Carmel's Indian children are "beginning to express themselves in Castilian."[55] He reflects on the merits of missionary life in a letter to Palóu:

> Those [missionaries] who come [to California] should be provided with a good stock of patience and charity, and their stay will be one of delight to them. It will enable them to amass riches—a wealth of sufferings. But what becomes of the ox that does not plough? And without plowing, can there be a harvest? . . . I put my trust in God that everything will turn out well.[56]

Monday 24 August 1772

Serra departs by land for San Diego, making his first trip along California's El Camino Real. He travels with Father José Cavaller, Fages, some soldiers, and Juan Evangelista, a Carmel Indian boy (approximately ten-to-twelve years old) baptized and named by Serra on 19 March 1771.

Tuesday 1 September 1772

Serra establishes California's fifth mission, San Luís Obispo de Tolosa. He leaves Cavaller behind as first resident missionary.

Saturday 17 October 1772

After Serra and his party pass through the Santa Barbara Channel, local "gentile" Indians try to force-fully impede their progress. One Indian is killed and another wounded. Serra and Juan visit Missions San Gabriel and San Diego, and then sail from San Diego for San Blas. Serra wishes to personally discuss mission matters with the new viceroy in Mexico City, Antonio María Bucareli y Ursúa. Presaging the future, he writes: "If only . . . [we] could go there and fly back immediately."[57]

Saturday 6 February 1773

The two weary travelers arrive at Mexico City's Franciscan San Fernando College. Both had been stricken with severe fever during the overland journey from San Blas to Mexico City. Serra was twice "at the gates of death,"[58] received the Last Sacraments, and later wrote: "This trip to Mexico has broken me down considerably. . . . It was some time before I recovered my strength, and I suffered much from loss of appetite."[59]

Saturday 13 March 1773

Ordered by Viceroy Bucareli, Serra drafts a thirty-two point *Representación* (*Petition*). The document outlines California's needs and problems, and provides input for a new *Reglamento* (*Regulation*). Effective 1 January 1774, the new *Reglamento* will increase the supply-line of food and improve its distribution, provide for expansion of the mission system, redefine presidio-mission relations, place Indian welfare exclusively under missionary control, and encourage Mexican emigration to California. Serra also obtains Fages' removal from office, and Viceroy Bucareli selects Fernando de Rivera y Moncada as new Monterey military commandant.

Wednesday 4 August 1773

Juan Evangelista is confirmed in the chapel of the archiepiscopal palace by Most Rev. Alfonso Núñez de Haro y Peralta, Archbishop of Mexico City.

September 1773

Serra possibly sits for a portrait, and also checks on the status of the mission paintings he had ordered in 1771. He diffuses talk of his being elected San Fernando College guardian by preparing to return to California, and repeats the same act of humility performed when leaving Palma twenty-four years prior. "Touch[ing] the hearts of all in such a way that they shed copious tears,"[60] he kneels and kisses the feet of each priest at the College, knowing that he will never see them again. With "the business for which I came . . . settled,"[61] Serra departs in mid-month for "that far distant vineyard of the Lord. And seeing that at present the state of my health is none too good, I will have to make the trip somewhat slowly."[62] He writes to his nephew in Mallorca: "[California] is the place for me to live in and, I hope to God, that is where I shall die."[63]

Retrato del Rev. Padre Fray Junípero Serra Apostol
e la Alta California, tomado del original que se conserva en
u Convento de la Santa Cruz de Querétaro.

Fray Junipero Serra Fundador de las Santas Misiones
de S. Diego, S. Carlos Boromeo de Monterrey, S. Gabriel, S. Luis
S. F.co de Asis y San Juan Capistrano de Alta California

Boceto de Pedro Pablo M.quez Conto de la Cruz
Prov. del St. Ev. Querela

32. San Fernando Serra portrait (page 56).

Original lost or destroyed. Oldest known copy an engraving for an article on Serra's life by M. Roa Barcena in *La Cruz* magazine, Mexico City, vol. III, no. 10, 9 October 1856, p. 303. Original possibly still in existence in 1904 when Franciscan historian Zephyrin Engelhardt acquired a photograph of the original oil painting while in Mexico City. The assumption is that Serra posed for the portrait while visiting San Fernando College in 1773. Considering that he was sixty years old and unlikely ever to return, his superiors would certainly want a man who had "brought honor to his college" to sit for a portrait. However, there is no record of this, hence no proof that his true likeness was captured without secondhand interpretation or passage of time. In the opinion of Southwest Museum founder Charles F. Lummis, who corresponded with Engelhardt concerning the print in 1924: "That characterless phiz doesn't in any way resemble the man who established civilization in California."[64]

33. Querétaro Serra portrait (page 57).

Original lost or destroyed. Late nineteenth-century oil on canvas copies at Mission Santa Bárbara and at the Franciscan Convento de Santa Cruz in Querétaro, Mexico, each 2' x 3.' Both bear the legend:

> Portrait of the Rev. Father Fray Junípero Serra, Apostle of Upper California, copied from the original which is kept in his convent of Santa Cruz in Querétaro. Painted by Father José Mosqueda

Mosqueda (1870-1954) "an excellent copyist . . . that employed a magic lantern . . . in painting,"[65] made the copies from an

> original painting of Fray Junípero Serra [that] was for many years in the holy convent of Santa Cruz de Querétaro. From there it was transferred to the Convent of Santa Clara [also in Querétaro] and finally about the year 1900, it was in the Franciscan Convent of San Francisco in Querétaro. From there it disappeared during the first period of the Mexican revolution . . . (circa 1910).[66]

Nothing more is known of the original. The Querétaro portrait incorrectly portrays Serra with greenish-gray eyes (his were dark), and a ruddy complexion (his was olive *moreno*). However, he is correctly shown wearing the large crucifix that he brought from Mallorca, and the portrait's overall effect at least imparts a more lifelike impression than the San Fernando portrait. One theory is that both the Querétaro and San Fernando portraits are nineteenth-century copies of Serra's features from the 1785 *Serra's Viaticum* painting.

34. Zacatecas Serra portrait (page 58).

Tempera on paper. 12-1/2" x 9-1/2". Discovered by Mission Carmel Curator Harry Downie in a Zacatecas, Mexico second-hand store in January 1954. Omitting Mission San Antonio but including Mission San Juan Capistrano (founded three years after Serra's Mexican visit), placing the Convento de Santa Cruz in the wrong administrative jurisdiction, misspelling Junípero, Borromeo, Monterey, California, and with a seemingly unpronounceable artist's surname, the legend translates:

> Fray Junípero Serra Founder of the holy missions of San Diego, San Carlos Borromeo de Monterey, San Gabriel, San Luís Obispo, San Francisco de Asís and San Juan Capistrano of Upper California. Sketch by Pedro Pablo Mguez. Convent of the [Holy] Cross. Province of the Holy Gospel. Quéreta[ro]

Painted on mid-to-late nineteenth century paper, in light, delicate brush strokes indicative of copying, the sketch is presumed to be from an older, lost original. The countenance matches the weary, sick Serra of 1773 more than the other healthy, embonpoint renderings, but after extensive research, historian Maynard Geiger concluded:

I made great effort during my . . . [Mexican] tour of research . . . in 1955 to obtain some information as to the identity of Pedro Pablo Mguez. . . . The investigation proved fruitless as to the time and origin [of the sketch] and the identity of the painter. . . . [This] is an entirely different conception of Serra, . . . it cannot be the same man either in physiognomy or spirit as shown in the Guerrero [*Serra's Viaticum*], San Fernando or Querétaro paintings. Admittedly it is a fine face.[67]

Sunday 13 March 1774

After witnessing a burial at sea, "the first [body] whom, in all my time at sea, I ever saw thrown overboard,"[68] Serra and Juan arrive at San Diego aboard "His Majesty's new frigate . . . [the *Santiago*] in a shorter time than any other boat before."[69] Serra authorizes relocation of Mission San Diego to a site six miles inland from the presidio, in the Tipai (Diegueño) Indian valley of Nipaguay.

Monday 11 April 1774

Serra and Juan arrive at Mission San Gabriel, having traveled by mule from San Diego. The mission priests gratefully accept "a supply of chocolate, . . . flour," and a painting of the Archangel Gabriel that Serra commissioned in Mexico. They retire the previous image, a missal-page print, and hang the new painting above the altar. Serra performs California's first Caucasian wedding ceremony, that of José Lorenzo de Esparza, a carpenter from Aguascalientes, Mexico, to María Josefa Dávila, from Guadalajara, Mexico. Recruited by Serra while in Mexico, the Esparzas are one of the first families to resettle in California. They will make their home at Mission San Gabriel.

Thursday 28 April 1774

As Serra continues north, he meets Captain Juan Bautista de Anza near one of the Indian *rancherías* along the Santa Barbara Channel. De Anza is returning to Mexico, having reconnoitered an overland trail to connect the Mexican mainland with the Pacific coast. The two pioneers camp together that night and discuss California's future.

Friday 6 May 1774

Serra and Juan arrive at Mission San Antonio. The mission priests welcome a new painting of Saint Anthony, and are willing to pay an eighteen *peso* debt to acquire another painting, that of Saint Louis. The priests at Mission San Luís Obispo did not want the painting because they already had one, and despite Serra's appraisal that "it was nicely executed, but the one I had with me was still nicer,"[70] they did not even ask to see it unwrapped. Serra declines Mission San Antonio's offer, and takes the white elephant to Carmel where he forgets to pay the bill. When San Fernando College orders him not to trade goods between missions as part of a temporary curtailment of father-presidential power in 1775, he remembers the incident and writes:

> I never had to accuse myself of transgressions against the seventh commandment [Thou shalt not steal]. But, possibly, your information may have been occasioned by the story of a painting of San Luís Obispo, which cost eighteen *pesos*. . . . I *forgot* to . . . credit the eighteen *pesos* to the San Luís Mission, and charge them to this mission [Carmel]. If Your Paternities like to believe that my not writing was of set purpose, to swindle them out of the eighteen *pesos*, you certainly may do so. I assert that I forgot—let my word be worth what it may.[71]

✝

The Glory of Heaven

Along with its companion *Horrors of Hell* painting, the *Glory of Heaven* was commissioned by Serra in June 1771. After sending his *Memoria* (*Account*) list to San Fernando College, the College's syndic handled the details. The original request is preserved in the Mexican National Archives:

> Account of a request for goods made by the Fathers of the Mission of San Carlos de Monterey, with the following notation: MR—year of 1771. . . . Two canvases two *varas* long, almost square but greater in length than in width, one representing Heaven and the other Hell, their value not to exceed one hundred *pesos*.[72]

The paintings accompanied Serra to California on the *Santiago* in 1774, arrived in Monterey on 9 May, and were taken to Mission Carmel shortly thereafter. They appear in Serra's 1774 Mission Carmel *Informe:*

> Since December, 1773, . . . until the end of . . . December, 1774, this mission has had the following . . . additions to Church and Sacristy. . . . Two . . . large ones [paintings] with their reinforcing rods: one depicting the Glory of Heaven, and the other the Horrors of Hell; the work of a good painter.[73]

The *Glory of Heaven* is signed but not dated, leading to two theories concerning its exact date of execution. The first is that the *Glory* is an early José de Paez work that pre-dates the California missions. Why? Because the painting depicts the Holy Trinity as three separate persons. On 1 October 1745, Pope Benedict XIV issued the Epistle *Sollicitudini*, which prohibited representation of the Holy Spirit in human form. As a priest and Commissary of the Holy Office of the Inquisition, the theory holds that Serra would not violate canon law by ordering and accepting such a representation in 1771. Therefore, the painting must have been commissioned by San Fernando College before the law was promulgated in Mexico, c. 1750-60. Since it fit Serra's request, it was entrusted to him during his 1773 Mexican visit, and shipped to California when he returned in 1774. The second theory is simply that Paez painted the *Glory of Heaven* sometime between the 1771 order and 1774 shipment dates, specifically in response to Serra's *Memoria.*

Mission Carmel's first "foreign" visitor, Frenchman Jean François de Galaup, Comte de La Pérouse, mentioned the *Glory of Heaven* and *Horrors of Hell* paintings in 1786:

> There was a picture of Hell . . . absolutely necessary to appeal to the senses of these recent converts. . . . I doubt that the picture of Paradise which hangs facing that of Hell produces as good an effect on them. The quiet scene it represents and the sweet satisfaction of the blest who surround the throne of the Supreme Being are concepts too sublime for men like brutes, but there must be rewards along-side the punishments.[74]

The paintings appear in Mission Carmel's 1842 post-secularization inventory, listed as "a large painting of glory (heaven) . . . a large painting of hell . . . [both] in the body of the church . . . on the Gospel side.[75] They were taken to Monterey's Royal Presidio Chapel after Mission Carmel's roof collapsed in winter 1852. The *Glory of Heaven* was returned during the 1930s' restoration, reframed, and once again hangs in the sanctuary of the church, on the Gospel side. The *Horrors of Hell* had long since disappeared.[76]

35. *The* Glory of Heaven. *José de Paez. Oil on canvas. Mid-eighteenth century. Mexico. Signed* Jphs de Paez fecit en Mexico *(Jphs is an abbreviation for Josephus, the Latin form of José. Fecit is Latin for "executed" or "made this"). 6'5" x 5.'*

Key

1) Saint John the Baptist holding lamb (Jesus' forerunner/baptizer); holding scroll (*Ecce Agnus Dei* [Behold the Lamb of God]).
2) Adam and Eve naked (*nuditas naturalis* [the natural state of man]).

The Triune God

3) God the Father wearing white (holiness/purity/light) with pink circle on chest (infinity); aureole surrounding raised right *Manus Dei* (Hand of God) with three fingers extended (Creator's blessing/Trinity); holding blue globe/sphere (power/perfection) and scepter (authority).
4) God the Son wearing blue (earthly ministry) with reclining lamb on chest (wounded flesh sacrificed to save mankind/Good Shepherd); left palm Crucifixion wound; holding Crucifixion Cross.
5) God the Holy Spirit wearing red ("tongues of fire appeared, which parted and came to rest on each of them [Apostles]. All were filled with the Holy Spirit" Acts 2:3-4); hands clasped over heart (God's infinite love).

6) David with harp ("David and all Israel danced before God with . . . harps" 1 Chronicles 13:8).
7) Moses with tablets of stone (Ten Commandments).
8) Saint Peter with key ("I will entrust to you the keys of the kingdom of heaven" Matthew 16:19).
9) Joseph and Mary.
10) Joachim and Anne (Mary's parents).
11) Saint Dominic (1170-1221, founder Dominican Order), holding staff (pilgrim preacher), lily (purity), and book (education); right hand outstretched to Saint Francis of Assisi (camaraderie between Orders).
12) Saint Francis of Assisi (1181-1226), founder Franciscan Order, wearing gray San Fernando College habit; holding cross (identification with Jesus/suffering); right hand with Stigma outstretched to Saint Dominic.
13) Saint John of the Cross (1542-91, joint founder Discalced Carmelite Order), holding cross (mystery of the Passion/suffering).
14) Saint Ignatius of Loyola (1491-1556, founder Society of Jesus/Jesuit Order), wearing red chasuble (yoke of Christ); holding open book (education) with Jesuit motto on page: *Ad Majorem Dei Gloriam* (For the Greater Glory of God).
15) Saint Bonaventure (1221-74, Franciscan theologian and cardinal), wearing gray San Fernando College habit; raised right hand (blessing/sanctity); holding lily (purity) in left hand (partially obscured by frame).

16) Archangel Gabriel (announcing Angel), holding lily (Blessed Virgin Mary's Annunciation purity).

17) Archangel Michael (warrior angel), wearing blue, starred armor (Satan's expulsion from Heaven); holding staff/cross (leader of the heavenly host/protector of Christians).

18) Archangel Raphael (guiding/healing angel), holding pilgrim's staff ("I am Raphael, one of the seven angels who enter and serve before the Glory of the Lord" Tobit 13:15).

19) Martyrs wearing white (virginity), with red rose crowns (martyrdom/heavenly joy); holding palm fronds (triumph over sin/immortality).

Wednesday 11 May 1774

Serra and Juan arrive home. They have been gone for nearly two years. Crespí and Palóu greet them, Palóu having relocated to Mission Carmel after the Franciscan transfer of the Lower California missions to the Dominicans in 1773. The *Santiago* has also just arrived, ending Monterey-Carmel's worst supply shortage. Having subsisted on peas, herbs, and milk (unable to offer Anza even a cup of chocolate when he visited the mission in April), and with the priests "in need of habits, tunics, cloaks, mantles, coats, girdles, underwear and sandals, . . . snuff and chocolate"[77] the community celebrates as the *Santiago* dispenses supplies and alms sent by Viceroy Bucareli: ham, jerked beef, corn, beans, chickpeas, lentils, rice, flour, peppers, olive oil, lard, wine, brandy, brown sugar and chocolate. Total Baptisms have risen from only fifteen to seventy-four during Serra's absence, but with a full storehouse, Serra can now "cast the net among the pagans, inviting them to the mission."[78] Seventy-two Baptisms will be performed within the next two months

> on children not over eight years old; . . . to hear them pray, and answer questions—well versed in all the questions and answers of the Christian Doctrine; to hear them sing, to see them all dressed in worsted clothes and woolens; to see how happy they are at play, and how they run up to the Father; as if they had known him all their lives—all of this gladdens the heart, and impels one gratefully to give praise to God.[79]

The Indians are "applying themselves in earnest to work, some with hoe in hand, some with the mould making *adobe* bricks, others in reaping and harvesting the wheat, in housing it in the barns, and in any other occupation assigned to them."[80] With the help of these "new Christians," Crespí and Palóu have expanded the mission compound during Serra's absence. It now consists of a larger new *jacalón* church of logs/planks, thirty *varas* in length (this is Carmel's third mission church, first used on Christmas Day 1773). Also of the same construction, a new office, guardhouse, surgeon house, two servant houses, blacksmith shop/quarters (outfitted with a "forge of choice make, with thirty-four pieces; [and] five *quintals* and three *arrobas* of sheet iron"[81] donated by Viceroy Bucareli as per Serra's 1773 *Representación* request), carpenter shop/quarters, granary, (partially made of *adobe*), and an *adobe* oven. The 1774 garden is

> splendid . . . and as in no other mission it [Mission Carmel] grows its corn, wheat and other grain without any irrigation. Not that it would be difficult to put into operation, although some believe it would be, but because the land here does not need it, as can be seen by looking at the corn—and it has had no rain.[82]

The wheat harvest will set a new record at 125 *fanegas*, and barley and beans are also plentiful. A "corner" of the garden is

> set aside for tobacco plants. The reason is that . . . I experienced all the way from San Diego to here, without ceasing: "Love God, Father!" and then immediately: "*Chuqui, Chuqui!*" And, thinking that I did not understand, to make themselves clear they said: "Tobacco, *Padre!*" As I do not smoke, I had none.[83]

Serra sums up this turning point in mission prosperity when he writes that "Monterey and its missions" should no longer be looked upon "as the China or Cueta [a Spanish North African city known for its prison] of exile."[84]

Saturday 11 June 1774

The *Santiago* departs for the first Spanish voyage of scientific exploration along the Pacific northwest coast, with Crespí as chaplain and diarist. Serra writes: "Practically all I hear is, 'southeast, northwest, northeast,' etc., and I understand as much about it all as I do of making pottery."[85] He later sends Viceroy Bucareli

> four small wooden pieces, ornamented as is customary with Chinese art . . . brought . . . by the sea expedition from a place called Santa Margarita [northern tip of present Graham Island, Queen Charlotte Islands, British Columbia] in the latitude of 55 degrees, . . . [and] specimens [of weaving] that . . . can be found along the [Santa Barbara] Channel. All of these articles are being packed in a box of red wood—a tree which abounds in these parts. They tell me that the carpenters in San Blas did not know any name for it other than the "wood of Monterey."[86]

Monday 25 July 1774

Serra marries his first couple at Mission Carmel, "Don Lorenzo de Resa, European Spaniard, to María Theresa de Ochoa, young lady of Tepic [Mexico]."[87] He writes that he and his "humble chaplains [are] working with a . . . fervor in tilling the vineyard of the Lord. . . . Brambles and thorns are not wanting; and they are not small ones."[88]

True Cross Reliquary

In the absence of any hallmarks, two theories have developed regarding the provenance of this Mexican silver cross. First, if the three-sided base motifs are interpreted to represent Spain, Portugal, and the Franciscan Order, then the cross dates from the period of Iberian peninsular unification under Felipe II of Spain, 1580-1640. If this is the case, then the claw-on-ball feet would be a later addition. Second, if the symbol attributed to Portugal (the *Cinco Chagas*, the Five Wounds of the Crucifixion) is alternatively viewed in light of its popularity as a Franciscan motif in art, then dating becomes more difficult since it must simply be treated as a Franciscan work of art. In this case, the cross would date from the mid-eighteenth century, in conformity with the claw-on-ball feet which were commonly used during that period. Not listed in any of the original Lower California requisition inventories, the cross may have belonged to San Fernando College, and was donated as a gift to the Upper California missions when Serra visited in 1773. In any event, it was shipped to Monterey in 1774 along with the *Glory of Heaven* and patron saint paintings. Serra describes it in Mission Carmel's 1774 *Informe*:

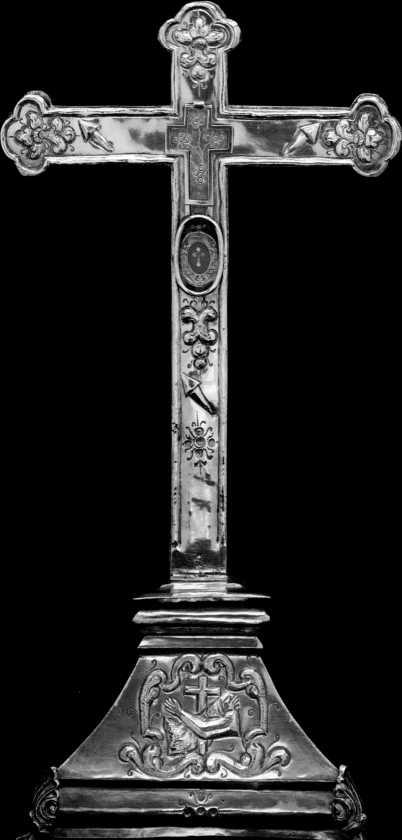

Since December, 1773, . . . until the end of . . . December, 1774, this mission has had the following . . . additions to Church and Sacristy. . . . A silver cross with its pedestal of the same metal, more than a third of a *vara*, with its *lingum crucis auténtico* [authentic True Cross relic] . . . in a little crystal crosspiece. Its weight is three *marcos*.[89]

37. True Cross reliquary profile.

Key

1) Reliquary number one (1-3/4" x 1-1/4"): outline of small cross formerly covered with crystal to hold the relic of Jesus' "True [Crucifixion] Cross" mentioned by Serra. The small inset-panel decorated with flowers/circles is a late nineteenth-century addition designed to cover the hollow of the missing original reliquary.

2) Reliquary number two (1-1/2" x 1"): nineteenth-century addition with another "True Cross" relic. The oval niche covered with beveled glass was cut into the hollow crosspiece, and together with reliquary number one, forms a one-piece detachable unit. The relic is housed within, in its own separate case. The alteration date can be determined from the relic-case design. The reverse is decorated with an image of the Miraculous Medal, bordered with the French *"O Marie concue sans peche priez pour nous"* (O Mary, conceived without sin, pray for us). These medals were first struck in 1832, and popularized in the ensuing decades. Therefore, the alteration was performed when Mission Carmel's furnishings were used at Monterey's Royal Presidio Chapel, from 1852—c. 1935. The obverse is bordered with a dove (Holy Spirit) over a triangle and rays (God/Holy Trinity); two of the Theological Virtues (Faith on the left with cross, Hope on the right with anchor), and the Sacred Heart below. The wooden Cross relic set on white fabric cross measures 1/4" x 3/16," and the case's wax canonical rubric is intact.

◄ *36. Silver True Cross reliquary. Repoussé decoration. 23 oz. Troy. 15" tall x 6-3/4" base, 7-1/2" crosspiece.*

3) First Order Franciscan coat of arms: arms of Jesus and Saint Francis of Assisi in saltire, both with Stigmata, surmounted by a cross. The complete coat of arms usually includes the cincture as a border, representing the Franciscan vows, and the Latin motto *Deus Meus et Omnia* (My God and My All).

4) Spain's "Santiago Matamoros" on horseback: Saint James the Greater/Apostle/"Moor-slayer," and patron saint of Spain. Legend relates that he is buried at the great medieval Spanish pilgrimage center of Compostela, and that he personally led the Spaniards to victory over the North African Moors, most notably at the Battle of Clavijo in 844.

5a) Portugal's *Cinco Chagas* (Five Wounds) of Jesus' Crucifixion, depicted as five hearts. The Portuguese national coat of arms bears five shields, commemorating the victory of Alfonso Henriques over five Moorish princes in 1139. Within each shield are five bezants (ornamental discs) symbolizing Jesus' wounds, in whose strength Alfonso was victorious and became the first King of Portugal.

5b) This symbol also has a purely Franciscan association, appearing in Franciscan art as an expression of the Order's traditional devotion to the Sacred Heart.

September 1774

Serra writes of the Indians' fondness for salmon and young sea birds "as big as a good-sized chicken:"

> They passed Sunday camping on the Carmel beach, divided into countless groups, each with its fire, roasting and eating what they had caught. Two of the Fathers and I went to watch them, and, as a relaxation, it was as as good as seeing a theater show.[90]

Great schools of sardines suddenly appear in Carmel Bay, and for the next three weeks the mission Indians are allowed a half-day wheat-harvesting schedule so that they can spend the afternoons fishing. News spreads fast, and many Indians arrive "from far-off places." The catch is so plentiful that one month later the mission still has twenty large barrels of the salted, dried fish. In the name of his people, Juan Evangelista sends Viceroy Bucareli one of the barrels, and Serra hopes that "his present, although a poor one, will be none the less appreciated."[91] Ten months later Juan receives a kind note of thanks from the Viceroy. In the tradition of his namesake (Saint John the Evangelist), Juan is gradually educating his people by sharing highlights of his Mexican sojourn, for example they are now "rid of their belief that the Spaniards are the offspring of mules, a notion they previously had, seeing that mules were the only members of the female gender they saw among us."[92]

Saturday 5 August 1775

The *San Carlos* enters San Francisco Bay, the first Spanish vessel to enter and explore the harbor.

Thursday 17 August 1775

Fabric to clothe the Indians is running low at Mission Carmel, and Serra pleads with Viceroy Bucareli for help:

> To supply them [the Indians] with food, there will be no trouble . . . but to cover in some fashion the nakedness of so many girls and boys, men and women, not so much against the cold—although we are cold enough for the greater part of the year—as for the sake of decency and modesty, especially with the gentler sex; that appears to me an almost impossible task. . . . Two large bolts of rough cloth, six of striped sackcloth, eight or more of wool, some of friezecloth, our habits, mantles and old tunics, and a whole heap of remnants given in exchange, or as gifts by godfathers to their spiritual sons, and more than a hundred blankets . . . all of this has been made over last year, and running into this year, as clothes for these poor people. Today, at this hour, there is almost nothing to be found, and when I look at my audience in church, I can scarcely see anything else than animal pelts, which the gentiles use, and which our Christians had thrown away when they received Holy Baptism. . . . Here we have not yet a single sheep, although I have already written to the Fathers at San Diego and San Gabriel to send some . . . perhaps if my lamentations could be heard by some of the rich and pious persons who frequent Your Excellency's drawing rooms, some of them might be moved to exercise one of the works of mercy—"to clothe the naked." We have already taken on ourselves the task of "feeding the hungry." But Your Excellency, from the love of God, will forgive me the annoyance I am causing you.[93]

Monday 27 November 1775

With Serra's assistance, Mission Carmel soldier Manuel Butrón and his Indian wife Margarita María receive the first private Spanish land grant in California, 140 *varas* square (406 square feet) at the mouth of Carmel Valley.

Saturday 2 December 1775

Serra marries Juan Evangelista and Thomasa María, both from the local Ichxenta *Ranchería.* The ceremony is performed at Mission Carmel.

Wednesday 13 December 1775

Couriers from Mission San Diego arrive at Monterey. Captain-Commander Rivera y Moncada immediately rides over Carmel Hill to relay the important dispatch to the missionaries. At 9 p.m., "in the vale of tears," Serra first learns that Mission San Diego was attacked and burned by nearly 1,000 Tipai-Ipai Indians on 5 November, and that Father Luís Jayme was brutally murdered. He says: "Thanks be to God, now indeed the land has been watered [with blood]; certainly now the conversion of the San Diego Indians will be achieved."[94] José Arroyo, a blacksmith, and José Urselino, a carpenter, are also killed. To Lasuén he later writes: "I would welcome such a fate, with God's grace and favor."[95] Serra writes to Viceroy Bucareli, asking for

> a formal statement drawn up by Your Excellency . . . in so far as it concerns me, and the other religious who at present are subject to me or will be in the future, . . . [that] if ever the Indians, whether they be gentile or Christian, killed [us], they should be forgiven.[96]

His request is granted. Around the same time, a rumor spreads that well-armed Salinas Valley Sanjone Indians are on their way to attack Mission Carmel. Envisioning martyrdom at the hands of "gentiles," Serra is "full of joy . . . the hour has arrived; . . . there is thus nothing else to do but to be courageous and prepare ourselves for whatever God shall decree."[97] Carmel's other priests receive no sleep that night, because Serra's "abounding joy did not allow him to stop talking. He recounted many similar situations in order to give us courage."[98] The attack does not occur.

Sunday 10 March 1776

With three births and one death (mother in childbirth) along the 1,500-mile trail from San Miguel de Horcasitas, Sonora, Mexico, the 242-member Anza party arrives at the Monterey Presidio in a driving rainstorm. Their ultimate destination is still 130 miles to the north, where they will establish the new Presidio-Mission San Francisco de Asís. The next day Anza and his diarist Father Pedro Font are welcomed at Mission Carmel, "with singular joy and festive peals of the good bells, especially a large one which they [Serra, et al.] had brought by sea."[99] Lodging there for twelve days, Font praises the location "so near the sea and in a country so charming and flower covered that it is a marvel . . . although the rest of the missions are very good, this one seemed to me the best of all."[100] He counts 400 Indians at the mission, and notes the "rather spacious and well made church . . . somewhat adorned with paintings, [and] three good-sized rooms of *adobe* for the dwelling of the fathers."[101] Anza is impressed by improvements made since his reconnoitering visit in 1774, noting that the vegetable garden "a stone's throw from the mission," is filled with squash, cauliflower, lettuce, herbs, wheat, barley, beans, chickpeas, peas and lentils, all watered "by hand, throwing on each plant a gourdful of water after transplanting and this suffices."[102] Having dined on fresh beef, lamb, chicken, vegetables, cakes and chocolate, the Anza party departs with a supply of fresh and cured salmon, vegetables, beans, spices, or as termed by Serra "a generous helping of all we have here."[103]

Saint Joseph

On 21 November 1768, Inspector General Gálvez declared Saint Joseph as patron of the "Sacred Expedition" to occupy California, and reserved a place for him at Monterey's new mission. Although

38. Saint Joseph. Mexico. Mid-eighteenth century. Estofado polychrome tunic and mantle over wood, encarnación brilliant finish face and hands, porcelain eyes. Original Infant Jesus, lily-staff and diadem lost or destroyed. 3' tall x 19" average width, 3' average circumference. ▶

San Carlos Borromeo would be patron and namesake of the mission, Saint Joseph would be titular patron of the mission church. He added that "Saint Joseph, being a very humble man, would not mind this sharing of honors."[104] The statue is first mentioned in Mission Carmel's 1774 *Informe*, where Serra writes:

> Since December, 1773, . . . until the end of . . . December, 1774, this mission has had the following . . . additions to Church and Sacristy . . . a niche more than two *varas* high [approximately 5' 6"] with its central cupola of redwood for the holy image of Saint Joseph.[105]

Only the niche was new, indicating that the statue was already present, possibly as far back as the mission's founding in 1770. The only connection with Gálvez as donor of the statue comes from Anza-expedition diarist Pedro Font, who saw it in 1776, and wrote:

> The patron of the presidio is San Carlos, and it is therefore called San Carlos de Monterey. In this title participates the nearby mission, which for this reason is called San Carlos y San Joseph, the latter in honor of the most Illustrious Señor Don Joseph De Galbes [*sic*], who gave the Mission a beautiful image of Señor San Joseph, as the principal patron whom he invoked for that whole establishment.[106]

The statue is listed in Mission Carmel's 1842 post-secularization inventory: "On the Gospel side [of the main altar] a statue of St. Joseph with the child (Jesus), 1 *vara* high with silver diadem."[107] As with most of Mission Carmel's other furnishings, the statue was taken to the Royal Presidio Chapel in Monterey after abandonment in 1852, and returned during the 1930s' restoration.

Tuesday 16 April 1776

Serra learns that San Diego's mission priests have excommunicated Captain-Commander Rivera y Moncada because he violated the right of sanctuary. He seized Carlos, an Indian implicated in the murder of Father Jayme, after he had been granted asylum within San Diego's presidio church. Serra supports the decision. Rivera y Moncada then restores Carlos to the church, is absolved from the censure of excommunication, and receives formal custody of the accused after making a polite request.

Thursday 11 July 1776

Having sailed on the *San Antonio*, Serra arrives in San Diego. He helps rebuild the destroyed mission, inscribes a new *Libro de Bautismos*, discovers an unburned Tipai (Diegueño) Indian catechism that Father Jayme had composed, and sends melted remnants of altar silver back to San Fernando College for recycling. All is not accounted for however, as Serra writes:

> It causes us considerable pain to hear the frequent rumors that various objects of the church and even images are to be found on the *rancherías* not very far away, and yet we are not able to persuade them [the soldiers] that an attempt should be made to recover them.[108]

Tuesday 17 September 1776

The San Francisco Presidio is established, followed by California's sixth mission, San Francisco de Asís, founded by Palóu in Serra's absence on 9 October.

Friday 1 November 1776

Serra arrives at the site chosen for Mission San Juan Capistrano, unearths the previously buried bells, and officiates at the "refounding" of California's seventh mission.[109] On the way back from a side trip to Mission San Gabriel, Serra is threatened by a large group of Indians "all painted and well-armed, emitting fearful yells, their arrows aimed in readiness."[110] He "firmly believed that they were going to kill [me]."[111] A Christian Indian in Serra's party threatens the "pagans" with retaliation, which subdues them. Serra then blesses the Indians, distributes glass beads, and leaves them after "having won their friendship."[112]

December 1776

On his way home to Carmel, rough sea blocks passage through a section of the Santa Barbara Channel. Local Indians carry Serra up the steep hill trail and along the cliffs. He later writes to Viceroy Bucareli:

> Tears welled up into my eyes when I saw with what good will they came to my assistance, . . . what a pleasure it was for me to see them, in great numbers, walking along the road with me, and breaking out into song each time I started a tune for them to take up. . . . Watching out for the opportunity, [they] would come up for me to make the sign of the Cross on their foreheads. Some followed me for many days.[113]

Sunday 12 January 1777

California's eighth mission, Santa Clara de Asís, is founded in Serra's absence. Spiritual daughter and contemporary of Saint Francis of Assisi, Saint Clare is the first woman so honored.

Wednesday 15 January 1777

Serra arrives at home and headquarters, Mission Carmel.

Monday 3 February 1777

Newly appointed Governor Felipe de Neve arrives in Monterey, bearing the royal edict that displaces Loreto, Lower California, and elevates Monterey to capital of both Californias. Serra's letter to Viceroy Bucareli expresses his "pleasure at seeing our own Monterey, whose birth I witnessed, now made capital of so large a province."[114]

May 1777

Agriculturally more self-sufficient, Mission Carmel's gardens are thriving, with "farmers, birdcatchers, field-clearers, grain cleaners, and every other kind of farm workers coming and going about their business."[115] The well-fed Indians have enough

> *pozole* and *atole,* cost what it may. When two sacks of cabbage are put in the pots, it saves us one or two *almuds* of wheat. When we run very short, some permissions [for the mission Indians to leave and feed themselves in the wild] are given, or we make the *pozole* and *atole* a little thinner. We manage as best as we can, and the population is fat and well satisfied.[116]

First-phase work also begins on the mission's irrigation system:

> This year has been extremely dry. . . . In order not to be dependent, as we have been until
> now, on the rains, and the excellence of the land, we have, for more than a month and a half
> now, been busy with the help of more than thirty [Indian] workmen leading off the water of
> the Carmel River. . . . As a result, we will be able to irrigate as much ground as the mission
> will be capable of putting under seed for many years to come.[117]

Saturday 27 September—Saturday 11 October 1777

Serra visits the two new "northern" missions and views San Francisco Bay for the first time, "a step-
ping-stone for future conversions . . . in higher altitudes,"[118] but "to go further on, ships will be
necessary."[119]

Saturday 29 November 1777

With fourteen colonizing families (mostly soldiers and their families from the San Francisco Presidio,
sixty-six persons total), El Pueblo de San José de Guadalupe, California's first civil settlement, is
founded "too close" to Mission Santa Clara. Serra is not present.

Monday 29 June 1778

After a High Mass and sermon, Serra administers California's first Confirmations, with seven-year
old Junípero Bucareli, son of the local Ichxenta *ranchería* chief, the first of ninety young Indians confirmed (the first adults will be confirmed on 9 July). Serra had personally selected the young
Junípero's baptismal name in 1774, and had asked the captain of the *San Carlos* to act as sponsor.

39. *Serra's leatherbound* Libro de Confirmaciones. *Although each mission had its
own Confirmation register, Serra used
Mission Carmel's* Libro de Confirmaciones *as a master record of all the confirmations he performed, a total of 5,308 by
the time his patent expired on 6 July 1784.
12" x 9" x 1" thick.*

40. *Serra's handwritten record of his first Confirmation. He lists Junípero Bucareli as number two because he counted Juan Evangelista as California's first confirmee, administered by Mexico City's archbishop on 4 August 1773.*[120]

Equally fond of the boy's parents, he had baptized his father "Antonio María Bucareli," and his mother "María Antonina de Ursúa."

Friday 31 July 1778

The Bucareli Monstrance arrives in Monterey aboard the *Santiago*.

The Bucareli Monstrance

Serra first asked Viceroy Bucareli for a new monstrance in a letter dated 27 June 1776, requesting it for the soon-to-be-founded Mission San Francisco:

> There is an . . . article I wish . . . to ask for, and even though I hesitate to do so, I will tell you what it is—a monstrance, however poor a one it may be. I can assure you that, were I to buy it with the blood of my own veins, they [San Francisco] would not go without one. With it, they will be able to have a procession of the Blessed Sacrament on the Feast of Corpus Christi, as I do here; and they will be able to expose the Blessed Sacrament, in front of that im-

mense multitude of gentiles in whose midst they live. Now, I have told you, Sir, what is on my mind, and I leave it in Your Excellency's hands.[121]

Viceroy Bucareli replied on 25 December 1776:

I have ordered the monstrance to be made, about which Your Reverence makes a suggestion in your letter of June 27. I will bear all expenses. If it cannot go in one the boats, it will assuredly go next year, 1778. I will see to it that it does.[122]

When it finally arrived in July 1778, Serra wrote the viceroy:

On the invoice . . . containing the supplies for the Mission here I read: "A monstrance which the Most Excellent Lord Viceroy sends to the Father President," a note which filled me with joy and happiness. A few days later the said supplies were brought ashore, and I at once had them open, before any other, the case which contained so precious a prize. And my comrade Fathers [Francisco Dumetz, Crespí, and the visiting Palóu from Mission San Francisco] were equally eager about it. Just the very sight of the neat packing box or casing in which it came—which alone indicated that it was much bigger than the one we have here in the Mission—was cause enough for much jubilant anticipation. But how much greater was our joy when we took off the coverings and looked and looked at it with wondering eyes. Everyone was highly delighted with it. We gave a thousand thanks to God, and for Your Excellency's kindness we begged a thousand blessings.[123]

Serra was momentarily perplexed. He had requested the monstrance for Mission San Francisco, yet he "found prominently engraved upon it—the inscription . . . in gilt characters which ran all around the base:"[124]

PERTENECIENTE A LA MISION DEL CARMELO DE LA NVEVA CALIFORNIA DONADA POR EL EXMO. SEÑOR B.^{o} FR. D.^{n} ANT.^{o} BVCARELI I VRCVA VIREI DE NVEVA ESPAÑA & EN EL AÑO DE 1777

[Belonging to Carmel Mission in New California, donated by the Most Excellent Lord Knight Commander (el Excelentísimo Señor Bailío Frey) Don Antonio Bucareli y Ursúa, Viceroy of New Spain, and in the year 1777]

"After talking the matter over a while," Serra and his associates solved the problem by

decid[ing] on what seemed to us the most likely intention of Your Excellency. I handed over the monstrance which the Mission had here—it is a large and serviceable one—to San Francisco; and the new one, which is larger and better, remains here for the Carmel or San Carlos de Monterey Mission in conformity with the inscription. And so at one and the same time both Missions were better off and happy about it; one had a good monstrance which it was without before, the other had a much better one than the one it had.[125]

"Keyed up to such a pitch of joy," Serra first used the new monstrance at Mission Carmel on Sunday 9 August 1778:

We had already made arrangements with the officers aboard ship and the crew [of the *Santiago*] . . . to hold solemn festivities for the blessing of a new statue of Nuestra Señora de Dolores. . . . And so we made up our minds to add an embellishment—that this should be done in the presence of Our Most Sacramental Lord. Thus we carried out our plans with the new monstrance which I had previously blessed. It was a day of high festivity. While Mass was being sung we had the salutes from our bronze guns we use at such celebrations. During my sermon I publicly announced, as indeed I should, Your Excellency's recent gracious benefaction to these new Christian lands. All of the Indians received, besides the ordinary rations, a portion of meat. In short it was a glorious day and Your Excellency was the recipient of prayers from each and every one of these poor people. . . . For all your goodness I give a thousand thanks to Your Excellency and do so from the bottom of my heart.[126]

◄ 41. *Bucareli Monstrance. Silver, gilt.* Repoussé *decoration on scalloped base and stem. 70 oz. Troy. 24" tall x 9-1/4" base diameter.*

In 1849 the monstrance was taken to the Royal Presidio Chapel in Monterey for safekeeping, shortly before Mission Carmel's roof collapsed. Returned to Mission Carmel in 1952, it once again serves as centerpiece of the mission's silver collection.

42. Monstrance custodia *(custody) holding unconsecrated Host. Detachable* custodia *incised and decorated with applied cherubs. 9-1/2" diameter.*

43. Monstrance profile.

44. Reverse side—monstrance custodia.

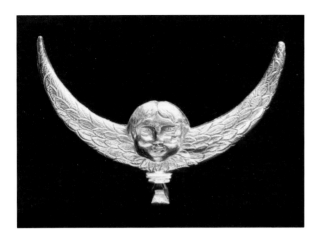

45. *Monstrance crescent* luna *(lunette). 1-1/2" tall x 2-1/2" wingspan.*

46. *Underside markings. 1) GŌSA LEZ—mark of Mexico's chief assayer from 1731-1778, Captain of Grenadiers Diego González de la Cueva; 2) crowned "M" Mexican tax mark; 3) eagle on cactus hallmark signifying quality/purity of metal; 4) 317—modern inventory number.*

47. *Chalice. Silver, gilt. Cup set in* repoussé *sleeve, with conforming scalloped stem and base. 22 oz. Troy. 9-1/4" x 5-3/4" diameter base, 3-1/4" cup. This alleged "Serra Chalice" and the Bucareli Monstrance are very similar in design, leading to the historical assumption that they were contemporaries, both gifts of Viceroy Bucareli, and both present at Mission Carmel in Serra's day. This is impossible. Required by a 1733* Cedula Real (Royal Decree), *every piece of legally produced silver in Mexico had to bear the mark of the chief assayer. The chalice bears the mark of Antonio Forcada y la Plaza, chief assayer from 1791-1818. Since Bucareli died in 1779, and Serra in 1784, neither lived to see this later addition, accession date 1805. This date is known because Mission Carmel's 1805* Informe *lists "two silver chalices, one of them gilded," as new additions to "church and sacristy." They are the only new chalices listed in Mission Carmel* Informes *between 1791-1825. Every other* Informe *merely states: "We have the same sacred vessels, jewels, vestments and decorations mentioned in the previous report."*

48. *Chalice markings. 1) eagle on cactus hallmark; 2) upside-down crowned "M" Mexican tax mark; 3) FCDA—mark of Mexico's chief assayer from 1791-1818, Antonio Forcada y la Plaza.*

Sunday 9 August 1778

Juan Evangelista is buried, victim of the measles. Serra writes: "My poor Juan, died on the ninth day after his wife, after receiving all the Sacraments, and I buried him in our habit."[127]

Monday 24 August—Wednesday 23 December 1778

Serra embarks on a Confirmation tour. Arriving in San Diego on board the *Santiago*, he will travel north by land, confirming "everybody from San Diego to San Antonio," a total of 1,716 new Indian confirmees. He arrives in Carmel "completely worn out."[128]

Monday 29 March 1779

Tension mounts between Serra and Governor Neve concerning the proposed election of Indian *alcaldes* for the missions. Serra describes the situation to Lasuén:

> Yesterday was Palm Sunday, and I said Mass at the [Monterey] presidio. Before Mass we exchanged a few words, and he brought up something so flatly contrary to the truth that I was shocked, and I shouted out: "Nobody has ever said that to me because they could not say it to me!" He answered, smiling, that he too was a logician and gave me thereby to understand that what he was telling me was inferred, even though in itself it was not [stated]. My reply was that his logic was very faulty, because such an inference was leagues away from it. And that is the way it is. He told me with irony in his voice not to worry and that the information was entirely confidential between us. I told him that it outraged me even if only a single individual knew of it. And so our exchange of words came to an end. That was the preparation I made for Mass on so solemn a day. I stood for a long time in front of the altar trying to calm my attention. . . . During the rest of the day I felt wretched, being quite incapable of throwing off the obsession, and arguing with myself, in a thousand ways, as to what I should do. I started a letter to the said Señor, . . . yet, with every sentence I wrote, something came up against it. So I stopped. I went over the matter again and again in my mind, and attributed my difficulty to my upset condition, and after wrestling with that letter until about midnight, to see if I could not calm myself, I took a fresh piece of paper and started to write a letter to Father Sánchez [at Mission San Gabriel]. It was a long one. . . . Then I began anew to argue, and the same thing happened to me as before. The thought came to me that the night was far spent, and that if I did not lie down for a while, even though I did not feel sleepy, I would be useless for anything today. So I made up my mind to lie down, fully dressed as I was. I got to the alcove, with the idea of finding some rest in sensible reflections and in fixing my mind on some religious subject. But it was all to no purpose. I just had to break out with: "What is the meaning of it all, O Lord?" And a voice within me seemed to reply in very clear words: *Prudentes sicut serpentes, et simplices sicut columbae* [Be clever as snakes and innocent as doves (Matthew 10:16)]. And I felt a new man again: "Yes, Lord, yes, Lord," I said, "thus it will be with Your grace." I fell off to sleep. At the usual time I arose to say my [Divine] Office. . . . And so the program I have outlined is this: whatever the gentleman wishes to be done should be done, but in such wise that it should not cause the least change among the Indians or disturb the routine.[129]

Sunday 15 August 1779

Serra finishes Mission Carmel's annual *Informe*, covering developments to the end of 1778. He mentions the *Jacalón grande*, the fourth mission church, which superseded the previous one at the end of 1778. With an *adobe* façade, a sacristy, and a whitewashed, painted interior, it is the largest of

Carmel's *jacalones*, "serving with all possible dignity . . . and it is large enough for the whole *pueblo*."[130] Also, conversion to an all-*adobe* compound begins with construction of

> three large rooms . . . of *adobe* . . . . One, with its alcove and large room with two windows, doors, latches, metal plates, and key, is . . . used as the carpenter shop. . . . The two others, their windows with gratings and shutters, . . . used for the time as a refuge for all the women without a husband and the dangerous ones, who spend the *siesta* hour and the night there under lock and key.[131]

The second phase of the irrigation system is completed

> in order that all our land may be irrigated should the need arise, . . . an embankment was made, on which all the people labored for some months, to hold back the water of a large lake, next to the houses. It offers much amusement and is of utility to the *pueblo* and to the garden, which is very close to it.[132]

Aided by "thirteen plows with their yokes, straps, etc.,"[133] wheat and barley production was "sufficient to keep our people the whole year,"[134] the bean harvest is still "in full swing,"[135] but the corn crop is down to fifty *fanegas* "because this is all the horses, cattle, the thieves and the crows have been pleased to leave us out of the splendid and plentiful crop of corn which God gave."[136]

49. Remnant of 1778 Mission Carmel adobe *wall, one of the oldest extant man-made structures in California. Originally part of the mission's first black-smith/carpenter shop, used later as a guest room, and incorporated into the present Blessed Sacrament Chapel in 1947. 27' long x 6' tall.*

✞

Our Lady of Sorrows

In Mission Carmel's 1778 *Informe,* Serra lists the following

improvement . . . in the church, there has been hung a beautiful painting of Our Lady of Sorrows seated at the foot of the Cross with her Divine Son laid on her lap. Its frame is a *vara*

50. Our Lady of Sorrows. *Martín Rodríguez.*[137] *Oil on canvas. 1777. Mexico. Signed Ma Rodríguez pinxit a 1777 (pinxit is Latin for "he painted this"). 5' 2" x 4' 3" canvas, 5'10" x 5'1" with frame.*

and a half high, and correspondingly wide. It has its altar, curtain, etc., very devotional.[138]

Serra was buried at the foot of this side altar (in Mission Carmel's "Serra *adobe*" church), in the sanctuary, on on the Gospel side. The painting appears in Mission Carmel's 1842 post-secularization inventory, above "the fourth altar, [the one] on the [Gospel side]. . . . A large painting of Our Lady of Sorrows."[139] Taken to the Royal Presidio Chapel in Monterey when Mission Carmel was abandoned in 1852, it was returned during the 1930s' restoration, and now hangs in the sanctuary, on the Epistle side. It is still in its original frame, although shortened along with the canvas by three inches during a 1940s' restoration.

Key

1) Our Lady of Sorrows (the Blessed Virgin Mary is venerated under this title to commemorate the sorrows she experienced during her Son's life) wearing red tunic (intense emotion/love for Jesus) and blue mantle (Heaven forthcoming); outstretched left hand (God's intercession); right hand over heart with dagger (grief/sorrow).

2) Jesus with nimbus (sanctity); wearing white shroud (Resurrection); five wounds/blood (Crucifixion/sacrifice); crown of thorns/nails/ointment jar with embalming spices (Instruments of the Passion); closed book (end of earthly ministry/Mystery of the Passion).

3) Saint John the Apostle/Evangelist wearing green tunic (charity); assisting Jesus and Mary ("Jesus said to his mother, 'Woman, there is your son.' In turn he said to the disciple, 'There is your mother.' From that hour onward, the disciple took her into his care." John 19:26-27).

4) Mary Magdalene wearing violet tunic (penance); assisting Jesus ("Near the cross of Jesus there stood . . . Mary Magdalene" John 19:25); ointment jar (also an attribute of Mary Magdalene, because she brought spices to the Sepulcher to annoint Jesus (Mark 16:1), and because of a medieval belief that she was the unnamed sinner who annointed Jesus' feet with ointment during the Supper at Simon Pharisee's (Luke 7:37).

Monday 11 October 1779

Serra arrives in great pain at Mission Santa Clara, and "the fact is that he did walk the entire journey,"[140] the only clearly documented walking trip that Serra made between Upper California missions. He declines medical assistance.

Thursday 21 October 1779

Serra administers Confirmation to soldiers, seamen, and Indians at Mission San Francisco, with "the entire *pueblo*, the greater part of the people living at the presidio, the officers, and many of the crewmen of *Nuestra Señora del Rosario* (alias *La Princesa*) and *Nuestra Señora de los Remedios* (alias *La Favorita*) in attendance."[141] While in San Francisco, a "deeply grieved" Serra learns of Viceroy Bucareli's death, and the outbreak of war between Spain and England.

Friday 19 November 1779

Via Mission Santa Clara, where he confirmed, Serra arrives at Mission Carmel.

Tuesday 24 October 1780

Embroiled in a "Confirmation controversy" with Governor Neve that questions the validity of his authority to confirm, Serra writes:

> At the time I was given notice from the secular arm that I was no longer to confirm, I had already administered 2,455 Confirmations. They are registered in the administration records reserved for such entries. There remained—and still are waiting in this mission of San Carlos—more than a hundred to be confirmed, not counting those that are being born. I put a stop to Confirmations, and will do so for some time to come—at any rate I shall confirm without any solemnity or publicity, as I did up to [now], on the principal feast day[s]. I was in the habit of confirming at the end of Mass, usually the principal Mass, attended by most people. Ordinarily it was a High Mass, and I would keep on the vestments I had worn during the Mass, and begin the ceremony with an address, explaining to the people about the holy Sacrament. But nevertheless, although I am not following this program for the present, I do not intend to forego the administration of Confirmation in a less solemn manner in case of sickness, or in danger of death, whether they be children or adult. Yet for me, the days in which the Sacrament will be either banished, or in hiding, will seem centuries. Countries such as this need this Sacrament badly. They have been waiting for it so many years, and during the two years in which they have had the privilege of receiving it, what a source of hapiness it has been to the entire population from San Diego to San Francisco. Another cross I have to bear and as hard as the aforesaid: it is that it may be published here that the Father [Serra] no longer confirms because the Governor deprived him of the power to do so, since he has found that his papers were not in order. What stories will not spring from that? The first would be: "Can it be possible that the Governor has power over the administration of the Sacraments? How can it be that, in a matter which is strictly the business of the Fathers, they are all together not as well informed on it as the Governor?" And finally, they will come to say: "According to that, the Confirmations administered up to now are not well made." Such remarks I expect from the soldiers and settlers and people, as they are called, *de razón* [of reason]. As for the Indians, all they may have to say is: "Confirmation is no good. The Captain [Governor Neve] does not like it, and that finishes the matter." I try to keep the affair hidden, but *nihil est occultum* [nothing is hidden].[142]

Thursday 8 March 1781

Junípero Bucareli, the first person confirmed by Serra, dies at age ten of an undisclosed illness.

Thursday 4 September 1781

With eleven colonizing families and four soldiers, forty-eight total, El Pueblo de Nuestra Señora de los Angeles is founded, soon known simply as Los Angeles. Serra is not present.

Saturday 8 September 1781

Serra confirms seventeen people at Mission Carmel, his first solemn administration of the Sacrament since 16 May 1780.

Thursday 27 September—Wednesday 3 October 1781

Serra travels to Mission San Antonio. He administers Confirmation after Masses on the 28th through 30th, confirming a total of 165 Indians.

Tuesday 9 October 1781

Central California experiences a slight earthquake at 7 a.m. At Mission Santa Clara, a flask of brandy breaks that the "poor Fathers there were jealously treasuring against some emergency."[143]

Tuesday 23 October—Thursday 22 November 1781

After comforting a Monterey Presidio soldier condemned to death for "not observing the seventh commandment [Thou shalt not stea],"[144] Serra and Crespí set out by mule for a northern Confirmation tour. At Mission Santa Clara Serra blesses the cross and dedicates the cornerstone of Santa Clara's third mission church, "plac[ing] in the sepulcher of the said cornerstone, a cross, medals, and various other coins, which symbolize the treasury of the church."[145] On the return trip Serra is thrown from his mule, or as he says, "I had a fall when the mule sent me up in the air."[146] The doctor from Pueblo de San José is called to attend to Serra's bruised ribs and "badly sprained hand," and after arriving home he writes: "Little by little relief came, and now it is a matter of the past. *Benedictus Deus* [Blessed be God]."[147]

Saturday 8 December 1781

Writing to Lasuén at Mission San Diego, Serra mentions that the last phase of Mission Carmel's irrigation system will be put into operation in "about a week or so . . . and that the water, should any remain over, will be stored in the pond near the granary. In this way it will never go dry and will serve as a fish pond."[148] He hopes that San Diego's new "vines will survive and bear fruit,"[149] thereby ending an "unbearable" dependence on imported wine. He also notes that chocolate and snuff are running low.

Sunday 1 January 1782

With no attending physician at Monterey, Serra consults his *Florilegium medicinal de todas las enfermedades* (*Medicinal Anthology of All Illnesses*), hoping to ease Crespí's "fatigue . . . chest trouble . . . and the swelling in his feet [that] continued to creep higher and higher."[150] To no avail, Crespí dies about 6 a.m., and is buried the next day in a redwood coffin, in the sanctuary of the church, near the main altar on the Gospel side.

Saturday 2 March 1782

Heading south by land, Serra begins another Confirmation tour.

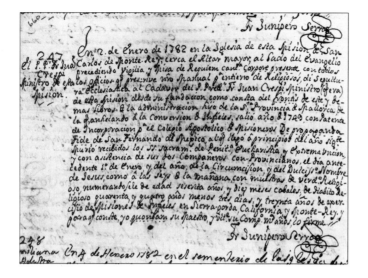

Tuesday 19 March 1782

Having spent the previous night at Pueblo de Los Angeles, Serra fasts, travels eight miles on foot to Mission San Gabriel, arrives before noon, sings High Mass on the Feast of Saint Joseph, preaches, and has enough energy to write letters in the afternoon.

Sunday 31 March 1782

On Easter Sunday, after the local 500-member Chumash Indian village has granted permission via interpreters, Serra establishes Mission San Buenaventura, California's ninth, and his tenth and last mission. A young bull is slaughtered and cooked, but the priests eat lamb, a Mallorcan Easter tradition. San Buenaventura was originally contemplated as one of the first missions to be founded, and Serra comments on the delay: "The saying which was connected with the canonization of [Saint Bonaventure] may be applied to his mission: The longer it took, the more solemnly did we celebrate."[152]

Sunday 21 April 1782

Serra establishes the Santa Bárbara Presidio. He assumes he is also establishing Mission Santa Bárbara, but Governor Neve will delay the mission's founding until 4 December 1786. He is the only priest present, and writes to Lasuén: "I send no . . . greetings from my companion religious because I have none. So I send them from my Guardian Angel."[153]

Saturday 18 May 1782

Having confirmed at Missions San Luís Obispo and San Antonio along the way, Serra arrives at Mission Carmel "on the Vigil of Pentecost, and my legs were badly inflamed. Medicine was recommended, but I used none of it. And now I am in good health, thanks be to God."[154]

Saturday 20 July 1782

Serra writes: "I have never seen the barley crop so poor as this year in this mission [Carmel]. . . . Prospects for wheat are fair, but the birds are causing horrible damage."[155]

Tuesday 10 September 1782

Neve formally transfers the California governorship to Pedro Fages, and secretly offers the following advice to the new governor:

> Concerning the treatment, management, and relationship with the Reverend Father President and the missionaries at the missions, . . . the safest procedure is to feign ignorance of everything that a question might involve.[156]

July 1783

Serra sails to San Diego for his last southern Confirmation tour, exact departure date unrecorded. Entrusting mission affairs to Palóu at Mission San Francisco, Serra writes: "I say all this, because my return may be only a death notice, so seriously ill do I feel. Commend me to God."[157]

Saturday 6 September 1783

After a short stop to baptize and confirm at the Santa Bárbara Presidio and Mission San Buenaventura, Serra arrives aboard *La Favorita* in San Diego. He confirms 233 persons at San Diego.

Friday 17 October 1783

Continuing to head north after confirming at Mission San Juan Capistrano, Serra arrives by mule at Mission San Gabriel. His health is very poor, and an Indian boy says: "The old Father . . . wants to die."[158] From San Gabriel, Serra writes to Father Juan Sancho, newly-elected San Fernando College guardian:

> I shudder at the thought of the hundred leagues or more that separate me from Carmel. . . . But, should God see fit to allow me to arrive home, I shall certainly try to go on to Santa Clara and San Francisco, to administer my last round of Confirmations before the time limit expires [on 10 July 1784]. . . . I look upon [this] as my last [tour]. May Our Lord be graciously pleased to allow me to finish it. . . . After that, or even right now, Your Reverence may look around for someone to succeed me—a man of more vigorous body and mind than this sinner.[159]

Monday 15 December 1783

After confirming en route, Serra arrives home during "this the happiest year of the mission [Carmel] because of the number of Baptisms."[160] He is welcomed by the sight of the newly completed *adobe* church. Preparation first began in 1779, when Serra wrote: "the timbers for the future church have been cut, squared, and transported. They are sixty large pine beams, more than twelve *varas* long."[161] In 1781 he wrote: "with the help of God, we will start work on the church. I have already got together any number of stone [foundation] blocks, quarried and dressed, and of a pleasing color."[162] The completed fifth Mission Carmel church, where the Indians "pray twice daily with the priest," measures "forty by eight *varas*, with a thatched roof,"[163] and contains three sandstone burial vaults.[164] The new all-*adobe* compound includes a "three room residence of the three priests. One [room is] large, with an alcove for a bed. The floor is plain earth and the roof thatched."[165] Also, new blacksmith and carpenter shops, several service and storage buildings, two granaries, and a long *"adobe* house" divided into guest quarters, Indian girls' dormitory, and storeroom. The resident Indian population has reached 645, and agricultural productivity continues to increase:

> The work of cleaning the fields once, sometimes twice, or even three times a year, is considerable because the land is very fertile. Every year we clear a little more [land]. Some of the land . . . was . . . covered with long tough grasses and thickets [and] also with great trees, willows, alders and so forth, and it has been hard work, . . . but we hope that it will pay off. . . . We also have a sizeable walled garden [which yields] abundant vegetables and some fruit.[166]

The mission has a

> serviceable *adobe* corral with sections for sheep and goats and next to this a separate pen for pigs. The rest of the corrals for horses and cattle, with their corresponding stud and bull stalls, are all made of pali[sades] and from time to time give us quite a bit of repair trouble.[167]

Mission livestock consists of

> 500 cattle, "large and small" 220 sheep and goats, 25 pigs, 8 "riding and draft mules," 20 "tame and broken horses," 90 "mares with their colts, also with them, two young mules from the time we had a jack," and 1 "old ass that may be with foal."[168]

Mission Carmel cattle brand (derived from Mision San Carlos de "Monte-Rey").

Saturday 17 April 1784

In a congratulatory letter to Lasuén when his mission becomes the first to administer 1,000 baptisms, Serra writes:

> I had a notion—a piece of excusable, self-complacency—that I would be the first, among the four who were close to the mark [Missions Carmel, San Diego, San Gabriel and San Antonio], to reach that milestone. But hail to San Diego! Here we are still eight short of reaching the thousand. But I am consoling myself with the thought that by [the end of] April we will reach the mark that San Diego reached in March. But, in either case, may the glory and honor be God's alone.[169]

Thursday 29 April 1784

Serra's last trip. Leaving Carmel for a northern Confirmation tour, he travels with "a litter. But I shall be looking on at it from the outside. . . the Governor['s] . . . wife . . . will be the one to occupy the inside."[170]

Saturday 15 May 1784

In the presence of Governor Fages, San Francisco Presidio Commandant José Moraga, Fathers Palóu and De la Peña, Serra dedicates Mission Santa Clara's new church "amid the ringing of bells, salutes from the muskets of the soldiers and with the fireworks of the Mission."[171] Joy and mourning intermingle because Father José Murguía, the mission's co-founder and builder of the church, had died suddenly on 11 May. He was buried "in the most beautiful church yet erected in California."[172] Serra makes a general Confession to Palóu,

> shedding many tears; nor did I [Palóu] shed fewer tears, for I also feared this would be the last time we would see each other. It looked as though we would not obtain what we both desired, namely, to die together, or at least that the last to die would be able to assist at the death of the one to go first."[173]

Wednesday 26 May 1784

Serra's last homecoming.

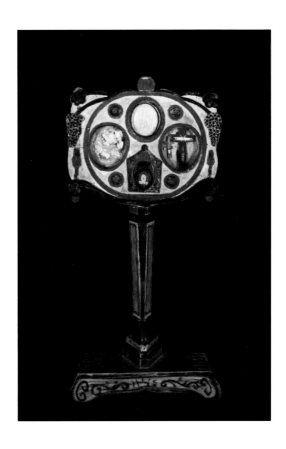

52. Serra Indian Reliquary, traditionally assumed to have been made by an Indian craftsman for Serra. 19-1/4" tall (contemporary base and stem).

53. Reliquary profile.

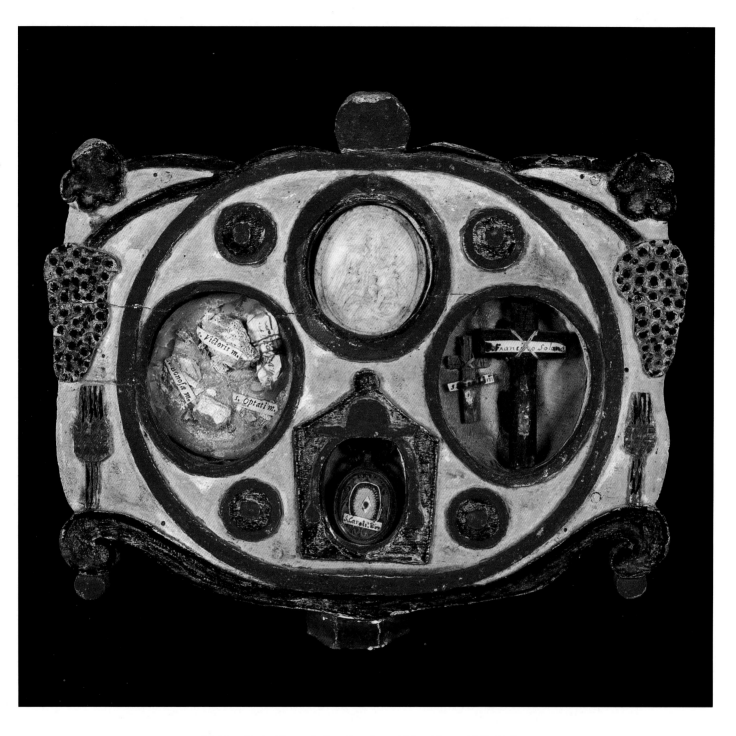

54. *Detail of relics sealed under glass. 10" x 8" x 1-3/4" thick.*

55. Reverse side of reliquary. Faded, barely decipherable legend is written in Serra's own hand. Translation:

Relics

Wax Agnus Dei *blessed by Pius VII.* Púrpura *of Saint Charles Borromeo. Bones of the martyrs Saint Victor, Saint ?, Saint ?, Saint Optatus, and Saint Bonosa. Cross, habit, and bone from the sepulcher of Saint Francis Solano, and cross and bone of Saint Rose of Lima . . .*

Key

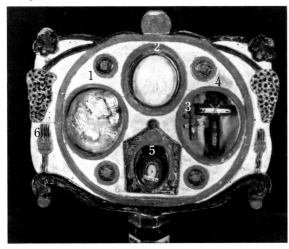

1) Bones of early Christian martyrs set in wax. Saint Optatus, martyred in A.D. 304 at Saragossa, Spain, and Saint Bonosa, martyred at Porto, Italy (date unknown), are clearly identifiable, but the number of martyred Victors precludes specific identification. The other two relics, wrapped in paper and tied with string, are also labeled (in Serra's hand), but the writing is obscured on both sides of the reliquary.

2) *Agnus Dei* sacramental depicting Our Lady of the Rosary and the Infant Jesus, from the pontificate of Pius VI (1775-99).

3) Relics of Saint Rose of Lima (1586-1617, Dominican tertiary, first New World saint, and patroness of South America). Label written by Serra.

4) Relics of Saint Francis Solano. Label written by Serra.

5) *Púrpura* (scarlet-red cardinal's cloth) relic of Saint Charles Borromeo, within decorative carved church and cardinal's hat. Label written by Serra.

6) Wheat and grapes representing bread and wine of the Eucharist.

Monday 14 June 1784

Serra's last marriage, performed at Mission Carmel.

Tuesday 6 July 1784

Serra's last Confirmation, performed at Mission Carmel.

Friday 30 July 1784

Serra's last funeral, performed at Mission Carmel.

Monday 2 August 1784

Serra's last Baptism, a baby girl, performed at Mission Carmel.

Sunday 8 August 1784

Written to San Fernando College Guardian Juan Sancho, Serra's last letter closes with:

> What I appreciate most of all are the prayers to Our Most Pure Superioress [the Blessed Virgin Mary] so that here we may achieve success and afterwards Heaven. . . . Your most affectionate and devoted subject, Fray Junípero Serra.[174]

Wednesday 18 August 1784

At Serra's request, Palóu arrives from Mission San Francisco. Upon hearing Serra's strong singing voice as he accompanies the Indians in afternoon hymns, Palóu optimistically assesses Serra's health. Replies a soldier who had known Serra since 1769: "There is no basis for hope: he is ill. This saintly priest is always well when it comes to praying and singing, but he is nearly finished."[175]

Thursday 19 August 1784

In honor of Saint Joseph, Serra has sung a High Mass on the nineteenth of each month for the last fourteen years. He is now too weak to perform his last, so Palóu acts as substitute, and Serra sings with the Indian choir.

Friday 20 August 1784

In the company of his Indian congregation, Serra walks the Stations of the Cross in the church.

Sunday 22 August 1784

The *San Carlos* anchors at Monterey harbor, and Doctor Juan García, the royal surgeon, immediately goes to Carmel to assist Serra. Hot poultices are applied to his chest, but the pain, congestion, and phlegm persist. Palóu describes the condition as "his old lung trouble."[176]

Tuesday 24 August 1784

Serra gives half of the blanket which covers his bed of planks to the "old chicken woman," so nicknamed in 1773 for having made a meal of the new mission's only hen.

Thursday 26 August 1784

Serra awakens much weaker, having spent a bad night. He makes his last Confession to Palóu, "amid many tears and with a clear mind just as if he were well."[177]

Friday 27 August 1784

Serra awakes at dawn, requesting the Viaticum. Rather than having the last Eucharist brought to him, Serra eschews tradition, stating that, "I want to receive Him in church, for if I can walk thither, there is no need for the Lord to come to me."[178] Having traveled 23,000 miles during his career, Serra now walks his last 100 yards to the church. Walking unaided to the sanctuary, he kneels on a *prie-dieu* set out for him, and prepares

> to receive the consecration of the Viaticum. As I [Palóu] began the hymn to summon the Host the sick father began the *Tantum ergo* . . . singing it with tears in his eyes, . . . [and] with the sonorous voice he always used, as if nothing were the matter, affecting us all so deeply that we could not follow him in the singing. I administered the holy Viaticum with the ceremonies of the manual of the [Franciscan] Order, and when the service was finished he remained in the same posture on his knees, thanking the Lord.[179]

After the ceremony, Nicolas Soler, visiting Inspector General of Presidios, the presidio soldiers, and the Indian community tearfully escort Serra back to his cell. Later that day he summons the carpenter to build his coffin. Palóu intercepts him on his way to Serra's cell, and so as to spare Serra, tells him to fashion a simple redwood coffin like the one he built for Crespí. Serra passes the rest of the day seated in silence, drinking only a bit of broth for dinner. He feels worse that evening, and Palóu administers the Last Sacraments. He does not sleep at all, spending most of the night on his knees and penitentially pressing his chest against the boards of his bed. Occasionally he sits on the floor, supported by Indians who have come to visit him. The surgeon says: "It seems to me that this blessed father wants to die on the floor."[180]

Serra's Viaticum

Shortly after Serra's death, Palóu wrote to San Fernando College Guardian Juan Sancho, suggesting that Serra be remembered in a painting:

> If you should wish to order it painted I should be very well pleased. . . . The most edifying scene would be to have him wearing his stole and kneeling before the altar of Our Lady, with the Child in her arms, and a priest vested with a cope before the altar, with a small Host for giving him the Viaticum, and coming from the lips of the dead father in verse *Tantum ergo*, with many Indians and Leather-jackets with their candles in their hands. In case you think well of it I will write by the land-post, suggesting the title that might be put beneath it. Pardon my annoying you, for if I am impertinent and important in this letter it is because of my confidence that your Reverence was very fond of our dead father.[181]

56. Serra's Viaticum. *Mariano Guerrero. Oil on canvas. 1785. Mexico. Signed*
Marianus Guerrero fecit a 1785 (fecit *is Latin for "executed" or "made this"). 5′ x 5.′*

Sancho approved the idea, writing to Palóu: "The picture of the deceased Fray Junípero is being painted at the expense of his Reverence, Bishop Verger."[182] The painting was displayed at San Fernando College until at least 1853, where American William Rich daguerreotyped Serra's face in that year. Turning up as Mexican government property in 1904, the painting now belongs to the National History Museum, Chapultepec Palace, Mexico City. Nothing is known about the artist except that he may have been a Franciscan. There is no proof if he knew Serra, worked from a more detailed description than Palóu's letter, or waited for Palóu's 1785 arrival in Mexico City to paint Serra's face. Therefore, the veracity of Serra's features in this keystone Serra portrait, possibly also the foundation for the San Fernando and Querataro portraits, must remain open to question. This applies to the likeness of Palóu as well, if he is the one administering Communion, which is not certain since Palóu merely suggested that "a priest" be shown "with a small Host." In historian Maynard Geiger's words:

> Its greatest defect is the artificiality of the poses. . . . All the facial features are wax-like and stereotyped. Serra's features do not portray a man of seventy years nor the face of a person in pain and approaching death.[183]

The churrigueresque-style *reredos* is depicted in conformity with early descriptions of Mission Carmel, and the rug is similar to one that belonged to the mission until recently stolen. However, the statue of Our Lady of Bethlehem above the altar, along with the six silver Loreto candlesticks on the altar, all appear highly stylized, further reminder that the painting's primary purpose was not historical perfection, but memorial to Serra.

Key[184]

1) Palóu vested in cope, stole, and surplice over habit; holding Host and ciborium.
2) Serra wearing stole over habit; holding Communion veil to catch any particles that might fall from the Host; intoning the *Tantum ergo Sacramentum.*
3) One of the priests is Father Matías de Santa Catalina y Noriega, Mission Carmel assistant missionary from July 1781—October 1787. The identity of the other two is unknown. Father Cristóbal Díaz, *San Carlos* royal chaplain, did not visit Serra until the morning of the 28th. Serra had written to the priests at Missions San Antonio and San Luís Obispo on the 25th, but they did not arrive until the 29th and 31st, respectively.
4) Assorted soldiers, sailors, and Indians holding lighted candles.
5) Churrigueresque *reredos* of Mission Carmel's fifth church, in which Serra was buried.
6) Set of six silver Loreto candlesticks.
7) Our Lady of Bethlehem statue.
8) Open tabernacle, with crucifix on top.
9) Burse in upright position, as prescribed when the Blessed Sacrament is removed from the tabernacle for Benediction/Viaticum. (This is rather large for a burse, and may instead be a tabernacle screen, placed in front of the door when closed.)
10) "Ooshaq" Turkish-style carpet.

Saturday 28 August 1784
Feast of Saint Augustine of Hippo—Confessor, Bishop, and Doctor of the Church

Appearing more at ease with the new dawn, Serra welcomes the officers and royal chaplain of the *San Carlos*. He thanks them for coming, and asks them for a "favor and work of mercy: throw a little bit of earth upon my body, and I shall be greatly indebted to you."[185] To Palóu he says: "I desire you to bury me in the church, quite close to Father Fray Juan Crespí for the present; and when the stone church is built, they may put me wherever they want."[186] He promises that "if the Lord in his infinite mercy grants me that eternal happiness, which I do not deserve because of my faults, . . . I shall pray for all and for the conversion of so many pagans whom I leave unconverted."[187] Palóu sprinkles his cell with holy water around noon, and a little while later Serra says: "Great fear has come upon me; I

57. *Palma Serra portrait. Fray Caymari. Oil on canvas. 1790. Mallorca. After reading Palóu's biography of Serra, Very Rev. Miguel Pellizer, Franciscan Provincial of Mallorca, suggested to Palma's mayor that Serra's portrait be painted for the Palma Hall of Famous Personages (where it still hangs). The commission was approved on 7 January 1790, and completed by the end of the year. The painting shows Serra holding a cross at the moment he expressed "great fear" before dying. Palóu holds the aspergill to sprinkle Serra' cell with holy water, and reads the "Commendation for a Departing Soul." Note the incongruous cane chair and Indian in full feather headdress peering over Palóu's shoulder! Legend reads: "Portrait of the Venerable Father Missionary Fray Junípero Serra, Founder of the Missions of Northern California. Born in Petra on 24 November 1713, and died at the mission of San Carlos on 28 August 1784."*

have a great fear. Read me the Commendation for a Departing Soul, and say it aloud so I can hear it."[188] The long, comforting prayer brings a calming smile to his face. The visitors leave the room, and Serra prays alone until one o'clock. Palóu brings him a cup of broth, and Serra whispers: "Now, let us go to rest."[189] It is *siesta* time and he has not slept for over thirty hours. Removing his mantle, he lies down on the rough bed of boards covered with a half-blanket, puts his head on the pillow, and clasps his crucifix against his breast, the same one he has carried since his Mallorcan days.[190] Palóu soon returns to check on Serra, and he

> found him just as we had left him a little before, but now asleep in the Lord, without having given any sign or trace of agony, his body showing no other sign of death than the cessation of breathing; on the contrary, he seemed to be sleeping. We piously believe that he went to sleep in the Lord a little before two in the afternoon, . . . and that he went to receive in heaven the reward of his apostolic labors. . . . *Anima ejus requiescat in pace* [May his soul rest in peace].[191]

So ends Junípero Serra's life. Aged 70 years, 9 months, 4 days, he will be buried exactly 35 years from the day he sailed for the New World. He had been a Franciscan for almost 54 years, a priest for 45, and an apostolic missionary for 35.

We all die, and like waters that return no more, we fall down into the earth[192]

58. *Serra's reconstructed cell. The foundation and first few feet of wall are original, as are the floor tiles, although gathered from other parts of the mission. The room is furnished as described by Palóu, with the replica bed and table constructed from original mission timbers. The Bible and discipline are original Serra possessions. 11'9" x 11'7."*

IV

Post - Mortem

1784 - 1987

59. Crespí assisting Serra at death. Detail from Mission Carmel's Serra Cenotaph.

28 August 1784

Immediately after Serra's death the Mission Carmel church bells begin to toll the *doble*, a mournful double stroke that brings everyone to the mission. Serra is placed in his coffin wearing gray habit, cowl, and cord. A stole is placed around his neck, and a small bronze reliquary cross in his clasped hands. His sandals are given to *San Carlos* Captain José Cañizares, and Father Cristóbal Díaz, the ship's royal chaplain. Mourners bringing wreaths of wildflowers file past the body until evening, when Serra's body is carried to the church for recitation of the Rosary. Surrounded by six lighted candles and two guards to keep mourners at a reverent distance, an all night vigil is maintained. Despite the guards, rosaries and medals are touched to the body, and small pieces of habit and hair disappear. Palóu admonishes against such "pious theft," reminding all present that relics are to be associated only with canonized saints.

29 August 1784

Palóu sings a Requiem High Mass in the morning, attended by officers and crew of the *San Carlos*, Monterey Presidio commandant and soldiers, mission guards, and 600 Indians. Among them is Bernardino de Jesús, the first person baptized by Serra in Upper California (he will live until 27 February 1792). "Melting the hearts of all," the bells continue the *doble* throughout the day, along with a cannon shot from the *San Carlos* every half-hour, answered by a volley from the Presidio. Burial begins at four in the afternoon. Military and naval officers alternate carrying Serra's coffin on their shoulders, in a procession led by cross-bearer and acolytes, Indians, sailors, soldiers, double rows of candle-bearing officers, and Palóu. They march out of the church, stop four times in the courtyard to sing a response, reenter the church, and place the coffin on a bier at the foot of the altar. The open grave is blessed and incensed, and following the final prayers, the coffin is lowered into the Gospel side of the sanctuary floor, in the vault next to the one containing the remains of his longtime friend Crespí. Palóu and several others throw in a farewell token of earth. A final response is sung, with "the tears, sighs and cries of those assisting drown[ing] out the voices of the chanters."[1] Immediately afterward, Palóu is besieged with requests for *recuerdos* (mementos). Serra's gray tunic is given to Captain Cañizares to cut into scapulars for the sailors. To the soldiers, underclothing and a handkerchief for the same purpose. Royal Surgeon Juan García, who treated Serra, also receives a handkerchief, and comments that "with this little cloth I expect to effect more cures than with my books and pharmacy."[2] He later places it on the head of a sailor who suffers from severe headaches and insomnia. Falling into a deep sleep, he awakens the next morning without any pain. Palóu offers Serra's hairshirt to Father Antonio Paterna, visiting priest from Mission San Luís Obispo. Gravely ill and contemplating the Last Sacraments, he puts on the garment, "and in a short time got well, . . . [and] was already saying Mass."[3] So begins the spread of Junípero Serra's fame.

5 September 1784

Palóu records Serra's death in Mission Carmel's *Libro de Difuntos*.

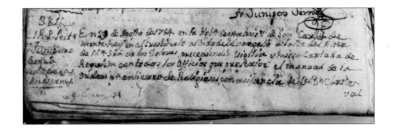

60. Entry number 381 in Mission Carmel's Libro de Difuntos, "The Reverend Father, Lector, Fray Junípero Serra, president of the missions."[4]

25 November 1784

San Fernando College Guardian Juan Sancho writes to the Franciscan Provincial of Mallorca, informing him of Serra's death:

> I have just received the news from our missions in Monterey of the death of our beloved countryman, the Reverend Father, Lector, Junípero Serra, who was the president, at San Carlos. I have been informed that he died the death of the just and in such circumstances that besides bringing tender tears to the eyes of all of those present, they all were of the opinion that his happy soul went directly to heaven to enjoy the reward for thirty-four years of great and continuous labors, undergone for our beloved Jesus, whom he ever kept in mind, suffering them in an inexplicable manner for our redemption. So great was his charity which he always manifested toward those poor Indians that not only the ordinary people, but likewise persons of higher condition were struck with admiration. All men said openly that that man was a saint and that his actions were those of an apostle. This has been the opinion concerning him ever since he arrived in this kingdom. This opinion has been constant and without interruption.[5]

14 September 1786

L'Astrolabe and *Boussole* enter Monterey Bay, bringing Spanish California's first official "foreign" visitors. Frenchman Jean François de Galaup, Comte de La Pérouse, and fellow scientists spend ten days in Monterey as part of a government-sponsored scientific and commercial expedition around the world.[6] He is welcomed at Mission Carmel by Serra's successor, Father President Fermín Francisco de Lasuén, where he notes:

Before entering the church we . . . crossed an open square in which the Indians of both sexes were ranged in line. Their faces showed no astonishment and left it doubtful whether we should even be a subject of their conversation during the rest of the day. . . . The president of the missions wearing his cope, his aspergill in his hand, was waiting for us at the door of the church, which was lighted up as though for a great feast day. He led us to the foot of the altar where he intoned the *Te Deum* as an act of thanksgiving for the happy outcome of our voyage. . . . The church is very clean, although thatched with straw. It is dedicated to Saint-Charles and decorated with good enough pictures copied from Italian originals.[7]

La Pérouse dines with Lasuén, reciprocated when he entertains Lasuén and his missionaries aboard ship a few days later. He procures supplies, and gifts are exchanged. For the mission, La Pérouse gives cloth, blankets, carpenter and blacksmith tools, wine, "perfectly sound" Chilean potatoes, and assorted herbs. Viscount de Langle, commander of *L'Astrolabe*, presents the mission with a hand-mill for grinding grain. La Pérouse also presents Lasuén with a painting of Mission Carmel by Gaspard Duché de Vancy, the expedition's artist. Lasuén makes a gift of "specimens of the most curious objects found in the countr[y] . . . three objects which are made of rush, and the one that is made of stone. All were fashioned by the Indians of the Santa Barbara Channel . . . [and] seventy *fanegas* of grain."[8]

61. Reception of the Count of La Pei Rus at the Mission of Carmelo of Monterei. *Tomás de Suría. A pen and ink and ink wash copy of the original oil painting by Gaspard Duché de Vancy of the La Pérouse expedition, attributed to Suría of the 1791 Malaspina expedition. To the right of Serra's courtyard cross stands Mission Carmel's fifth church (with Lasuén in the doorway), the* adobe *in which Serra was buried. To its right, Indian bell ringers announce La Pérouse's arrival.*

62. San Juan de la Crus 1781 *(Saint John of the Cross) bell. Bronze, three-eyeleted handle, with diamond-shaped scrolled cross, cast in Mexico. 20" tall x 19" diameter. Seven tower bells were originally requisitioned from the Lower California missions for the 1769 "Sacred Expedition" to California. Three were lost at sea with the* San José, *the remaining four evenly divided between Missions San Diego and San Carlos at Monterey (Mission Carmel after August 1771). Mission San Carlos somehow acquired another bell by June 1771, when Serra mentioned three bells. He wrote that one was cracked and exchanged for the* San Antonio's *ship bell, and that the other two were being set aside for the future missions of San Antonio and San Luís Obispo. The damaged bell eventually joined another cracked bell, both returned to San Blas for recasting. Always in demand during the early period, bells were frequently traded between missions according to supply and demand, making it impossible to trace provenance.* San Juan de la Crus *is certainly Mission Carmel's earliest remaining bell, most likely present during Serra's last years, and one of the trio appearing in the La Pérouse expedition sketch.*

63. *Woodcut engraving frontispiece from Francisco Palóu's* Relación historica. *Palóu was in Mexico City at the time of publication, but there are no known records to corroborate the authenticity of Serra's features as per his description. 6-1/2" x 5."*

Francisco Palóu's *Relación histórica de la vida y apostólicas tareas del Venerable Padre Fray Junípero Serra* (*Historical Account of the Life and Apostolic Labors of the Venerable Father Fray Junípero Serra*) is published by the firm of Don Felipe de Zúñiga y Ontiveros in Mexico City, at the expense of San Fernando College.[9] Copies are distributed in Mexico, California, Mallorca, and the royal palace in Madrid.

Key

V. R. DEL V. P. F. JUNIPERO SERRA

1) Legend reads: True portrait of the Venerable Father Fray Junípero Serra son of the Holy Province of Our Seraphic Saint Francis on the island of Mallorca; Doctor and Ex-Professor of Theology, Commissary of the Holy Office, Missionary of the Apostolic College of San Fernando in Mexico, Founder and President of the Missions of Northern California—He died with great fame of holiness on August 28, 1784 at the age of 70 years 9 months 4 days having spent half of his life as an apostolic missionary.

2) Serra wearing Franciscan habit, holding crucifix (suffering/sacrifice/conversion of souls) and stone in right hand (mortification of the flesh/penance); tears (pathos for the unredeemed).

3) Serra's Spanish/European (Christian) and Indian (neophyte/pagan) congregation.

4) Birds (redeemed souls).

5) Chalice with snake (attribute of Saint John the Evangelist, in reference to miraculous escape from death by poisoning). Serra's life was threatened on eight occasions: At the hands of a skipper en route to Málaga in 1749; in a storm off the coast of Mexico in 1749; from a mysterious plot against his life while in the Sierra Gorda during the early 1750s'; a poisoned wine incident while giving a mission in the early 1760s'; during an insurrection at San Diego in 1769; when Santa Barbara Channel Indians obstructed his passage in 1772; when Sanjone Indians threatened to invade Mission Carmel in 1775; and when "well-armed" Indians near Mission San Juan Capistrano threatened to attack his party in 1776.

6) Chain (flagellation/chastity).

7) Scallop shell (attribute of): a) Saint Augustine of Hippo, on whose feast day Serra died; b) Santiago, patron saint of Serra's Spanish homeland; c) pilgrims.

8) Lighted candle (life).

9) Skull (death/mortality).

12-25 September 1791

Spanish naval captain Alessandro Malaspina's scientific expedition includes Mission Carmel on its tour of the Monterey Peninsula.

2 December 1792

With the *Discovery* and *Chatham* at anchor in Monterey harbor, explorer and English naval captain George Vancouver visits Mission Carmel. He notes preparation for the new church of stone and mortar. The former material appeared to be of a very tender friable nature, scarcely more hard than indurated clay; but I was told, that on its being exposed to the air, it soon becomes hardened, and is an excellent stone for the purpose of building. It is of a light straw colour, and presents a rich and elegant appearance, in proportion to the labour that is bestowed upon it. It is found in abundance at no great depth from the surface of the earth; the quarries are easily worked, and it is I believe the only stone the Spaniards have hitherto made use of in building.[10]

He tours the grounds and:

On our return to the convent, we found a most excellent repast served with great neatness, in a pleasent bower constructed for that purpose in the garden of the mission. After dinner we were entertained with the methods practiced by the Indians in taking deer, and other animals, by imitating them.[11]

During his second visit to California in late 1793, Vancouver presents Lasuén with

a handsome barrelled organ, which, notwithstanding the vicissitudes of climate, was still in complete order and repair. This was received with great pleasure, and abundant thanks, and was to be appropriated to the use and adornment of the new church at the presidency of the missions at San Carlos.[12]

After a third trip to California in late 1794, which includes a second visit to Mission Carmel in November, Vancouver sails with

six hundred large abalone shells, six sheep, and six otter skins, in addition to many sacks of different kinds of vegetables, and of [Chilean] potatoes, besides frequent gifts that had some kind of value.[13]

64. The Mission of St. Carlos, near Monterey. *William Alexander. A 1798 watercolor copy of the original sepia wash drawing by John Sykes of the 1792 Vancouver expedition.*

1) *Site of present church.*
2) *Crespí and Serra graves marked after dismantling of "Serra adobe" church.*
3) *Present sacristy, erected before the church to train Indian craftsmen.*
4) *Serra's 1771 founding cross.*
5) *Tile kiln.*
6) *Mission Carmel's provisional sixth church, dedicated 2 February 1793.*
7) *Cattle stockade.*
8) *Indian huts.*

7 July 1793

Under the supervision of Mexican "master-mason and stonecutter" Manuel Ruíz, the first Santa Lucía sandstone block is laid in position for Mission Carmel's new church, the exterior measuring 165' x 37.' Crespí and Serra's burial vaults will be incorporated into the sacristy of the new structure.

29 October 1796

Under the command of Boston sea Captain Ebenezer Dorr, the *Otter* arrives at Monterey seeking provisions. Involved in the "China trade," the *Otter* is the first U.S. vessel to anchor in a California port.

16 July 1797

Mission Carmel priest Julian López is buried in the sanctuary of the new stone church, on the Gospel side, in the vault closest to the wall.

September 1797

Mission Carmel's new church (the seventh, last, and present) is blessed and dedicated after being "whitewashed and decorated inside."[14] Exact September date unrecorded.

27 June 1803

Lasuén is buried "in the sanctuary of the church of this Mission of San Carlos of Monterey in New California, on the Gospel side and in the stone vault nearest the high altar."[15]

24 November 1813

Centennial of Serra's birth.

1814-19

After extensive repairs and enlargement, Mission Carmel's compound is complete, with the quadrangle entirely enclosed, and the church assuming its final form. The elliptically vaulted plaster/stone arched ceiling is removed under danger of collapse (except for the three major stone arches over the Doric pilasters, i.e. the decorative columns set into the walls), and replaced with wooden timbers and planking. The stone is used to build the side mortuary or "Crucifixion" chapel (present Our Lady of Bethlehem Chapel) and an outside staircase to the belltower.

27 September 1821

Mexico acquires formal independence from Spain.

65. Mission Carmel's present stone church as it appeared when first completed in 1797, with open espadaña *bell-tower.*

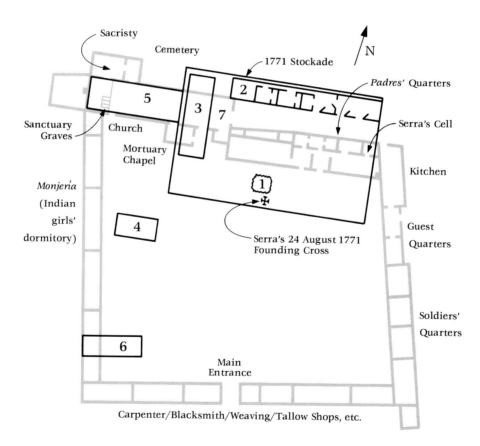

Mission Carmel's seven churches:

1) *Enramada* church of 24 August 1771.
2) *Jacal* church of 1771-73.
3) *Jacalón* church of 1773-78.
4) *Jacalón grande* church of 1778-83.
5) "Serra *adobe*" church of 1783-93.
6) Provisional *adobe* church of 1793-97.
7) Present stone church, dedicated September 1797.

9 April 1822

The Mexican flag is raised at Monterey.

1-5 January 1827

Fredrick W. Beechey, commander of the British exploring vessel *Blossom*, visits the Monterey Peninsula and Mission Carmel, where he counts 260 Indians, and writes:

> Before the valley of San Carmelo opens out, the traveler is apprised of his approach to the mission by three large crosses erected upon Mt. Calvary, and further on by smaller ones placed at the side of the road, to each of which some history is attached. In the church is a drawing of the reception of La Pérouse at the mission, executed on board the *Astrolabe*, by one of the officers of his squadron. I much wished to possess this valuable relic, with which however the *padre* was unwilling to part.[16]

66. Mission of San Carlos—Upper California. William Smyth (Beechey expedition artist). 1827. Watercolor. Mission Carmel at its developmental peak, showing:

1) *Point Lobos.*
2) *Workshops/soldier quarters.*
3) *Priest quarters.*
4) *Terminus of road from Monterey.*
5) *One of fourteen crosses along the* Via Crucis *(Latin for "Way of the Cross") between Monterey and Carmel, commemorating the Stations of the Cross.*
6) *Cemetery.*
7) *Doctor's house.*
8) *Indian adobe houses.*

9 August 1834

As an extension of overall Mexican government policy, the Mexican California Assembly passes the *Reglamento Provisional* (*Provisional Regulation*), a decree of secularization authorizing civil confiscation of all California mission properties. Mission Carmel is inventoried by Father José Suárez del Real, last resident missionary (who remains until 1840), and assessed at "46,022 *pesos, 7 reales,* and 10 *granos.*"[17]

3 January 1836

Nineteen-year old American Harvard undergraduate/temporary seaman Richard Henry Dana, Jr. provides a record of Mission Carmel hospitality:

> On Sunday morning, . . . we procured horses, and rode out to Carmel Mission, . . . where we got something in the way of a dinner—beef, eggs, *frijoles, tortillas,* and some middling wine—from the *mayordomo* [majordomo, a soldier-overseer] who, of course, refused to make any charge, as it was the Lord's gift, yet received our present, as a gratuity, with a low bow, a touch of the hat, and *Dios se lo pague!* [May God reward you!][18]

18 October 1837

The French exploratory frigate *Venus* anchors at Monterey, and commander Abel Du Petit-Thouars makes a side-trip to Mission Carmel:

> Upon our arrival at the mission of San Carlos we were struck by the solitude of the place and by the state of ruin in which the buildings were found. . . . A large wooden cross still stood in the center of this enclosure. . . . We saw no one upon entering the court of the mission: it was deserted! . . . On visiting the part at the north of the mission we entered a large room, dark and without furniture, where we met Father José María del Real, the sole surviving ecclesiastic at the mission. . . . Afterwards we went to visit the church. . . . Upon entering the chapel I noticed several paintings on wood which represented subjects delineated in the holy scriptures; but my attention was particularly attracted by the sight of a large painting of *San Isidro el Labrador* [*St. Isidore the Laborer*], which is at the left upon entering the chapel [and still hangs on the left side of the nave]. It was hanging at an angle by one of the upper corners of the frame. In this position the saint and his plough looked upside down. . . . The reverend father, in a tone of great sorrow and in a deep voice, informed me that during an earthquake this picture had been thus disarranged and that surely this catastrophe had been the manifestation of the will of God and a definite prediction of the ruin of the missions.[19]

25 April 1840

Thomas J. Farnham, an American lawyer from Illinois, visits Mission Carmel and writes:

> The valley of the mission is a charming one . . . and in its bends are many stately groves, between which lie the forsaken fields of the missions, overgrown with wild grass and brush. . . . Here and there is found an Indian hut, with its tiled roof, mud walls and floor, tenanted, but falling into decay. . . . There was an outside stairway to the tower of the church. We ascended it . . . and saw the ruined mission of San Carmelo. . . . On the timbers overhead, hung six bells of different sizes—three of them cracked and toneless. . . . The walls of the church are of stone masonry; the roof of brick tiles. . . . An oaken arm-chair, brown and marred with age, stood on the piazza, proclaiming to our lady of Guadaloupe [*sic*] [Guadalupe] and a group of saints rudely sketched upon the walls, that Carmelo was deserted by living men.[20]

27 April 1840

The Diocese of Both Californias is established by Papal decree. Most Rev. Francisco García Diego y Moreno, O.F.M., will be installed as first bishop in Mexico City's Basilica of Our Lady of Guadalupe on 4 October, arrive in San Diego on 10 December 1841, and reside in Santa Barbara, the diocesan See.

January 1846

Mission Carmel and furnishings are slated to be auctioned (which is postponed and does not take place), squatters begin to occupy the premises, and Monterey residents help themselves to mission *adobe* bricks, roof tiles, and timbers for their homes. William Garner, American correspondent for the Philadelphia *North American and United States Gazette*, writes:

> Redwood . . . is not subject to the worms. . . . I have seen some of it taken out of the old buildings in the mission of San Carlos, . . . and it appears in every respect as sound as the day it was hewn out of the tree. It makes most excellent shingles, perhaps the best in the world.[21]

7 July 1846

Under the direction of Commodore John D. Sloat, Commander of the Pacific Squadron of the United States Navy, the American flag is raised at Monterey during the war with Mexico (May 1846—February 1848).

2 February 1848

The signing of the Treaty of Guadalupe Hidalgo ends the Mexican War, and California is formally ceded to the United States.

October 1849

New York *Tribune* correspondent Bayard Taylor, an observer at Monterey's convention to draft a new California State Constitution, describes nearby Mission Carmel:

> The mission building is in the form of a hollow square, with a spacious court-yard, over-looked by a heavy belfry and chapel-dome of sun-dried bricks. The outbuildings of the Indian retainers and the corrals of earth that once herded thousands of cattle, are broken down and tenantless. We climbed into the tower and struck the fine old Spanish bells, but the sound called no faces into the blank windows. . . . The interior of the church was lofty, the ceiling, a rude attempt at a Gothic arch, and the shrine a faded mass of gilding and paint, with some monkish portraits of saints. A sort of side-chapel near the entrance was painted in Latin mottos and arabesque scrolls. . . . The walls were hung with portraits of saints, some black and white, some holding croziers, some playing violins, and some baptizing Indians. Near the altar is the tomb of Padre Junipero Serra, the founder of Monterey, and the zealous pioneer in the settlement and civilization of California.[22]

9 September 1850

California is admitted to the Union as the thirty-first state.

67. California grizzly bear cub resting at Serra's feet, symbol of the nascent State of California that he nurtured at birth. Detail from Mission Carmel's Serra Cenotaph. 20" x 7" x 7-1/2" tall.

Winter 1852

All movable Mission Carmel church goods are taken to Monterey's Royal Presidio Chapel. The heavy stone/wood/tile roof begins to collapse, and the interior is badly damaged and exposed to the elements. Services are limited to one Mass per year, held in the sacristy on the 4 November Feast of Saint Charles Borromeo, "San Carlos Day."

10-12 March 1856

Prompted by an awakening of interest in California's past, and requested by Most Rev. Joseph Alemany, Archbishop of San Francisco, the pastor of Monterey's Royal Presidio Chapel, Rev. Cayetano Sorrentini, spends three days attempting to reestablish the location of Serra's forgotten grave at Mission Carmel. Assisted by Francisco Pacheco and other interested parishoners, he concentrates "where Mr. Pacheco and other longtime inhabitants indicated as points to be examined."[23] Several twelve foot deep trenches produce nothing on the first day. The second day yields

> vaults [near the sanctuary on the Epistle side] in which were found various coffins as many as three in each and the greater part of the remains wearing habits of religious [Franciscan tertiaries], we continued excavating, and then we found the grave of a governor [José Antonio Romeau, governor from 1791 until his death in April 1792], his wife, and child.[24]

On the third day he clears

> all the earth which was in the area of the main altar on the Gospel side. . . . We found a vault well sealed in which there was a coffin wherein were the remains of a priest wearing a stole and garments in a good state of preservation, as may be seen from the fact that the stole had braid of fine gold. This finding of a priest so richly vested, a thing which none of the others had [the day before,] convinces me that perhaps there are the remains of the one for whom we are looking [Serra]. . . . I considered it prudent to cover the said vault and the said exterior with stones and earth so that the devil would not tempt the squatters to do the same to the ashes of those remains as they did to the holy water and baptismal fonts, the altars and confessionals.[25]

In 1882 Sorrentini will clarify what he found: "I unearthed and discovered for the first time the bodies of the four pioneer fathers buried there, one of whom I believed to be the sacred remains of the Apostle, Father Junípero Serra."[26]

112

19 October 1859

Following a decision by the United States Land Commission, President Buchanan signs the patent that confirms Catholic Church ownership of Mission Carmel and a fraction of its original land (nine acres), described as:

> The Church and the buildings adjoining the same erected on three sides of a quadrangle, being the same known as the Church and Mission Buildings of the Mission of El Carmelo situated in Monterey County, together with the land on which the same are erected and curtilage and appurtenances thereto belonging and also the Cemetery adjoining the same, with the limits fixed and defined by the stone wall enclosing the same. Also the garden of said Mission which is situated about southeast from said Church, with the limits as the same is enclosed by the hedge of willows surrounding it.[27]

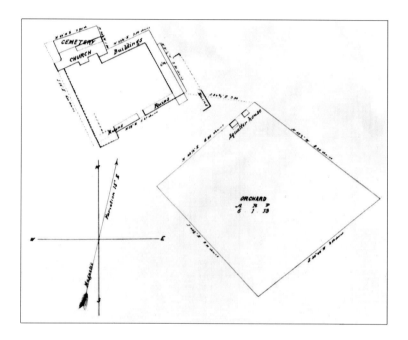

Mission Carmel church/compound, 1859. From original U.S. government survey of land restored to the Catholic Church.

31 May 1861

Geologist William H. Brewer, Principal Assistant to the Whitney Geological Survey of California, notes the condition of Mission Carmel:

> The main [church] entrance was quite fine, the stone doorway finely cut. The doors, of cedar, lay nearby on the ground. . . . About half of the roof had fallen in, the rest was good. The paintings and inscriptions on the walls were mostly obliterated. Cattle had free access to all parts; the broken font, finely carved in stone, lay in a corner; broken columns were strewn around where the altar was; and a very large owl flew frightened from its nest over the high altar. I dismounted, tied my mule to a broken pillar, climbed over the rubbish to the altar, and passed into the sacristy. There were remnants of an old shrine and niches for images. A dead pig lay beneath the finely carved font for holy water. I went into the next room, which had very thick walls—four and a half feet thick—and a single small window, barred with stout iron bars. Heavy stones led from here, through a passage in the thick wall,

to the pulpit. As I started to ascend, a very large owl flew out of a nook. Thousands of birds, apparently, lived in nooks of the old deserted walls of the ruins, and the number of ground squirrels burrowing in the old mounds made by the crumbling *adobe* walls and the deserted *adobe* houses was incredible—we must have seen "thousands" in the aggregate. This seems a big story, but "hundreds" were in sight at once. The old garden was now a barley field, but there were many fine pear trees left, now full of young fruit. Roses bloomed luxuriantly in the deserted places, and geraniums flourished as rank "weeds." So have passed away former wealth and power even in this new country.[28]

24 November 1863

Sesquicentennial of Serra's birth.

1870

Rev. Angelo Casanova, Royal Presidio Chapel Pastor, hires Portuguese whaler Christiano Machado as resident caretaker of Mission Carmel. Machado repairs the "orchard *adobe*" house, cultivates the original pear orchard, and begins clearing three to four feet of dirt, weeds and debris from within the church.

68. *Mission Carmel interior, c. 1870. Cross on left marks approximate site of Serra's grave. Rooted pine trees initially introduced as San Carlos Day decorations.*

August 1877

"So that Mass could be said there on San Carlos Day and on other occasions,"[29] Casanova re-roofs Mission Carmel's sacristy at a cost of $44.

Robert Louis Stevenson attends San Carlos Day Mass at Mission Carmel, and writes:

> The church is roofless and ruinous, sea-breezes and sea-fogs, and the alteration of the rain and sunshine, daily widening the breaches and casting the crockets from the wall. . . . Only one day in the year, . . . the *"padre"* drives over the hill from Monterey; the little sacristy, which is the only covered portion of the church, is filled with seats and decorated for the service; the Indians troop together, their bright dresses contrasting with their dark and melancholy faces; and there, . . . you may hear God served with perhaps more touching circumstances than in any other temple under heaven. An Indian, stone-blind and about eighty years of age, conducts the singing; other Indians compose the choir; yet they have the Gregorian music at their finger ends, and pronounce the Latin so correctly that I could follow the meaning as they sang. . . . I have never seen faces more vividly lit up with joy than the faces of these Indian singers. It was to them not only the worship of God, nor an act by which they recalled and commemorated better days, but was besides an exercise of culture, where all they knew of art and letters was united and expressed.[30]

69. *Mission Carmel with shingled sacristy, c.1877.*

1880

Casanova begins charging tourists ten cents each to view the ruins of Mission Carmel. Setting the money aside for a proposed "restoration," he writes: "When this will be possible God knows."[31] He raises $11.75 the first year.

14 January 1882

Using Serra's death entry in Mission Carmel's *Libro de Difuntos* as a guide, Casanova privately:

> locates the spot, . . . as near as it was possible to tell, right over Serra's grave. After digging down about three feet through accumulated dirt and rubbish the pick, in the hands of the workman, struck a board and immediately surmising that this was what he sought, he went to work carefully and uncovered several redwood boards set in evenly, and immediately

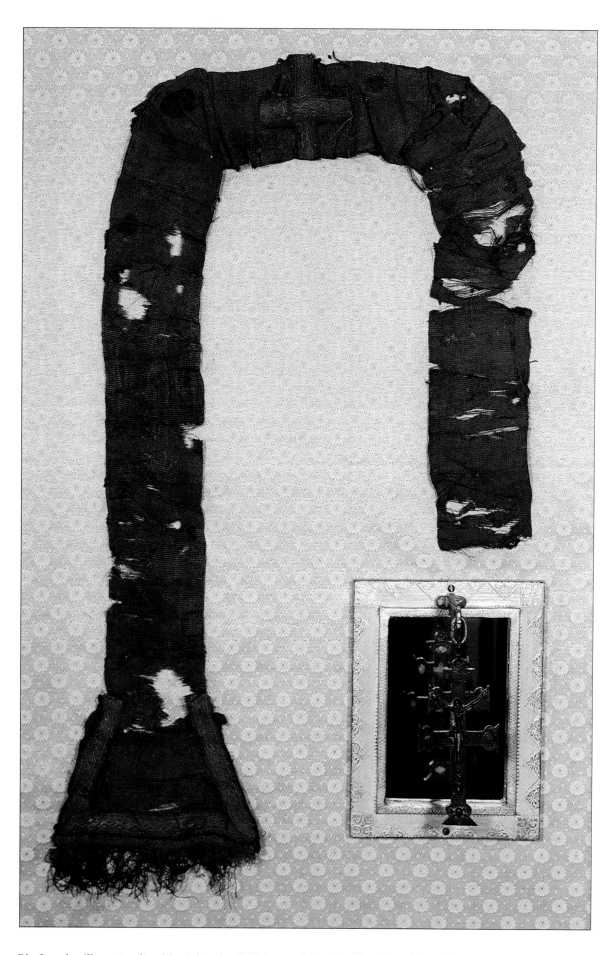

70. *Serra's silk, cotton-lined burial stole. 4' 8" long x 3" wide. 6" wide at fringe (see page 135 for burial reliquary cross).*

over stones, which evidently covered a grave. The coffin had been placed in a narrow tomb which was covered with stone slabs, and over the slabs were the boards struck by the workman while digging. One of the stone slabs at the foot of the grave was broken, and the weight of the dirt and rubbish above had forced the board covering the slab to give way, filling the foot of the coffin with earth. The upper portion or head of the coffin, and contents, were in a splendid state of preservation. . . . The tibiae of the legs were calcined, the ribs of the breast were arched, yet not fallen in, the skull was unbroken and intact, and pieces of the stole (violet color) and fringes were taken up, and I [Casanova] have preserved them. After this discovery . . . the man I have there to take care of the place [Machado] reported two more graves discovered, precisely as the records say of the two other friars there buried, both in the sanctuary and on the Gospel side.[32]

Serra Stole Chronology

Key

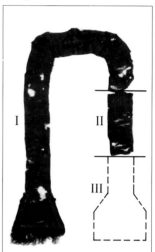

14 January 1882

Casanova removes Serra's stole from his grave.

3 July 1882

Along with the other stoles found on this day, Casanova cuts section III of Serra's stole into very small pieces and distributes them to those in attendance at the public viewing. He cuts off section II for Mr. and Mrs. Machado, devoted admirers of Serra. He displays section I at the Royal Presidio Chapel in Monterey.

1882-1893

Sometime before his death in 1893, Casanova places section I in Machado's custody.

1906

During a serious illness, Machado receives several visits from friend and fellow-Portuguese countryman Right Rev. Msgr. Henrique Ribeiro, pastor of Five Wounds Church in San Jose. Machado entrusts section I to Ribeiro, who takes it to San Jose. Machado may have done this because

> he and Fr. Mestres [Casanova's successor as Royal Presidio Chapel pastor] had some difficulty in regard to Fr. Mestres taking old pictures and relics away from Carmel Mission. He may have given the larger piece to Monsignor Ribeiro for safekeeping.[33]

1930

Having inherited it from her parents, Mary Ann Machado Goold gives section II to Rev. Michael Murphy, first Mission Carmel resident priest (from 1929-33). She also returns the "Serra discipline" at this time.

1933

Father Murphy turns section II over to Harry Downie, Mission Carmel Curator.

September 1938

Sparked by Serra cell-rededication publicity, and a call for the return of Mission Carmel property, the sexton at Five Wounds Church (Monsignor Ribeiro's nephew, Frank Bettencourt) returns section I to Mission Carmel. Downie compares section I and section II. The fabric, texture, and color match. Mrs. Goold identifies section I as part of the original.

September 1945

Downie obtains a small piece of section III, accompanied by a letter of authenticity written by Casanova in 1882. Sections I, II, and III match.

3 July 1882

"After giving notice in the papers of San Francisco, over 400 people from the city, and from the [Monterey] Hotel Del Monte, at the hour appointed, went to [Mission] Carmelo:"[34]

> To satisfy the desires of many people who wanted to see the graves of the Reverend Fathers buried in the sanctuary of the Church of San Carlos in Carmel, and to determine by means of the very burial registers their location and remains, we [Casanova and Machado] opened the graves and found the remains in a good state of preservation. Three of the deceased were wearing their violet stoles still in a very good state and (in one vault) one coffin was resting above another, the top coffin lying to one side (a person had already examined the tombs and perhaps could not place the coffin back again in place with care). Others say that Father Cayetano Sorrentini in the year 1856 also found the vault and, disturbed by one of the squatters who had taken possession of the orchard (which was held for about twelve years), ordered it to be replaced as it was, and the coffins covered quickly and in the best manner the workers were able to do it. The stoles we found them wearing on July 3 we took up and distributed pieces of them as mementos which the people desired. It appeared that

71. Mission Carmel, 3 July 1882, showing extent of roof and structural damage.

the bodies had been buried in lime, for there was much lime in the coffins and the remains were, one might say, encased in it. . . . After the examination of the remains we again covered the vaults with the same stone slabs which they had before. The vault in the middle, because there were not sufficient stone[s] to cover it, we filled with earth and it was covered like the others with the same stone flags. In order to bear witness of this investigation, I sign my name in Monterey, this Fourth of July, 1882. Angelo D. Casanova. It is to be noted that no coffin was removed or transferred.[35]

72. *3 July 1882 public viewing of Serra's grave, showing Father Casanova holding Mission Carmel's* Libro de Difuntos; *mission caretaker Christiano Machado sitting on the edge of Serra's vault; California National Guard "Legion of Saint Patrick" Cadets; California National Guard Third Regiment Band; and audience.*

1883-1884

Casanova's fundraising campaign and "restoration" project continues. Most Rev. Francis Mora, Bishop of Monterey-Los Angeles, contributes $500, part of $4,000 raised by June 1883. More is needed, and "irrespective of creeds," a statewide campaign for additional funds is launched, endorsed by California Governor George Stoneman, four ex-governors, the mayors of San Francisco and Los Angeles, and fifty prominent citizens. A proclamation addressed "to the people of California" asks that

> this building, one of the first fruits of civilization in our beloved state, may be restored, and the centennial anniversary of Junípero Serra's death commemorated in a manner worthy of the good pioneer priest.[36]

With the money received, Casanova installs a new ceiling and high-pitched roof, seventeen-feet higher than the original tile roof. Also, new doors, iron gates, stained glass for the façade star window, and among several interior "restoration" projects, burying the sanctuary graves underneath a foot of concrete and stone when he raises the level of the sanctuary floor.

28 August 1884

Centennial of Serra's death. "Fully 2,000" attend Mission Carmel's rededication, including Governor Stoneman, General Mariano Vallejo, four bishops, and "some old, old Indian[s], . . . wrinkled like pippins, . . . in their brightest colored garments."[37] Ceremonies begin at 10:45 a.m. with an outdoor procession of

> altar boys, swinging censers and bearing holy water; then Archbishop Alemany in full robes, and miter, the two chief Franciscans (P. Ferdinand Bergemeyer of Indianapolis, Visitor-General of the Franciscan Order in the United States, and Father Romo, Superior of the Franciscan Convent at Santa Barbara) bearing the embroidered hem of his garment. He sprinkles the walls as he proceeds, and is followed by the clergy in canonicals. . . . The circuit of the building having been as nearly completed as possible, room for his Grace is called at the main entrance and the procession enters the church and passes up to the altar, intoning the litany. . . . A catafalque covered with black velvet and the *Mementi Mori* (*Memento for the Dead*, a prayer of remembrance) which had stood before the steps of the chancel [sanctuary], is now borne into the sacristy and the pontifical requiem mass is begun.[38]

Several addresses follow the Mass until 4 p.m., with a break at 1 p.m. for an

> ox roast . . . barbecue . . . held within an *adobe* ruin across the enclosure and . . . under the management of the Santa Clara [present Santa Clara University] collegians. . . . The various booths, too, did a flourishing business. . . . Much listening had made the people thirsty and keg after keg [of beer] was thrown aside with nothing left of its contents.[39]

At another booth

> not twenty yards from the main entrance, were three-card monte, Spanish monte, chuck-a-luck and other games prohibited by law. These games proved more attractive to their votaries than the solemn chant of the priests or the ritual that accompanied the ceremonies of blessing the sacred shrine.[40]

73. Serra centennial "pilgrims" arriving at Mission Carmel, 28 August 1884. Note Casanova's new high-pitched roof.

74. "Pilgrims" at Serra centennial celebration. Members of Monterey Hilby family include Mr. and Mrs. Francis M. Hilby, Jr. (far right), and Mrs. Agatha Hilby Few (fourth from right).

75. Schumacher Crayon Serra portrait, excerpted from Serra's Viaticum by San Francisco artist Arthur Nahl, and executed at the Los Angeles studio of Frank G. Schumacher in 1884.

76. Mission Carmel, c. 1885.

3 June 1891

The "pretty old town" of Monterey is "elaborately decorated. . . . All along the principal streets pine and cypress boughs . . . [are] interlaced, and there [is] a goodly show of bunting.[41] The occasion is the unveiling of the world's first public Serra monument, a granite statue of Serra located on Monterey's Presidio Hill. Spectators begin arriving "almost before dawn . . . [in] the smartest of smart phaetons, . . . [in] wagons, . . . on horseback, . . . [and] on foot.[42] By 11 a.m. more than 5,000 people crowd the grassy knoll approximately 100 yards from the Vizcaíno-Serra landing site, and after several speakers eulogize Serra, Casanova says: "We are here to do honor to Father Junipero Serra. Mrs. Stanford has presented us with this monument and now it shall be seen."[43] To the strains of *Hail Columbia*, four baby hands pull the flag aside [belonging to five-year old María Antonia Field and her four-year old brother Estéban, members of Monterey's pioneer Munras family]. The banners dropped about the base of the statue and the figure of the hero priest glistened in the sun.[44]

77. Stanford Serra monument shortly after dedication, c. 1891. Donated by Jane (Mrs. Leland) Stanford, and sculpted from a sixteen-ton block of Crystal Lake granite by Peter Bisson, Jr. at Western Granite and Marble Company, San Jose (exact source of Serra's facial features unknown). The cross in the boat bears the date of Monterey-Carmel's 3 June 1770 founding, and Serra's book is inscribed Scripta Sacra *(Sacred Scripture). The legend contains two errors: Mission Santa Clara was founded on 12 January 1777, and Mission San Buenaventura on 31 March 1782. 9'6" tall, 9'6" x 6'8" base.*

6 July 1904

The oak tree under which Serra said Monterey's founding Mass on 3 June 1770 is declared

dead. In former years the waters of the bay came up to the historic landing place where the tree stands, at the mouth of a small ravine [just south of the present Artillery Street entrance to the Monterey Presidio]. The building up of the railroad embankment [1889] and the road to Pacific Grove shut out the surf, and water coming down the ravine in winter was drained to the bay through a culvert [now under present Pacific Street/Lighthouse Avenue]. The collapse of this culvert last winter caused the water to back up about the roots of the tree, where it stood for several months. The backing up of this water has resulted in the death of the old tree, which stood for so long as a living monument commemorating the coming of Viscaino [*sic*], . . . and of Serra, the man who brought civilization to the west.[45]

122

78. *Vizcaíno-Serra* Quercus agrifolia *(coast live oak) in full growth, c. 1880 (looking west).*

79. *Vizcaíno-Serra oak, rivulet, culvert, and commemorative cross, c. 1900 (looking east toward Monterey Harbor).*

4 October 1905

The Vizcaíno-Serra oak

is being preserved through the efforts of H. [Harry] A. Greene, who has always taken a great interest in the landmarks of the romantic history of early California. . . . The trunk is being preserved with crude oil and creosote. Where the trunk has been eaten away, it is being filled with concrete, and a wire frame holds trunk and branches. The whole thing will be mounted on a concrete pedestal, and, for the present at least, will be kept in the rear of San Carlos Church [Royal Presidio Chapel, Monterey]. W. K. Yorston is doing the work [for the Chapel's Pastor, Rev. Ramón Mestres]. The old tree is probably the most noteworthy of California's landmarks, and the effort to preserve it the most praiseworthy that has been made.[46]

80. Vizcaíno-Serra oak tree stump at present location, rear of Royal Presidio Chapel, c. 1906. Rev. Ramón Mestres, Pastor, stands near plaque inscribed:

The Junipero Oak. At Monterey, June 3rd, 1770. The ceremony of taking possession of California for Spain was enacted by Father Junipero Serra under the shade of this tree. Placed here for preservation by R. Mestres, H. A. Greene, 1905.

24 March 1908

As reported in the *Monterey Daily Cypress*, a

monument given by James A. Murray to mark the landing place of Father Junipero Serra is being placed in position. It arrived yesterday from San Francisco, and most of the day was occupied in unloading it and hauling it to where it is to be erected. It is a granite shaft sixteen [*sic*] [twelve] feet long and about four feet square. It is the largest piece of granite ever brought to Monterey county. Heavy trucks and sixteen horses were required in its transportation. The monument is in the shape of a shaft. On its face is a raised cross . . . [and] the face of Junipero Serra. At the foot of the cross is a carving of Carmel Mission. It bears the simple inscription "[Junipero] Serra." The monument will be in place about Saturday [28 March] but it will not be unveiled until June third, the anniversary of the landing of the Franciscan father.[47]

81. Celtic Cross marking approximate site of Vizcaíno-Serra oak tree and Serra's 1770 landing site shortly after its dedication, c. June 1908. Bas-relief of Serra (which won a gold-medal at Seattle's 1909 Alaska-Yukon Exposition, 15" diameter) by Oakland deaf-mute sculptor Douglas Tilden (exact source of Serra's facial features unknown). Mission Carmel at base (22" x 19," with proper roofline) most likely also by Tilden. The monument was executed by M. T. Carroll and Sons Co., Colma, from a fifteen-ton block of Vermont granite. 11'10" x 4'5" x 2.'

24 November 1913

Bicentennial of Serra's birth. "In weather that reached the acme of . . . perfection, . . . more than 2,000 pilgrims"[48] attend a Mission Carmel Mass and celebration, filling "the sacred edifice to overflowing. The altar before the gospel side of which is the tomb of Serra, was blazing with candles and thickly decorated with flowers."[49] Telegrams arrive from King Alfonso XIII of Spain, and the Bishop of Mallorca. California Governor Hiram Johnson declares the date "Serra Day," and proclaims: "To the memory of Junípero Serra, California owes an everlasting tribute. He brought civilization to our land, and in deed and character he deserves a foremost place in the history of our state."[50]

82. Mission Carmel "pilgrims" celebrating bicentennial of Serra's birth one day early, Sunday 23 November 1913.

83. Mission Carmel interior, c. 1915, showing the Casanova-Mestres restoration efforts. The original corpus was returned from Monterey (with a new cross) and placed in the original reredos ventilation niche. Casanova had the two small windows cut, also note new marble altar, altar rail, pulpit, ceiling, plastered walls, and plank floor.

24 November 1919

Mestres breaks ground for reconstruction of Mission Carmel's "Serra cell." He erroneously estimates that the cell is closer to the church than originally located, and accordingly places the commemorative cross in the wrong place.[51]

84. Serra cell groundbreaking ceremony, 24 November 1919.

85. *Quadrangle ruins viewed from the belltower, c.1920. Cross marks approximate site of Serra's cell. A more accurate marking would be farther back toward the fence, and to the left near the adobe ruins.*

2 October 1921

Mestres baptizes Alejandro, Berthold, and Juan Onesimo, the last full-blooded Carmel Valley Rumsen Indians (the Onesimo surname was adopted from their great-grandfather Onesimo Antonio, who was baptized at Mission Carmel on 17 February 1796). Afterward, a cornerstone ceremony marks the location of the future "Serra Cenotaph Room," site of the original mission living/reception room.

86. Onesimo family at Serra Cenotaph Room cornerstone ceremony, 2 October 1921. Manuel Onesimo and grandson Berthold, bearing cornerstone. Alejandro stands at far right.

12 October 1924

The Serra Cenotaph is unveiled. Bronze figures designed and executed at Mission Carmel by sculptor Joseph Mora (1876-1943) depict the recumbent Serra (based on a composite of the San Fernando,

Serra's Viaticum, and Palou Woodcut Serra portraits) attended by Crespí, with Lasuén and López kneeling at his feet.[52] The California travertine-marble base depicts scenes from Serra's life.

87. Sculptor Joseph Mora at unveiling of Serra Cenotaph, 12 October 1924, which he considered "the supreme professional effort in my life."[53] Large crucifix in background also designed by Mora, with figures of Christ (top), Saint Francis of Assisi (left), Saint Anthony of Padua (right), and Saint Charles Borromeo (bottom). Note six silver Loreto candlesticks, two altar cards, and missal stand on altar. They were still kept at Monterey's Royal Presidio Chapel, but had been brought to Mission Carmel for the unveiling.

1 March 1931

Pursuant to an 1864 Act of Congress that created a national statuary hall and invited each state to donate two statues (in bronze or marble) of citizens "illustrious for their renown because of distinguished civil or military service, . . . [and] worthy of . . . national commemoration,"[54] a statue of Serra is unveiled in Statuary Hall, the U.S. Capitol Building, Washington, D.C. The Congressional delegation from California includes U.S. Senator Hiram Johnson, U.S. Senator Samuel Shortridge, ten Congressmen and one Congresswoman. U.S. Secretary of the Interior Ray L. Wilbur, "speaking on behalf of President Hoover," says:

> Junípero Serra, imbued with divine spirit, charged with an exalted mission and sustained by an unfaltering faith, . . . [carried] the message of salvation over unknown paths along the unchartered shores of the Pacific. . . . He was the torch bearer of civilization. . . . The tide of

mental enlightenment and spiritual uplift that followed in his wake still rises with the passing of years. His name is reverent, his work enduring, his influence is ever living.[55]

88. Bronze statue of Serra shortly before shipment to Washington, D.C., late 1930. Designed and executed by sculptor Ettore Cadorin of Santa Barbara, and based on the San Fernando Serra portrait. Serra holds a miniature replica of Mission Carmel with Casanova's 1884-1936 high-pitched roof. 8′ 9," and displayed in the Hall on a 3′ 6" marble base with the simple inscription: "Junipero Serra—California."

27 October 1933

Mission Carmel is granted parish church status, ending eighty years of dependence on the Royal Presidio Chapel, Monterey.

89. Mission Carmel sanctuary graves, c. 1931. Contemporary statue of Saint Thérèse of Lisieux. Memorial plaque on wall installed by Casanova, c. 1884 (removed 1943). Latin inscription translates:

Here repose the earthly remains of the Very Reverend Father Junípero Serra, O. [Order of] S. [Saint] F. [Francis], Founder and President of the California Missions who was peacefully interred here on 28 August 1784. Together with his associates R.R.P.P. [Reverend Fathers] Juan Crespí, Julian López and Francisco Lasuén. May they rest in peace.

28 August 1934

Sesquicentennial of Serra's death. The California State Senate declares 28 August 1934 "Junípero Serra Day." Most Rev. Philip Scher, D.D., Bishop of Monterey-Fresno, and Very Rev. Novatus Benzig, O.F.M., Provincial of the Franciscan Province of Santa Barbara, formally propose Serra as a candidate for sainthood to Rome's Sacred Congregation of Rites. Rev. Augustine Hobrecht, O.F.M. is appointed first "vice-postulator" to coordinate and promote the "Serra Cause."

5 July 1936

A Solemn Pontifical Mass is celebrated at Mission Carmel by Bishop Scher, marking the reopening of the church after extensive restoration, which included installation of a new tile roof and vaulted ceiling, returning the roofline to its original appearance.

90. Mission Carmel during re-roofing, May 1936, and with new tile roof, July 1936.

91. Mission Carmel museum display, c. 1937. Note Serra Indian Reliquary on earlier base than present, although probably not the original.

29 August 1937

After a Solemn High Mass at Mission Carmel, Serra's restored cell is blessed and dedicated. Rev. Augustine Hobrecht, O.F.M., Serra Cause Vice-Postulator, delivers a speech about Serra's "life and labors," and members of the Indian Onesimo family place a wreath of flowers on his replica bed of planks. Afterward, "as a happy and blessed ending to the day, solemn Benediction of the Blessed Sacrament . . . [is] given at the grave of Fr. Serra."[56]

7 May 1943

Mission Carmel Curator Harry Downie begins preliminary work to lower the church sanctuary floor to its original level. He locates the foundation of the fifth mission church of *adobe* in which Serra was buried. He begins to examine the two coffins in the vault nearest the wall of the church, but is prevented from opening the central vault because Bishop Scher has ordered a canonically recognized exhumation of Serra's remains as part of his canonization process.

30 August—7 December 1943

Serra's secret canonical exhumation begins. As preparatory work on 30-31 August, Downie uses a compressor to break through the heavy stone slabs and concrete placed over the three sanctuary vaults by Casanova in 1883. He carefully removes and saves the dirt Casanova placed in the central vault, which was filled within inches of the top. On the morning of 1 September, with the church doors locked, the sanctuary draped from view, the tombs covered and canonically secured with wax seals, and the "oath of fidelity and secrecy" administered by Very Rev. John Durkin, V.F., Bishop's Delegate, and Rev. Lucien Arvin, Promoter of the Faith, the official proceedings begin with the assistance of: Rev. Constantine Badeson, Notary; Rev. Eric O' Brien, O.F.M, Serra Cause Vice-Postulator; Major Richard F. Berg., M.D., U.S.A., Fort Ord, and Clemens Naglemann, M.D., both recorded on the official list of those present as "skilled anatomical physicians;" Rev. Maynard Geiger, O.F.M., Ph.D., Mission Santa Bárbara Archivist and Historian of the Franciscan Province of Santa Barbara; Harry Downie, "custodian of the church and sepulcher . . . [and] skilled workman;" several "witnesses designated to point out the traditional site of Serra's burial," including "Joseph Mora, skilled artisan, . . . George Marion, retired actor, . . . and Mrs. Mary Goold, daughter of Christian Machado;"[57] Sergeant Joe Hinojos, U.S.A., Fort Ord, official photographer; and several "supplementary witnesses" and church officials also present on the first day. As the investigation proceeds, two anthropologists are called in to assist in identifying the remains: Theodore McCown, Ph.D., Professor of Anthropology, University of California, Berkeley; and Mark Harrington, Ph.D., Curator, Southwest Museum, Los Angeles.

Vault Key

92. Mission Carmel sanctuary graves shortly before Serra's exhumation, c. 1943. Natural tree-growth cross marks Serra's grave.

VAULT I (each vault measures 7′ long x 2′ 4″ wide x 5′ 2″ deep) yields the remains of three bodies:

A) Julian López: Mission Carmel's *Libro de Difuntos* clearly states that he was buried in this vault on 16 July 1797.

B) Juan de la Guerra y Carrillo: A well-preserved skeleton in a newer coffin poses initial confusion. The mystery unravels when Mary Ann Goold, Christiano Machado's daughter, recalls that during the private January 1882 Casanova opening, a man wearing a black suit was discovered in vault I. Unable to offer an explanation at that time, Casanova had her father burn the suit to avoid detracting from the credibility of Serra's burial place. With this information, Downie searches Mission Carmel's *Libro de Difuntos*, and entry number 2,851 solves the mystery:

> On October 22, 1840, the remains of the body of the said Juan de la Guerra y Carrillo were exhumed from the cemetery of this mission of San Carlos—whose body had been (first) buried there on Sept. 6, 1833—and on the above mentioned date, his remains were placed in the church of the said mission in a sepulcher . . . the first on the Gospel side and it is covered with wood.[58]

C) Unidentified bones of a child (possibly De la Guerra family member): Machado's daughter also remembers hearing about the body of a small child in vault I. Clandestine burials often took place in the abandoned church, and before Casanova sealed the sanctuary with cement in 1884, vault I was the easiest to open.

VAULT II contains two bodies:

A) Junípero Serra: After five feet of dirt is removed, the sides of a badly deteriorated redwood coffin appear in the middle of the floor of the vault, along with a skeleton in alignment with the coffin. A small bronze reliquary cross is found with the remains. The bones are carefully removed and placed in a secretly numbered box, the same procedure used with the other skeletons. The anonymous bones are examined and studied by the two physicians and two anthropologists, and in a thirty-six-page report, Dr. McCown (an expert in identifying prehistoric and historic human remains) concludes:

Tradition, historical fact, anthropology, and archaeology combine overwhelmingly in establishing the identity of the cranium of the skeleton of Individual A as Father Serra . . . a short-statured, small-boned, white male European . . . over sixty years at death. He was about five feet, two inches tall, at the most . . . [a] small and wiry but well-proportioned man. . . . We can clearly identify Individual A of grave 2, the traditional Serra grave, as being the earthly remains of Father Junípero Serra. The only possible basis for a reinterpretation would be detailed and contradictory evidence regarding the physique and physiognomy of Fr. Serra based upon the records or upon descriptions of him by others of his contemporaries. Until and unless this is forthcoming, I believe we may consider the identification proved.[59]

B) Juan Crespí: His remains are found on the left side of the vault, next to Serra's redwood coffin. Apparently he had been moved to vault II when López was buried in vault I in 1797. The McCown report notes that

skeleton B of grave 2 . . . was taller, much stronger and with robust bones, all of them features which do not agree with what we are led to believe were the bodily characteristics of Fr. Serra. Moreover, the position of the remains is not to be ignored. The skull of B lay beside the thorax of skeleton A more or less in the region of the elbow. Moreover, the preserved part of the cranial vault lay base upward, as is evident from the photograph taken. These facts all demonstrate that B's bones, not the corpse, had been placed in the [vault] of Individual A.[60]

VAULT III holds one body:

A) Fermín Francisco de Lasuén: Mission Carmel's *Libro de Difuntos* clearly states he was buried in this vault on 27 June 1803. Neither the coffin nor the remains appear to have been disturbed, and they are left untouched.

Final interment is at 9:30 a.m. on 7 December. Juan de la Guerra and the unidentified child are placed in a newly opened vault, located between vault I and the rear wall of the sanctuary. Crespí and López are placed in new terra-cotta coffins with copper inscription plates, and placed in vault I. Serra receives a new copper coffin with an air-tight inner glass lid. At the foot of his remains, a sealed copper tube contains the following record in Latin:

The remains of the Servant of God Reverend Father Junípero Serra, Apostle of California and Founder of the Missions, buried on 29 August 1784, exhumed and identified in 1943, and reinterred in this new coffin on 7 December of the same year, by authority of the Most Reverend Philip G. Scher, Bishop of Monterey-Fresno.[61]

The coffin is canonically sealed with brass wire wound through the latches and crimped with small lead rubrics (impressed with a cross on one side, and an image of the Blessed Virgin Mary on the other), and then lowered into vault II. Lasuén remains undisturbed in vault III. All three vaults are covered with inscribed, interlocking slabs of composition stone/concrete designed and installed by Downie.

✝

Serra's Burial Reliquary Cross

Discovered during Serra's 1943 exhumation, this bronze burial reliquary cross played an important role in the scientific study to conclusively identify Serra's remains:

> There is one prime piece of . . . archaeological [evidence]. This is the reliquary found in association with the bones of burial A in grave 2. One of the neck vertebrae is stained with green by the verdigris from a bronze cross.[62]

After removal from the grave, it was:

> cleaned . . . [and with] the verdigris removed, it was found to be of bronze. Within, when opened scissors-wise, there was found more verdigris and lime. The small thin pieces of glass covering the relics were removed after which some of the writing on thin strips of

94. Reverse side of open reliquary showing nine cloth relics under glass.

◄ *93. Serra's bronze burial reliquary cross (enlarged). Actual size 4-3/4" tall (5-1/4" with eyelet) x 1-1/2" upper arm, 2-1/4" lower arm, 1" base.*

paper covering the relics could be read. One of these inscriptions read: "B. Raydi M" and another "Raydi M" both . . . meaning Blessed Raymond Lull of Mallorca.[63]

The conclusion was:

> The reliquary itself was so clearly the product of a European craftsman, probably an Italian or Spaniard, and the revelation of the object's connection with the Blessed Raymond Lull— the eponym of Serra's University of Mallorca—is evidence which no qualified archaeologist could hesitate to stress in the strongest possible way as being critical to identifying the remains with which it was found as those of a priest, a native of Mallorca.[64]

Key

1) Legend credits the medieval *cruz de Caravaca* (Caravaca cross) with winning battles and converting Moors after a supernatural vision in 1232 revealed the distinctive design to Gines Pérez, a priest imprisoned in the southern Spanish town of Caravaca during the Moslem occupation (711-1492). The cross is also associated with Saint Teresa of Avila (1515-82).
2) INRI: acronym for the Latin *Iesus Nazarenus Rex Iudaeorum* ("Pilate had an inscription placed on the Cross which read, JESUS THE NAZAREAN THE KING OF THE JEWS. The inscription in Hebrew, Latin, and Greek, was read by many." John 19:19-20).
3) Jesus on the Cross.
4) IHS: first three letters of Ihsus, the Greek word for Jesus.
5) AM: monogram for the Latin *Ave Maria, Regina* (Hail Mary, Queen).
6) Our Lady of Sorrows at the foot of the Cross.
7) Skull and crossbones: reference to Golgotha ("Jesus was led away, and carrying the cross by himself, went out to what is called the Place of the Skull (in Hebrew, Golgotha). There they crucified him." John 19:16-18); and to a medieval belief that the Cross was implanted over Adam's grave, with Christ's sacrifice serving to redeem mankind from Adam and Eve's Original Sin.

95. Serra's remains, 7 December 1943.

96. Serra's reinterment, 7 December 1943. L-R: Rev. Constantine Badeson, Notary; Rev. Eric O' Brien, O.F.M, Serra Cause Vice-Postulator; Very Rev. John Durkin, V.F., Bishop's Delegate; Rev. Michael O'Connell, Mission Carmel Pastor; Harry Downie, Mission Carmel Curator; Rev. Lucien Arvin, Promoter of the Faith; Very Rev. Gregory Wooler, O.F.M, Provincial of the Franciscan Province of Santa Barbara.

97. Mission Carmel sanctuary graves of Crespí, López, Serra, and Lasuén.

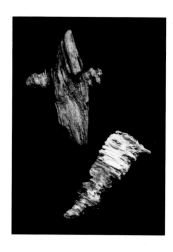

98. *Serra's grave and remnants of original 1784 redwood coffin. Epitaph reads: "Father Junípero Serra—Apostle of California—1713-1784."*

99. *Redwood-encrusted nails from Serra's original redwood coffin.*

17 December 1943

Bishop Scher institutes the Diocesan Historical Commission for the Canonization Cause of Junípero Serra, in order to gather all important historical sources concerning Serra's life, character and reputation. The three appointed members are: Herbert E. Bolton, Ph.D., Professor Emeritus of History, University of California, Berkeley; Rev. Maynard Geiger, O.F.M., Ph.D., Mission Santa Bárbara Archivist and Historian of the Franciscan Province of Santa Barbara; and Right Rev. Msgr. James Culleton, D.D., J.C.D., Chancellor-Secretary of the Diocese of Monterey-Fresno. Serra's philosophy and sacred theology lectures, sermons, diary, letters, and official reports are culled from over 100 libraries and archives in California, Mexico and Mallorca, and when combined with the canonical depositions of 200 California pioneers, a total of 7,500 pages of documents are collected.

12 December 1948—July 1949

From the historical documents and depositions, the vice-postulator draws up the *articuli*, a series of statements about Serra's virtue and sanctity to be proven in ecclesiastical court. The locked-door proceedings begin in Fresno, the Monterey-Fresno Diocesan See, where judges are empowered to interrogate witnesses with questions submitted by the promoter of the faith. The court reconvenes at Mission Carmel, with Harry Downie as the first witness, followed by several descendants of families familiar with Serra. Testimony is limited to what each person knows about Serra, for example, Abel Espinosa, 92, discusses what was handed down from his grandfather Caetano, Portolá-expedition member and contemporary of Serra. The court also holds sessions at San Gabriel, Santa Barbara, Santa Clara, and San Francisco, and in all, fifty witnesses are questioned. After final testimony by Diocesan Historical Commission members and the vice-postulator, some 8,700 pages of documents weighing half a ton are boxed, stamped with the Monterey-Fresno episcopal seal, and sent to Rome's Sacred Congregation of Rites. There they will be scrutinized to ascertain if Serra lived a life of heroic virtue, if in life and death he enjoyed a reputation for holiness and miracles, and to make sure that he has not been the object of any unauthorized religious devotion.

100. Serra Cause Canonical Court at Mission Carmel, 17 December 1948. L-R: Rev. Eric O'Brien, O.F.M., Serra Cause Vice-Postulator; Harry Downie, Mission Carmel Curator, witness; Rev. Lucien Arvin, Promoter of the Faith; Right Rev. Msgr. Michael Sullivan, Vicar General of the Diocese of Monterey-Fresno, Judge; Rev. Michael O'Connell, Mission Carmel Pastor, witness (testifying); Very Rev. James Bolger, C.Ss.R., Vice-Provincial of the Redemptorist Province of Oakland, Judge; Very Rev. Joseph O'Brien, S.J., Provincial of the Jesuit Province of California, Judge; Very Rev. Msgr. James Dowling, Notary; Rev. John Ryan, Judge. Note Our Lady of Bethlehem statue on Gospel side of altar. Statues of Our Lady of Sorrows and Saint John on either side of crucifix are copies carved by Harry Downie. The originals were returned from Montery's Royal Presidio Chapel in 1967.

April 1956

Downie finishes designing/constructing/installing Mission Carmel's new *reredos* altarpiece at his Mission Carmel workshop, built in seventeen sections over a period of seven months.

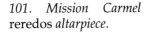

101. Mission Carmel reredos altarpiece.

26 August 1956

Arriving to a crowd of 3,000 shortly after 10 a.m. Sunday Mass ends, President and Mrs. Dwight D. Eisenhower tour Mission Carmel and visit Serra's grave. They are spending the weekend in Pebble Beach after attending the Republican National Convention in San Francisco. Right Rev. Msgr. Michael O'Connell, Mission Carmel Pastor, remarks that early mission records refer to "the experimental government of George Washington." "It was an experiment!" replies the President. "But it lasted," adds Mrs. Eisenhower.[65]

102. President and Mrs. Eisenhower at Mission Carmel, with Right Rev. Msgr Michael O'Connell, Pastor. Sisters of Charity of the Blessed Virgin Mary in background.

103. Mission Carmel by Dwight D. Eisenhower. During his visit, the President "asked photographers to record the scene in color so he could paint it later."[66] The small oil on canvas (9" x 12") was presented to Msgr. O'Connell and Mission Carmel in March 1957. The statue flanking the doorway (eighteenth-century Istrian stone Saint Francis of Assisi, donated c. 1925 along with a companion Saint Anthony of Padua) and the courtyard cross (replica commemorating the terminus of Monterey-Carmel's mission-period Via Crucis) have since been relocated to provide an unobstructed façade view.

28 August 1959

The 175th annivernsary of Serra's death. A commemorative ceremony is held in Statuary Hall, the U.S. Capitol Building, Washington, D.C. The Hon. John F. Shelley, U.S. Representative, Fifth District, delivers the following address:

> The Capitol of the United States derives a profound sense of the spiritual and the sublime in dedicated service from a simple but impressive statue of Father Junipero Serra, O.F.M. The statue embodies . . . the selflessness of this saintly Franciscan Father on his historic mission of dangerous, pioneering adventure. To achieve the greatness that immortalizes him . . . he traveled more than 8,000 miles from his native Spain, finding in Calfornia a hospitable soil and climate, both physically and spiritually, for the influence of his work and teaching. The observance of the 175th anniversary of his death, August 28, 1959, marks one of the high points in the history of the Capitol of the United States.[67]

29 May 1960

On his forty-third birthday, U.S. Senator and Mrs. John F. Kennedy attend 10 a.m. Sunday Mass at Mission Carmel, and visit Serra's grave. To the photographer who takes his picture as he enters the mission courtyard, presidential-candidate Kennedy says: "I am not in the habit of having my picture taken when I go to church."[68]

104. Senator and Mrs. Kennedy entering Mission Carmel courtyard, with friends Mr. and Mrs. Paul Fay of San Francisco.

26-27 April 1961

Two days of solemn ceremonies mark the elevation of Mission Carmel Church to the rank of minor basilica, ordered by Papal decree, to honor Mission Carmel's special historical and artistic sig-

105. Solemn Pontifical Mass at Mission Carmel Basilica, 27 April 1961. His Eminence James Cardinal McIntyre, Archbishop of Los Angeles; Most Rev. Aloysius Willinger, C.Ss.R., D.D., Bishop of Monterey-Fresno; and Most Rev. Egidio Vagnozzi, D.D., Apostolic Delegate to the United States, officiating. Note the Ombrellone *to left of altar,* Tintinnabulum *to right.*

nificance.[69] The specially designed *Tintinnabulum* and *Ombrellone* are blessed, symbols of Papal recognition that will be permanently displayed in the church.

29 May—4 June 1963

The Spanish government officially celebrates the approaching 250th anniversary of Serra's birth. Twenty distinguished Californians fly to Mallorca to attend special observances. President Kennedy sends the following telegram:

> I send best wishes to the people of Spain and particularly those gathered on Mallorca on the occasion of the 250th Anniversary of the birth of Father Junípero Serra, Founder of California. This celebration is the reminder of our Spanish heritage whose values were exemplified in the piety, courage and vision of Father Serra.[70]

Addressing a group of Mallorcans at Serra's birthplace in Petra, U.S. Supreme Court Chief Justice Earl Warren says:

> It has been said, and rightly, that the history of the world is the history of great men. This thought moves us to revere the memory of Fray Junípero Serra, so that it may persist in the minds and hearts of our people.[71]

24 November 1963

The 250th anniversary of Serra's birth. By Act of Congress signed into law by President Kennedy on 16 October 1963, a national medal is struck in honor of Serra.[72] The California State Legislature declares 24 November 1963 "Junípero Serra Day," but celebrations planned throughout the state, and most extensively at Mission Carmel, are canceled due to the assassination of President Kennedy only two days before.

106. Bronze U.S. national Junípero Serra medal designed by Chief U.S. Engraver Frank Gasparro, showing Serra as depicted in the U.S. Capitol's Statuary Hall. Reverse side erroneously attributes founding of tenth mission to Serra (Mission Santa Bárbara was founded by Lasuén on 4 December 1786, two years after Serra's death). Minted in quantities of 5 fourteen-carat gold (proof); 25 platinum (proof); 10,000 silver (1,000 proof); and 82,000 bronze (1,000 proof) at the U.S. Mint in Philadelphia. 1-5/16" actual size diameter (shown enlarged).

21 September 1966

First Lady Mrs. Lyndon B. Johnson tours Mission Carmel, and visits Serra's grave. "It is a privilege to see this enchanting spot of history," she writes in the mission's guest book. The First Lady is visiting the Monterey Peninsula as part of her "Beautify America" program, and later that day she will dedicate Big Sur's Highway 1 as the first scenic highway in California.

107. Mrs. Johnson signing Mission Carmel guest book. L-R: Stewart L. Udall, U.S. Secretary of the Interior; Harry Downie; Mrs. Edmund G. Brown, Sr.; Fred S. Farr, California State Senator; Edmund G. Brown, Sr., Governor of California; Most Rev. Harry A. Clinch, D.D., Auxiliary Bishop of Monterey-Fresno and Mission Carmel Pastor; Rev. David Hill, Pastor, All Saint's Episcopal Church, Carmel; Rev. Roger Dieudonne, Mission Carmel Assistant Pastor; and Junípero Serra School students in background. Photograph inscription reads: "To Bishop Clinch with warm appreciation for sharing with me the history and tranquility of the Carmel Mission and School—Lady Bird Johnson—September 1966."

24 November 1970

The National Conference of Catholic Bishops unanimously passes a resolution requesting His Holiness Pope Paul VI to proceed with all proper haste toward the beatification and canonization of Serra.

August 1981

The first of three volumes of the nearly 1,000-page Serra Cause *Summarium* is completed in Rome by Rev. Jacinto Fernández, O.F.M., Ph.D., Spanish-American historian from Valencia, Spain. Printed in Latin, Italian, and Spanish, and composed from the 8,700 pages of documents sent to Rome in 1949, the highly technical dissertation presents Serra as a candidate for sainthood to the Sacred Congregation for the Causes of Saints. If accepted, Serra's name will be submitted to the Pope with the petition that His Holiness declare him "Venerable," the last major step toward beatification and canonization.

Bicentennial of Serra's death. In the company of Most Rev. Pio Laghi, S.T.D., J.C.D., Apostolic Pro-Nuncio in the United States; Very Rev. John Forman, O.F.M., Minister General of the Franciscan Order; twenty-one western U.S and three Mexican bishops; and 125 other priests; His Eminence Timothy Cardinal Manning, D.D., J.C.D., Archbishop of Los Angeles, is principal celebrant and homilist for the liturgical celebration honoring Serra at Mission Carmel Basilica. In his homily he says:

> It can probably be asserted, without contradiction, that the greatest single event that has occurred since the death of Junípero Serra, two hundred years ago today, occurs in this ceremony. . . . The seed must die in order to bear fruit. . . . This holy seed, which is the mortal remains of Junípero Serra . . . lies buried here beneath us, and out of that burial has come the flowering of the Church in California. And so we, representing all of the dioceses of California, assemble here today to recognize this particular gift that God has given to this fair land, to make an affirmation of the sanctity of this holy friar, [and] to petition our Heavenly Father that the Cause of his elevation to the ranks of the beatified or the canonized may be accelerated by our presence, and certainly that this event would be brought to the notice of the Sacred Congregation.[73]

108. *Commencement of Serra Bicentennial Concelebrated Mass at Mission Carmel Basilica, 28 August 1984. L-R (seated): Most Rev. Thaddeus Shubsda, D.D., Bishop of Monterey in California; Most Rev. Pio Laghi, S.T.D., J.C.D., Apostolic Pro-Nuncio in the United States; His Eminence Timothy Cardinal Manning, D.D., J.C.D., Archbishop of Los Angeles; Most Rev. John Quinn, D.D., Archbishop of San Francisco; Most Rev. Harry Clinch, D.D., Former Bishop of Monterey in California. Altar screen/dais (designed by Monterey Diocesan Curator Richard-joseph Menn) surmounted by Diocese of Monterey in California coat of arms (bishop's mitre over Serra's 3 June 1770 Monterey founding cross, planted on hill over crown signifying See City etymology [Monte-Rey (King's Mountain)], flanked by the mission's two founding bells announcing Christianity's arrival). Note* Tintinnabulum *on left side of sanctuary,* Ombrellone *on right. Book of Gospels stands on altar.*

9 May 1985

His Holiness Pope John Paul II declares Junípero Serra "Venerable."

28 August 1985

Official closing of the international "Serra Year" marked by outdoor Mass at Mission Carmel, performed by Cardinal Manning, once again in the company of twenty-four bishops. President Reagan sends the following telegram, read by Bishop Shubsda, Chairperson and Episcopal Moderator of the Serra Bicentennial Commission:

> I am pleased to send warm greetings to everybody participating in the solemn religious ceremonies concluding the bicentennial of the Venerable Father Junípero Serra's death. Father Serra is one of the heroes of our land. His tireless work for the Indians of California, despite distances and physical disabilities that would have daunted a lesser man, remains a shining page in our history. His missions stand as a monument to his powerful religious convictions. I am proud that my own State of California has erected, in our Nation's Capitol, a statue in his honor. Mrs. Reagan joins me in wishing all of you a memorable event. God bless you.[74]

109. Outdoor Mission Carmel Concelebrated Mass marking close of "Serra Year," 28 August 1985. L-R: Most Rev. Thaddeus Shubsda, D.D., Bishop of Monterey in California; Most Rev. Roger Mahoney, D.D., Archbishop-designate of Los Angeles; His Eminence Timothy Cardinal Manning, D.D., J.C.D., Archbishop of Los Angeles; Most Rev. Harry Clinch, D.D., Former Bishop of Monterey in California; Most Rev. John Quinn, Archbishop of San Francisco. Baldachin designed by Monterey Diocesan Curator Richard-joseph Menn. Note the alleged "Serra Chalice" on altar.

Also, the U.S. Postal Service issues a forty-four cent airmail stamp honoring Serra,[75] and U.S. Postmaster General Paul N. Carlin presides at the "first day of issue" ceremony in San Diego on 22 August 1985. A special "second" day of issue is held on 28 August at Carmel.

110. Junípero Serra commemorative airmail stamp, designed by Richard Schlecht of Richmond, Virginia, and modeled by Frank Waslick of the U.S. Bureau of Engraving and Printing. The design was based on Spain's forty peseta stamp issued in October 1984, with Serra's likeness patterned after the Querétaro Serra portrait against a silhouette of Upper and Lower California, and Mission San Gabriel's campanario. The stamp won the Italian Philatelic St. Gabriel Art Prize for best religious stamp of 1985. 1.44 x .84 inches image area, 1.56 x .99 inches overall (shown enlarged).

4 November 1986

On the Feast of Saint Charles Borromeo, the Vatican Secretariat of State officially announces that His Holiness Pope John Paul II will visit Mission Carmel Basilica at 12:45 p.m. on 17 September 1987, to honor Venerable Junípero Serra and pray before his grave.

Prayer for Serra's Canonization

Eternal God, moved by the promptings of Your divine grace, Fray Junípero Serra, a priest of the Order of Friars Minor, went "ever forward" from his native Mallorca to Mexico and to California to extend the kingdom of Christ to the shores of the sunset sea. Because he planted the seeds of the true faith, watered them with his sweat and tears, and lived a life of penance petitioning You to give the people of his western rim of Christianity growth in their faith, we humbly beseech You to grant that he be found worthy to have his name entered on the list of those whom the Church calls saints. We ask this, O God, in the name of Your divine Son, Jesus. Amen.[76]

The longer it took, the more solemnly did we celebrate
Serra—31 March 1782[77]

17 September 1987

Notes

PREFACE/ACKNOWLEGMENTS

[1]Maynard J. Geiger, *The Life and Times of Fray Junípero Serra, O.F.M.*, 2 vols. (Washington, D.C.: Academy of American Franciscan History, 1959), 1:22.

[2]Maynard J. Geiger, *Palóu's Life of Fray Junípero Serra* (Washington, D.C.: Academy of American Franciscan History, 1955), p. 257. "Unfading will be his memory" (Sirach 39:9), which Palóu quoted to characterize Serra's reputation.

[3]Antonine Tibesar, ed., *Writings of Junípero Serra*, 4 vols. (Washington, D.C.: Academy of American Franciscan History, 1955-66), 1:27 (Serra to Fr. Miguel de Petra, 29 September 1758).

I. MALLORCA: 1713-1749

[1]Geiger, *The Life and Times of Fray Junípero Serra, O.F.M.*, 1:59.

[2]A duplicate baptismal register in the Mallorcan capital of Palma records Serra's arrival at 1 p.m.

[3]Serra's birthplace is now a museum open to the public. The house is

> built of stone, with a frontage of twenty-eight feet, . . . a typical farmer's house of the early 18th century. An ample doorway, with a rounded arch, served as the entrance for the mule, as well as the family. A corridor leads from the parlor, arranged with period furnishings, to a long narrow garden in the rear. That passageway divides the mule's corral on the right from the small kitchen and bedroom on the left. The second story, reached by a staircase from the parlor, contains another bedroom and an area for storage. Two small windows admit light and air. The bakeoven and woodshed are in the rear garden. Today there is a plaque on the façade of the home indicating its role in the life of its famous son, Fray Junípero Serra. [Weber, *Some Fugitive Glimpses at Fray Junípero Serra*, p. 264]

From 1932-80, the City of San Francisco, California owned legal title to Junípero Serra's birthplace. Petra's "sister city" maintained and administered the property until "Proposition 13" public-service cutbacks prompted the San Francisco Board of Supervisors to return title to the City of Petra. Carmel, California is Petra's "sister-city." The relationship was described by Rev. Noel Moholy, O.F.M., S.T.D., Serra Cause Vice-Postulator:

> It is not too unusual for some community in these United States to adopt a foreign hamlet or village . . . as a sister-city. The relationship . . . between Petra, Mallorca, and Carmel, California, however, finds historic basis, seldom, if ever equalled. . . . The secluded village of Petra on the largest of the Balearic Islands cherishes his cradle; Carmel-by-the-Sea in the most populous of the United States contains his grave. [McCarty, "Anniversary of Birth of Fray Junípero Serra," *The Americas* 20 (October 1963):204]

[4]Geiger, *Palóu's Life of Fray Junípero Serra*, p. 5.

[5]Bodo, Murray, *Juniper: Friend of Francis, Fool of God* (Cincinnati: St. Anthony Messenger Press, 1983), p.1.

[6]Serra's name does not appear on the 31 May 1737 record of ordination for his deacon class, because he had not reached the canonically required age of twenty-four. Most likely he was ordained shortly after reaching the proper age on 24 November 1737, although there are no known documents to substantiate this. He was certainly a priest by 21 February 1739, if not by the earlier date of 19 March 1738. On the former date he received faculties as diocesan confessor from the Bishop of Mallorca, and on the latter, those of preacher.

[7]Geiger, *The Life and Times of Fray Junípero Serra, O.F.M.*, 1:28.

[8]Geiger, *Palóu's Life of Fray Junípero Serra*, p. 6.

[9]Tibesar, *Writings of Junípero Serra*, 1:3 (Serra to Fr. Francesch Serra, 20 August 1749).

[10]Geiger, *Palóu's Life of Fray Junípero Serra*, p. 263.

[11]Ibid., p. 12.

[12]Geiger, *The Life and Times of Fray Junípero Serra, O.F.M.*, 1:58. Serra was only 5' 2." He was described as "of medium height" in relation to the Spanish eighteenth-century standard of height. 5' 6" to 5' 8" would have been considered tall.

[13]Ibid., pp. 59-60.

II. MEXICO: 1749-1769

[1]Tibesar, *Writings of Junípero Serra*, 1:139 (Serra to Fr. Juan Andrés, 3 July 1769).

[2]Geiger, *Palóu's Life of Fray Junípero Serra*, p. 15.

[3]Tibesar, *Writings of Junípero Serra*, 1:13 (Serra to Fr. Francesch Serra, 14 December 1749).

[4]Ibid., pp. 15, 17. Serra added:

After disembarking the ship was found to be most unseaworthy—the main mast gone and holes of such size as to make it impossible to survive another day at sea. On December 10, the celebration took place in the monastery of our Seraphic Father Saint Francis. The prior of the Dominicans sang the Mass in the presence of the two communities saved from the sea, and, despite my inability, I was appointed to preach the sermon. [Ibid., p. 17]

[5]Ibid., p. 17.

[6]Geiger, *Palóu's Life of Fray Junípero Serra*, p. 44.

[7]Ibid., p. 30.

[8]Ibid.

[9]Ibid., p. 236.

[10]In his Serra biography, Palóu recorded all that is known about this attempt on Serra's life:

One night when he [Serra] was with his companion, who is at present the Bishop of Mérida in Maracaybo, His Excellency Don Fray Juan Ramos de Lora, both were sitting on the steps at the base of the cross in the cemetery of his Mission Santiago de Jalpan. It was about eight o'clock at night, and they were enjoying the evening air. All of a sudden he [Serra] said to his companion priest: "Let us leave here. Let us go inside the house, for we are not safe here." They went inside. On the following day, they learned with certainty that a plan was afoot to take their lives, so that if they had not gone away from there, both would have been killed. [Geiger, *Palóu's Life of Fray Junípero Serra*, p. 276]

[11]Tibesar, *Writings of Junípero Serra*, 1:25 (Serra to Fr. Miguel de Petra, 29 September 1758).

[12]Palóu elaborated:

> In one of those towns in which [Serra] gave a mission, . . . when he was consuming the Precious Blood [consecrated wine], he had imbibed a heavy weight as if it were lead, so that he visibly changed color . . . and lost his speech altogether. . . . [But for] one of those attending the Mass, [he] would have fallen to the floor. They took him immediately to the sacristy, where his vestments were removed, and they placed him on a bed. As soon as the people learned of the occurrence, all believed that someone had put poison in the wine-cruet in order to kill him. . . . An antidote, . . . quite effective in such cases was offered him in a water glass and, smiling, [he] signified that he did not want to drink it. The brother, taken aback, asked him if he wanted some oil in order to empty his stomach. Giving an affirmative sign, he drank it and was then able to say a few words, the first being . . . *Si mortiferum quid biberint, non eis nocebit* [They will be able to drink deadly poison without harm (Mark 16:18)]. . . . The oil did not cause him any nausea or make him vomit, but it cured him either by virtue of its healing power or because of the faith of the venerable patient. [Geiger, *Palóu's Life of Fray Junípero Serra*, pp. 46-47]

When asked why he refused an antidote, Serra replied:

> It was not . . . because I believed in its ineffectiveness, nor because I had any horror of it, for in other circumstances I would have taken it. But I had just received the Bread of Angels [the Eucharistic Host], which by the power of Consecration ceased to be bread and was changed into the Body of my Lord Jesus Christ. . . . How could you ask me to take so nauseating a drink, after tasting the Divine Morsel which had been bread and then no longer was? [Ibid., p. 47]

[13]Entitled *Novena de Alabanzas en Honrra de la Puríssima Concepción de María SSma, con el Título de Prelada* (*Novena of Praises in Honor of the Most Pure Conception of Mary, Most Holy, bearing the title of Prelatess*), the work is a nine-day novena of prayers to the Immaculate Conception. The Novena was first published by D. Xavier Sánchez, Mexico City, 1765, and a second-edition by Don Felipe de Zúñiga y Ontiveros in 1770. Authorship is anonymous, except for title-page data that attributes the work to *"la balbuciente lengua de un menor subdito de la Sra. del Colegio Apostólico de S. Fernando la ofrece a sus devotos"* (the sweet [or child-like] tongue of a minorite [Franciscan] subject of the Seigniory [or Dominion] of the Apostolic College of San Fernando—he offers it [the novena] to its [the college's] devoted). Prominent Mexican bibliographers have interpreted this as a reference to Serra, most notably José Mariano Beristain y Souza in *Biblioteca Hispano Americana Septentrional* (*Northern American Hispanic Library*), Mexico City, 1796, and José Toribio Medina in *La Imprenta de México, 1539-1821* (*The Mexican Press, 1539-1821*), Mexico City, 1907. According to historian Francis J. Weber:

> If the *Novena* was indeed authored by Fray Junípero Serra, and its stylistic composition lends credence to that supposition, then it has the distinction of being the only one of the friar's writings published during his lifetime. [Weber, *Some Reminiscences about Fray Junípero Serra*, p. 114]

The Santa Bárbara Mission Archive-Library possesses an incomplete thirty-three page copy of the diminutive *Novena* (3" x 4"), cataloged as item number twelve in the Junípero Serra Collection of Documents.

[14]Geiger, *The Life and Times of Fray Junípero Serra, O.F.M.*, 1:201.

[15]Geiger, *Palóu's Life of Fray Junípero Serra*, p. 55.

[16]Ibid., p. 80. At this time the present San Francisco Bay lay undiscovered. Gálvez refers to "old" San Francisco Bay (present Drake's Bay), familiar through previous explorer's records.

[17]Herbert E. Bolton, *Historical Memoirs of New California*, 4 vols. (Berkeley: University of California Press, 1927), 1:64.

[18]Ibid., pp. 46, 53.

[19]Ibid., p. 56. *Palabrero* (from the Spanish *palabra* [word], and the Latin *parabola* [speech]), refers to the largest altar card in the customary set of three, containing the words of consecration and other prayers said by the priest during Mass. Mission Carmel does not presently have this card, nor do any of its secularization inventories mention it. The *palabrero* was centrally placed on the altar (altar cards are no longer used), the Saint John's Gospel card to its left (on the Gospel side of the altar), and the *lavabo* card to its right (on the Epistle side).

[20]Tibesar, *Writings of Junípero Serra*, 1:185-87 (Serra to Inspector General José de Gálvez, 2 July 1770).

[21]Translation: At the beginning of time the Word already was; and God had the Word abiding with him, and the Word was God. He abode, at the beginning of time, with God. It was through him that all things came into being, and without him came nothing that has come to be. In him there was life, and that life was the light of men. And the light shines in darkness, a darkness which was not able to master it. A man appeared, sent from God, whose name was John. He came for a witness, to bear witness to the light, so that through him all men might learn to believe. He was not the light; he was sent to bear witness to the light. There is one who enlightens every soul born into the world; he was the true Light. He, through whom the world was made, was in the world, and the world treated him as a stranger. He came to what was his own, and they who were his own gave him no welcome. But all those who did welcome him he empowered to become the children of God, all those who believe in his name; their birth came, not from human stock, not from nature's will or man's, but from God. And the Word was made flesh, and came to dwell among us; and we had sight of his glory, glory such as belongs to the Father's only-begotten Son, full of grace and truth. [Knox, trans., *The Missal in Latin and English*, p. 717]

[22]Translation: With the pure in heart I will wash my hands clean, and take my place among them at thy altar, Lord, listening there to the sound of thy praises, telling the story of all thy wonderful deeds. How well, Lord, I love thy house in its beauty, the place where thy own glory dwells! Lord, never count this soul for lost with the wicked, this life among the bloodthirsty: hands ever stained with guilt, palms ever itching for a bribe! Be it mine to guide my steps clear of wrong: deliver me in thy mercy. My feet are set on firm ground; where thy people gather, Lord, I will join in blessing thy name. Glory be to the Father, and to the Son, and to the Holy Ghost. As it was [in the beginning, is now, and ever shall be, world without end, Amen]. [Knox, trans., *The Missal in Latin and English*, p. 691]

To be added to the final Collect

And protect from all adversity our Pope, our Bishop, and our King, together with the royal offspring, the people, the army, who have been committed to your care; grant your peace in our times and drive all evil from your Church. Through Our Lord [Jesus Christ, your Son, who lives and reigns with you in the unity of the Holy Spirit, God, forever and ever. Amen.]

[23]Robert Archibald, *The Economic Aspects of the California Missions* (Washington, D.C.: Academy of American Franciscan History, 1978), p. 35.

[24]Tibesar, *Writings of Junípero Serra*, 1:145 (Serra to Fr. Francisco Palóu, 3 July 1769).

[25]Tibesar, *Writings of Junípero Serra*, 3:359 (Serra Report on the Missions, 15 August 1779).

[26]"Carmel Mission Bible to be Used by Reagan," *Monterey Peninsula Herald*, 28 December 1966, p. 1.

[27]Geiger, *Palóu's Life of Fray Junípero Serra*, p. 63.

[28]Ibid., p. 62.

[29]Bolton, *Historical Memoirs of New California*, 1:60.

[30]Tibesar, *Writings of Junípero Serra*, 1:49 (Serra Diary, 9 April 1769).

[31]Ibid., p. 367 (Serra to Viceroy Antonio Bucareli y Ursúa, 21 May 1773).

[32]Ibid., p. 51 (Serra Diary, 16 April 1769).

[33]Ibid., p. 57 (Serra Diary, 5 May 1769).

[34]Ibid., p. 59 (Serra Diary, 11 May 1769).

[35]Ibid. (Serra Diary, 12 May 1769).

[36] Ibid., p. 61 (Serra Diary, 14 May 1769).

[37] Ibid.

[38] Ibid., p. 63 (Serra Diary, 15 May 1769).

[39] Ibid., p. 65 (Serra Diary, 17 May 1769).

[40] Geiger, *Palóu's Life of Fray Junípero Serra*, p. 67.

[41] Ibid.

[42] Tibesar, *Writings of Junípero Serra*, 1:67 (Serra Diary, 19 May 1769).

[43] Ibid., p. 65 (Serra Diary, 18 May 1769).

[44] Ibid., pp. 67, 69 (Serra Diary, 21 May 1769).

[45] Ibid., p. 71 (Serra Diary, 25 May 1769).

[46] Ibid., p. 73 (Serra Diary, 26 May 1769). Serra adds that "we could not guess from where it [the ribbon] came." Possibly Rivera y Moncada's land contingent, which had already passed through the area, could have given it to the Indian.

[47] Ibid., pp. 75, 77, 79 (Serra Diary, 28 May 1769).

[48] Ibid., pp. 79, 81 (Serra Diary, 30 May 1769).

[49] Ibid., p. 83 (Serra Diary, 2 June 1769).

[50] Ibid., p. 85 (Serra Diary, 3 June 1769).

[51] Ibid., p. 87 (Serra Diary, 6 June 1769).

[52] Ibid., p. 91 (Serra Diary, 10 June 1769).

[53] Ibid.

[54] Ibid., p. 97 (Serra Diary, 14 June 1769).

[55] Ibid., p. 99 (Serra Diary, 15 June 1769).

[56] Ibid., p. 107 (Serra Diary, 22 June 1769).

[57] Ibid., (Serra Diary, 23 June 1769).

[58] Ibid., (Serra Diary, 24 June 1769).

[59] Ibid., p. 111 (Serra Diary, 26 June 1769).

[60] Ibid., p. 113 (Serra Diary, 26 June 1769).

[61] Ibid., p. 115 (Serra Diary, 27 June 1769).

[62] Ibid.

[63] Ibid., p. 135 (Serra to Fr. Juan Andrés, 3 July 1769).

III. CALIFORNIA: 1769-1784

[1]Geiger, *The Life and Times of Fray Junípero Serra, O.F.M.*, 2:372.

[2]Tibesar, *Writings of Junípero Serra*, 1: 121 (Serra Diary, 1 July 1769).

[3]Ibid., p. 145 (Serra to Fr. Francisco Palóu, 3 July 1769).

[4]Ibid., p. 143.

[5]Ibid., p. 137 (Serra to Fr. Juan Andrés, 3 July 1769). Serra alludes to Genesis 9:20-21 ("Noah, a man of the soil, was the first to plant a vineyard. When he drank some of the wine, he became drunk and lay naked inside his tent").

[6]Tibesar, *Writings of Junípero Serra*, 1:155 (Serra to Fr. Juan Andrés, 10 February 1770). Three years later Serra wrote:

> The entire *ranchería* which made war on us on the Feast of the Assumption of Our Lady, 1769, is now Christian—with the exception of a few old men who . . . [are] still under instructions . . . but they never fail . . . to be present each day at daily prayers. [Ibid., p. 369]

[7]Geiger, *The Life and Times of Fray Junípero Serra, O.F.M.*, 1:237.

[8]Bolton, *Historical Memoirs of New California*, 1:229, 236-237, 239. Due to a combination of storms and termites, Downie's 16' tall replica cross fell during the winter of 1983. A replacement was erected in January 1984.

[9]Tibesar, *Writings of Junípero Serra*, 1:153 (Serra to Fr. Juan Andrés, 10 February 1770).

[10]Ibid., 2:71 (Serra to Fr. Francisco Pangua, 14 June 1774).

[11]Ibid., 1:167 (Serra to Fr. Juan Andrés, 12 June 1770).

[12]Bolton, *Historical Memoirs of New California*, 2: 289.

[13]Ibid., 2:89 (Serra Memorandum, 22 June 1774). Serra went on to recount Juan Evangelista's explanation of the offerings:

> They [the Indians] had done so, that the cross—*porpor* was the name they gave it—might not be angry with them. And to explain why they were afraid, he [Juan] said that the sorcerers and priest-dancers who roam through the night saw the cross, each night, going up high in the heavens—not of dark material as wood is, but resplendent with light, and beautiful to behold; and for that reason they regarded it with great respect, and made presents to it of all they had. [Ibid.]

Serra also learned that

> the same thing was true as regards the crucifixes on the breast of the Fathers, and the rosary crosses worn by the soldiers. The story goes that when our men appeared on the scene, and were coming towards them, they saw on their breasts crosses as tall as the one they planted afterwards on the coast. They wondered how they could carry something so big and bright. As they approached, those who were bold enough to stay there saw that the nearer they came, the smaller the crosses appeared, until, on arrival, they saw them in their natural size, or as they are in fact. This, they say, inspired them with much good will towards our men, especially seeing that, when they got near, they did them no harm; on the contrary, they treated them kindly and gave them presents. Another occurrence which inspired in them considerable respect for our men is this: According to their story, at different times, they saw, coming from the sky, a great flock of birds of variegated and beautiful colors, such as they had never seen before; the birds flew as if to meet and welcome our men, and, on reaching them, they accompanied them for quite a distance. [Ibid., pp. 113, 115]

[14]Tibesar, *Writings of Junípero Serra*, 1:169 (Serra to Fr. Juan Andrés, 12 June 1770).

[15]Alexo Niño. Listed as entry number one in Mission Carmel's *Libro de Difuntos*, he is described as *"moreno libre, soltero y natural de Acapulco"* (free black, single and native of Acapulco). A simple wooden cross above the Vizcaíno-Serra landing site commemorates his burial, Monterey's first non-Christian one, although the exact gravesite is unknown. During excavations for the Lighthouse Avenue tunnel in 1977, a skeleton was unearthed near the landing site, but was not analyzed.

[16]Translator's error. Serra uses the word *imagen* to mean image, statue, or effigy, and *not* painting.

[17]Tibesar, *Writings of Junípero Serra*, 1:169, 171 (Serra to Fr. Juan Andrés, 12 June 1770). This was actually Spain's third official exercise of all the "formalities according to law" that included Monterey. Cabrillo had claimed California for Spain in 1542, and Vizcaíno in 1602.

[18]Ibid., p. 171. The site chosen was approximately 8/10ths of a mile from the Vizcaíno-Serra landing site, and next to a small *estero* (saltwater inlet), roughly bounded by present Webster and Fremont Streets between Camino El Estero and Abrego Street.

[19]Ibid., p. 391 (Serra to Fr. Miguel de Petra, 4 August 1773).

[20]Ibid., p. 173 (Serra to Father Juan Andrés, 12 June 1770).

[21]Ibid., p. 183 (Serra to Inspector General José de Gálvez, 2 July 1770).

[22]Bolton, *Historical Memoirs of New California*, 4:50. The title "La Conquistadora" is not unique to Mission Carmel's statue of Our Lady of Bethlehem. When settling new territory, the Spanish traditionally invoked the protection of the Blessed Virgin Mary as "Our Lady of the Conquest." Mission Loreto, Lower California's first permanent settlement (1697), still possesses its original Conquistadora statue brought by its founder, Fr. Juan Salvatierra, S.J. In Santa Fe, New Mexico, an earlier Conquistadora brought by Fr. Alonso de Benavides, O.F.M. in 1625, is displayed in the *reredos* of Saint Francis Cathedral's Conquistadora Chapel.

[23]Tibesar, *Writings of Junípero Serra*, 1:188-89 (Serra to Inspector General José de Gálvez, 2 July 1770).

[24]Ibid., p. 186.

[25]Ibid., p. 189.

[26]Ibid.

[27]Ibid.

[28]Ibid., 2:61 (Serra to Viceroy Antonio Bucareli y Ursúa, 29 May 1774).

[29]Ibid., p. 67 (Serra to Melchor de Peramas, 14 June 1774); p. 73 (Serra to Fr. Francisco Pangua, 14 June 1774); and p. 87 (Serra Memorandum, 22 June 1774). "Two" ships refers to the additional presence of the *San Antonio* in Monterey harbor.

[30]Bolton, *Historical Memoirs of New California*, 4:50.

[31]Ibid., p. 175.

[32]"Four Thousand Attend Carmel Mission Marian Rites," *Monterey Peninsula Herald*, 10 May 1954, p. 2.

[33]Bolton, *Historical Memoirs of New California*, 2:300.

[34]Ibid.

[35]Ibid.

[36]Tibesar, *Writings of Junípero Serra*, 1:222 (Serra to Fr. Rafael Verger, 20 June 1771).

[37]Ibid., 1: 179 (Serra to Fr. Francisco Palóu, 13 June 1770).

[38]Ibid. p. 197 (Serra to Viceroy Carlos de Croix, 18 June 1771).

[39]Geiger, *Palóu's Life of Fray Junípero Serra*, p. 99.

[40]Ibid., p. 101.

[41]Tibesar, *Writings of Junípero Serra*, 1:197, 199 (Serra to Viceroy Carlos de Croix, 18 June 1771).

[42]Ibid., p 209; and pp. 241, 243 (Serra to Fr. Francisco Palóu, 21 June 1771).

[43]Ibid., p. 243.

[44]Geiger, *Palóu's Life of Fray Junípero Serra*, pp. 110-11.

[45]Tibesar, *Writings of Junípero Serra*, 2:140-41 (Serra to Viceroy Antonio Bucareli y Ursúa, 24 August 1774). The area did not receive its own mission, Nuestra Señora de la Soledad, until 1791. Palóu also commented on Indian salutations:

> This practice was so widely propagated that even the pagans were accustomed to use it, not only when addressing the fathers but also when greeting the Spaniards. The practice became the custom throughout the whole vast region. It softened the hardest heart to hear the pagans, on meeting their fellow Indians or Spaniards along the road, saying the words: "Love God." [Geiger, *Palóu's Life of Fray Junípero Serra*, p. 116]

[46]Tibesar, *Writings of Junípero Serra*, 4:259 (Serra-Noriega Report on the Missions, 1 July 1784).

[47]Ibid., 1:171 (Serra to Fr. Juan Andrés, 12 June 1770).

[48]Ibid., 4:259 (Serra-Noriega Report on the Missions, 1 July 1784). Palóu mentions this cross in his Serra biography:

> The first thing he [Serra] ordered done was the making of a large cross. This he blessed and raised, with the aid of soldiers and servants, fixing it in the center of the area selected for the mission. This was next to the cabin where he lived and the other cabin which served temporarily in place of a church. That sacred symbol was his companion and the source of all his delights. As soon as morning dawned, he venerated it while the soldiers sang the *Alabado* [a traditional Mexican hymn sung at dawn, from *alabar*, to praise]. Before it, the servant of God recited his Matins and Prime, and immediately afterwards he celebrated the Holy Sacrifice of the Mass, at which all the soldiers and servants assisted. Afterwards all began to work, each one at his assigned occupation, the Venerable Father acting as engineer and overseer. Frequently during the day he venerated the holy cross, reciting his Divine Office before it. This I heard from the lips of the corporal [Mariano Carrillo] who was in charge of the guard at that place. At night he did the same when he finished reciting the Franciscan Rosary. The soldiers, following his example, did likewise, while the Indians were also instructed. . . . When the pagans came to visit the Venerable Father . . . the first thing he did was to make the Sign of the Cross over them with his own hand, after which he had them venerate the cross. [Geiger, *Palóu's Life of Fray Junípero Serra*, p. 116]

[49]"Site of First Mission Cross is Located," *Monterey Peninsula Herald*, 19 December 1939, p. 7.

[50]Tibesar, *Writings of Junípero Serra*, 1:255 (Serra to Fr. Rafael Verger, 8 August 1772); and p. 353 (Serra to Viceroy Antonio Bucareli y Ursúa, 21 May 1773).

[51]Ibid., p. 257 (Serra to Fr. Rafael Verger, 8 August 1772); and pp. 351, 353 (Serra to Viceroy Antonio Bucareli y Ursúa, 21 May 1773).

[52]Ibid., 4:259 (Serra-Noriega Report on the Missions, 1 July 1784).

[53]Ibid., pp. 259, 261. Palóu elaborated on the difficulty of irrigating Mission Carmel's fields (not until 1777 would an irrigation project be started):

> The mission has at this site plenty of good land, although not for irrigation, for the river runs too low, and in the rainy season it is very rapid, and if it is retained by a dam it is sure to carry it away. But, according to what has been observed, seasonal crops can be raised, of wheat as well as corn, by the humidity of the earth and the constant fogs that prevail after the cessation of the rain. [Bolton, *Historical Memoirs of New California*, 3: 231]

[54]Ibid., 1:261 (Serra to Fr. Rafael Verger, 8 August 1772).

[55]Ibid., p. 267 (Serra to Fr. Francisco Palóu, 18 August 1772).

[56]Ibid., p. 269. Serra offered a slightly different version in 1779: "Be sure that He Who sends or permits these hardships will send us also such a measure of patience as is needed. Where will the ox go, which does not fare forth to plough, but to the block?" (Ibid., 3:307).

[57]Ibid., p. 257 (Serra to Fr. Rafael Verger, 8 August 1772).

[58]Bolton, *Historical Memoirs of New California*, 3:1.

[59]Tibesar, *Writings of Junípero Serra*, 1:393 (Serra to Fr. Miguel de Petra, 4 August 1773). Serra elaborated:

Because of the fatigue of the journey, I arrived in the city of Guadalajara [at the Convento de San Francisco, 360 miles northwest of Mexico City] burning with fever A few days later I was advised to receive the Last Sacraments, and was in real danger. Later on the constant fever turned into an intermittent one, and I continued my trip in that condition. On arriving at Querétaro [at the Convento de Santa Cruz, 130 miles northwest of Mexico City] I again was so ill, that they, too, advised me to receive the Last Sacraments. But in a short time I recovered, and finally I arrived at this our holy College. [Ibid.]

[60]Geiger, *Palóu's Life of Fray Junípero Serra*, p. 143.

[61]Tibesar, *Writings of Junípero Serra*, 1:393 (Serra to Fr. Miguel de Petra, 4 August 1773).

[62]Ibid., p. 327 (Serra to Viceroy Antonio Bucareli y Ursúa, 13 March 1773). Father Pablo Font, O.F.M., San Fernando College member when Serra visited in 1773, wrote the following account of Serra's health to Father Jayme Axaló, O.F.M., in the province of Catalonia, Spain. He offers a succinct, vivid portrait of Serra at age sixty, very ill yet still imbued with remarkable zeal and stamina:

San Fernando College, Mexico, 26 August 1773

The President (Observant Religious Junípero Serra), former professor *de prima* at the University of Palma, is very venerable in his old age and has never in all his twenty-four years as a Missionary at this College spared himself any effort to convert the faithful and unfaithful. Despite his many long and difficult years he is like a lion, giving in only to fever, for none of the ailments that constantly afflict him, especially shortness of breath, chest pains, and sores on his legs and feet, have ever kept him from his apostolic duties. During his stay here he has amazed us, for although in very bad health he has never missed choir either by day or night except when stricken by fever. Often he has seemed dead and suddenly brought back to life, and whenever he has gone to the infirmary for care it has been because he was obeying an order to do so. At times his sores and other afflictions have made him so ill as he went along the road among the faithful and unfaithful that he had to be carried, not wanting to stop and take care of his half-dead body; and then he would be seen well again by the sole virtue of Divine Providence. For the austerity of his life, his humility, charity and other virtues, he is truly worthy of being counted among the imitators of the Apostles. Now he is returning to Monterey, covering a thousand leagues by land and sea as if they were a mere nothing, to visit the Missions there, bring them joy and divine guidance, preside over them, and continue to found others until he dies. May God give him many years of life. I could say much more about this holy man. He has often been elected Guardian but never confirmed as such, either because he was away or because the Prelates felt that such an extraordinary man should not be held back from his apostolic duties. [translated from the Spanish version in Geiger, *Palóu's Life of Fray Junípero Serra*, p. 415]

[63]Ibid., p. 389 (Serra to Fr. Miguel de Petra, 4 August 1773).

[64]Maynard Geiger, *Representations of Father Junipero Serra in Painting and Woodcut: Their History and Evaluation*, (Santa Barbara: The Franciscan Fathers, 1958), p. 17.

[65]Ibid., p. 24.

[66]Ibid., pp. 20-21.

[67] Ibid., pp. 25-26. Regarding all the early Serra portraits (San Fernando, Querétaro, Zacatecas, *Serra's Viaticum*, and the Palóu Woodcut), historian Geiger concluded:

On the assumption that we are dealing here with portraiture and because of the tenuous evidence at our disposal, based mostly on assertion rather than conclusive proof, my opinion is that we cannot point out to any of the extant Serra paintings or prints and say that this one to the exclusion of all others represents Serra as he really was. I would go even further and state that we do not really know if we have an authentic likeness of Serra at all. The best that we can do now . . . is to photograph and reproduce the paintings and consider various claims for what they might be worth. The only answer that an honest historian today can give to the question: "Is there an authentic likeness of Serra?" is "I do not know." And if a second question be asked: "Which of the paintings do you think most likely represents Serra?" the answer is: "I do not know." [Ibid., p. 35]

[68] Tibesar, *Writings of Junípero Serra*, 2:35 (Serra to Fr. Antonio Zamudio, 26 March 1774).

[69] Ibid., pp. 35, 49.

[70] Ibid., p. 431 (Serra to Fr. Francisco Pangua and the Discretorium, 13 April 1776).

[71] Ibid., pp. 431, 433.

[72] *Memoria*, Archivo General de la Nación, Mexico City, p. 1. Regarding the other mission paintings ordered in 1771, Serra wrote the San Fernando College guardian:

The requests that I would like to make of Your Reverence are . . . that you should order the five patron saints of the missions to be painted, for each mission its own. That is to say, for Fathers [Pedro] Cambón and [Angel] Somera: the Archangel Gabriel. For Fathers [Domingo] Juncosa and Cavaller: Saint Louis, the Bishop, with his episcopal insignia, showing below the level of his rochet [ceremonial linen outer vestment], the Franciscan habit and cord plainly to be seen, a mitre on his head, the cope, decorated with flowers and his royal crown and scepter at his feet. For Fathers [Miguel] Pieras and Buenaventura [Sitjar]: Saint Anthony of Padua, the Preacher, attractive in appearance, and, above all, with the Infant Jesus. For the other two missions that do not yet have ministers here [nor have been founded yet], the paintings may be sent to me, or the Fathers that come may bring them: Saint Clare, with her Franciscan habit, and her veil, not as the nuns here wear it, but falling on the shoulders, as she is painted in Europe. And for the other mission, Our Father Saint Francis receiving the Stigmata, or as Your Reverence may prefer, so long as they do not paint him in [a] blue [habit]. [Tibesar, *Writings of Junípero Serra*, 1:221]

When ordering paintings, Serra's meticulousness even extended to the type of frame to be sent: "with a gilded frame; let the frame come in separate pieces and let there be a reinforcing middle stick " (Tibesar, *Writings of Junípero Serra*, 2: 279).

[73] Tibesar, *Writings of Junípero Serra*, 2:241, 243 (Serra to Viceroy Antonio Bucareli y Ursúa, 5 February 1775).

[74] Charles Rudkin, ed., *The First French Expedition to California: Laperouse in 1786*, (Los Angeles: Glen Dawson, 1959), pp. 62-63.

[75] "General Inventory of . . . Mission of San Carlos of Monterey, June 22, 1842," Mission Carmel Archives, Carmel, p. 5.

[76] One theory suggests that the *Souls in Hell* painting at Mission Santa Bárbara is the misplaced Mission Carmel original. This is impossible because Carmel's *Horrors of Hell* appears in the mission's 1842 post-secularization inventory. Santa Bárbara's *Souls in Hell* is listed in its 1835 inventory, which proves that Santa Bárbara already had its painting before Carmel's was lost. Mission Carmel's *Glory of Heaven* and *Horrors of Hell* may have been taken to Monterey's Royal Presidio Chapel earlier than 1852, if they are the same pair described by Bayard Taylor in 1849:

Near the door hung opposite pictures of heaven and hell—the former, a sort of pyramid inhabited by straight white figures, with an aspect of solemn distress; the latter enclosed in the expanded jaws of a dragon, swarming with devils, who tormented their victims with spears and pitchforks. [Taylor, *Eldorado, or, Adventures in the Path of Empire*, p. 118]

[77] Bolton, *Historical Memoirs of New California*, 4:315.

[78]Geiger, *Palóu's Life of Fray Junípero Serra,* p. 157.

[79]Tibesar, *Writings of Junípero Serra,* 2: 139 (Serra to Viceroy Antonio Bucareli y Ursúa, 24 August 1774).

[80]Ibid., p. 177 (Serra to Viceroy Antonio Bucareli y Ursúa, 9 September 1774).

[81]Bolton, *Historical Memoirs of New California,* 3:123.

[82]Tibesar, *Writings of Junípero Serra,* 2: 147 (Serra to Viceroy Antonio Bucareli y Ursúa, 24 August 1774).

[83]Ibid.

[84]Ibid., 1:383 (Serra to Viceroy Antonio Bucareli y Ursúa, 11 June 1773).

[85]Ibid., 2:329 (Serra to Fr. Francisco Pangua, 10 October 1775).

[86]Ibid., p. 349 (Serra to Viceroy Antonio Bucareli y Ursúa, 20 October 1775). The Peréz expedition's original objective had been to reach the 60th parallel. In 1775, a two-vessel Pacific coastal expedition sailed a bit farther north, although falling short of its 65th-parallel goal. The *Sonora,* under Juan Francisco de la Bodéga y Quadra, reached the 58th parallel at present Chichagof Island, Alaska. The *Santiago,* under Bruno de Hezeta, only reached the 49th parallel at present Nootka Sound, Vancouver Island, British Columbia, forced to reverse course for Monterey due to illness among the crew.

[87]Ibid., p. 447 (The Marriage Records at San Carlos—Serra entry of 25 July 1774).

[88]Ibid., p. 83 (Serra to Viceroy Antonio Bucareli y Ursúa, 21 June 1774); and p. 167 (Serra to Fr. Guardian Francisco Pangua and the Discretorium, 31 August 1774).

[89]Ibid., pp. 241-43 (Serra to Viceroy Antonio Bucareli y Ursúa, 5 February 1775).

[90]Ibid., p. 145 (Serra to Viceroy Antonio Bucareli y Ursúa, 24 August 1774).

[91]Ibid., p. 181 (Serra to Melchor de Peramas, 11 September 1774).

[92]Ibid., p. 67 (Serra to Melchor de Peramas, 14 June 1774).

[93]Ibid., pp. 307, 309 (Serra to Viceroy Antonio Bucareli y Ursúa, 17 August 1775).

[94]Geiger, *Palóu's Life of Fray Junípero Serra,* p. 167.

[95]Tibesar, *Writings of Junípero Serra,* 3:191 (Serra to Fr. Fermín de Lasuén, 22 April 1778).

[96]Ibid., 2:405, 407 (Serra to Viceroy Antonio Bucareli y Ursúa, 15 December 1775).

[97]Ibid., 3:191 (Serra to Fr. Fermín de Lasuén, 22 April 1778); and Geiger, *Palóu's Life of Fray Junípero Serra,* pp. 285-86.

[98]Geiger, *Palóu's Life of Fray Junípero Serra,* p. 286.

[99]Herbert E. Bolton, *Font's Complete Diary* (Berkeley: University of California Press, 1933), p. 300.

[100]Ibid., pp. 301-02.

[101]Ibid., p. 301.

[102]Ibid., p. 303.

[103]Tibesar, *Writings of Junípero Serra,* 2:435 (Serra to Fr. Francisco Pangua and the Discretorium, 13 April 1776).

[104]Geiger, *Palóu's Life of Fray Junípero Serra,* p. 370.

[105]Tibesar, *Writings of Junípero Serra*, 2:243 (Serra to Viceroy Antonio Bucareli y Ursúa, 5 February 1775).

[106]Bolton, *Font's Complete Diary*, pp. 290-91.

[107]"General Inventory of . . . Mission of San Carlos of Monterey, June 22, 1842," p. 3.

[108]Tibesar, *Writings of Junípero Serra*, 3:31 (Serra to Fr. Francisco Pangua, 24 September 1776).

[109]The first attempt had been hastily terminated when Mission San Diego was burned in November 1775.

[110]Geiger, *Palóu's Life of Fray Junípero Serra*, p. 178.

[111]Ibid.

[112]Ibid.

[113]Tibesar, *Writings of Junípero Serra*, 3:113, 115 (Serra to Viceroy Antonio Bucareli y Ursúa, 1 March 1777).

[114]Ibid., p. 111.

[115]Ibid., p. 81 (Serra to Fr. Fermín de Lasuén, 6 April 1778).

[116]Ibid., p. 99 (Serra to Fr. Francisco Pangua, 26 February 1777).

[117]Ibid., pp. 145, 147 (Serra to Viceroy Antonio Bucareli y Ursúa, 1 June 1777).

[118]Ibid., 2:267 (Serra to Viceroy Antonio Bucareli y Ursúa, 2 July 1775).

[119]Geiger, *Palóu's Life of Fray Junípero Serra*, p. 201.

[120]Translation:

Jesus, Mary and Joseph
In the name of Christ, Amen.

On 29 June 1778, in the Church of the Mission of San Carlos de Monterey belonging to the Apostolic College of San Fernando in Mexico and to the Minorite Order of Our Lord Saint Francis, after attending to the formalities noted at the beginning of this book, I the undersigned Fray Junípero Serra, vested in the same priestly vestments in which I had just finished chanting High Mass on that solemn day, dedicated to the Holy Apostles Saint Peter and Saint Paul, and assisted by Fray Juan Crespí and Fray Francisco Dumetz, both of them Apostolic Fathers of the College and co-Ministers of this Mission, with the newest holy chrism to be had, prepared and blessed by the Right Reverend Lord Bishop of Guadalajara, solemnly confirmed according to the Roman Pontifical Ritual, the following:
2. Junípero Bucareli—First, I confirmed the child Junípero, of about seven years of age, the legitimate son of Antonio María Bucareli, at that time Chief of the heathendom of these parts, and María Antonina Ursúa. The parents were a newly baptized couple from the Ichxenta *Ranchería*, called by us San José. The child's godfather was Fernando Chamorro, a Mexican, married, and a blacksmith for Our Lord the King of these Missions.

[121]Tibesar, *Writings of Junípero Serra*, 3:13 (Serra to Viceroy Antonio Bucareli y Ursúa, 27 June 1776).

[122]Ibid., p. 269 (Serra to Fr. Rafael Verger and the Discretorium, 17 October 1778).

[123]Ibid., p. 227 (Serra to Viceroy Antonio Bucareli y Ursúa, 19 August 1778).

[124]Iid., p. 269 (Serra to Fr. Rafael Verger and the Discretorium, 17 October 1778).

[125]Ibid., p. 229 (Serra to Viceroy Antonio Bucareli y Ursúa, 19 August 1778). The monstrance that Serra gave to Mission San Francisco remained there until stolen in 1982. A replica is on display in the mission museum.

[126]Ibid.

[127]Ibid., 3:247 (Serra to Fr. Rafael Verger, 19 August 1778). Juan was a "tertiary" member of the Secular or "Third" Order of St. Francis.

[128]Ibid., p. 321 (Serra to Fr. Rafael Verger, 6 April 1779).

[129]Ibid., pp. 293-95 (Serra to Fr. Fermín de Lasuén, 29 March 1779).

[130]Ibid., p. 357 (Serra Report on the Missions, 15 August 1779).

[131]Ibid. One of these rooms soon became the new blacksmith shop.

[132]Ibid., p. 247 (Serra to Fr. Rafael Verger, 19 August 1778); and p. 357 (Serra Report on the Missions, 15 August 1779).

[133]Ibid., p. 359.

[134]Ibid., p. 213 (Serra to Fr. Fermín de Lasuén, 10 July 1778).

[135]Ibid., p. 369 (Serra to Fr. Fermín de Lasuén, 16 August 1779).

[136]Ibid., p. 389 (Serra to Fr. Fermín de Lasuén, 28 September 1779).

[137]Extensive research has so far proved futile in uncovering any biographical data for Martín Rodríguez. The painting is faintly signed "Ma Rodríguez," and the surname spelling is not clear (Rodríguez/Rodríquez, etc.). The name Martín is taken from Ferdinand Perret's 1958 "La Perret-enciclopedia de arte Hispano-Americano de la época colonial" ("The Perret Encyclopedia of Hispanic-American Colonial Art," an unpublished manuscript in the Santa Barbara Historical Society Library that inventories California mission art), which lists "Martín Rodríguez" as artist of *La Pieta de la Misión Vieja de San Carlos Borromeo*" (The Pietà [sic] [*Our Lady of Sorrows*] of Old Mission San Carlos Borromeo). Mission Carmel tradition suggests that Rodríguez was founder of the Fine Arts Academy of San Carlos in Mexico City, and that he donated the painting to Mission San Carlos (Carmel) in honor of their common namesake. This is impossible because the Academy was not founded until November 1785, eight years after *Our Lady of Sorrows* was painted. Furthermore, the name Rodríguez (in any form) does not appear on the founders roll, nor is it listed among the original academy professors.

[138]Tibesar, *Writings of Junípero Serra*, 3:357 (Serra Report on the Missions, 15 August 1779).

[139]"General Inventory of . . . Mission of San Carlos of Monterey, June 22, 1842," p. 4. Mission Carmel had five altars in 1842: the main altar; two small altars on the Epistle side wall (one in the sanctuary); one small sanctuary altar on the Gospel side wall (Our Lady of Sorrows); and one in the mortuary chapel (present Our Lady of Bethlehem Chapel).

[140]Geiger, *Palóu's Life of Fray Junípero Serra*, p. 208. Serra traveled the eighty miles between Missions Carmel and Santa Clara in two days, leaving Carmel on 10 October, and arriving at Santa Clara on the 11th. Only two weeks before, on 28 September he had written:

The trouble with my legs gets worse, rather than better. It is with difficulty that I rest, even for a short time, and for this reason I did not say Mass yesterday. Today, however, I celebrated with much difficulty, . . . the nights I pass without much sleep. [Tibesar, *Writings of Junípero Serra*, 3:391]

[141]"San Carlos Book of Confirmations, volume 1, 1778-1896," 21 October 1779, Mission Carmel Archives, Carmel.

[142]Tibesar, *Writings of Junípero Serra*, 4:53-55 (Serra to Fr. Francisco Pangua, 24 October 1780).

[143]Ibid., 4:145 (Serra to Fr. Francisco Pangua, 17 July 1782).

[144]Ibid. Serra goes on to say: "The Commandant General had sentenced the man to the gallows. But the Governor, for want of a hangman, had commuted the sentence—he was to be shot by the firing squad. His name was Juan Antonio Labra" (Ibid.). This was Monterey's first clearly recorded legal execution, and probably California's, too.

[145]Geiger, T*he Life and Times of Fray Junípero Serra, O.F.M.*, 2:236. This was a new location for the mission, moved one-half mile to higher ground to escape periodic flooding by the Guadalupe River. The cornerstone was

accidentally discovered in 1911 by workmen digging for a gas main along Franklin Street near Campbell Avenue in Santa Clara. With contents intact, it is now on display in the Mission Room of Santa Clara University's de Saisset Museum.

[146]Tibesar, *Writings of Junípero Serra,* 4:99 (Serra to Fr. Fermín de Lasuén, 8 December 1781).

[147]Ibid., pp. 146-47 (Serra to Fr. Francisco Pangua, 17 July 1782).

[148]Ibid., p. 101 (Serra to Fr. Fermín de Lasuén, 8 December 1781). Serra also noted that "some salmon have been placed in the pool and so we have it handy" (Ibid., p. 273). The project had been delayed in its last phase by

> the famous steward of San Luís Obispo [Ignacio Vallejo, father of Mariano and Salvador], [who] came to our house offering to take the . . . job at this mission. He started May 1, at a salary of two hundred *pesos* in cash, etc. He saw and approved the work that the two Fathers were doing toward extracting water and, after stating that within three days we would see corn irrigated, he went out one morning and without saying anything to us, he took the people from the work and set them digging another ditch a few yards further up the river, claiming that what had been done previously was valueless and, with that, the corn sown was lost and he spent seven months and used all the workmen in the ditch. Not a grain of corn was gathered and they got a little over 400 *fanegas* of barley. Because of the folly of this man, a great part of the wheat was lost in the fields. But finally the water was extracted. . . . Thanks be to God! [Ibid., 4:269]

[149]Ibid., 4:101 (Serra to Fr. Fermín de Lasuén, 8 December 1781). Maintaining an adequate supply of altar wine was frequently a problem, as in 1774, when "all the barrels arrived all completely empty, and we each tried to evolve a theory to account for it" (Ibid., 2:379). Or in 1783, when "we met with an accident—when the barrel was being brought here from San Juan Capistrano it fell off the mule, broke into pieces, and all the wine was lost. But the neighboring missions came to our rescue" (Ibid., 4:195).

[150]Ibid., 4:147 (Serra to Fr. Francisco Pangua, 17 July 1782).

[151]Translation:

247
Father Preacher Fray Juan Crespí
Minister of this Mission

On 2 January 1782, I buried Father Preacher Fray Juan Crespí in the Church of the Mission of San Carlos de Monterey, next to the pulpit from which the Gospel is read near the high altar. The burial was preceded by a vigil and a High Requiem Mass, with the body present, which included all the liturgical prayers prescribed by the Constitution of our Order for the burial of members of religious communities. Father Crespí had been a Minister of the Mission from the time of its foundation, as recorded on the first page of this and all other books belonging to the administration. He was born in the holy province of Mallorca, which he left in 1749 to devote himself to the conversion of the heathen. Having obtained the appropriate license to join the Apostolic Missionary College of San Fernando for the Propagation of the Faith in Mexico, he arrived there early the following year. He died after receiving the holy Sacraments of Penance, the Viaticum and Extreme Unction the previous day, the first day of January and of the year, that is on the day of Our Lord's Circumcision and the Sweet Name of Jesus, at around six in the morning. His two fellow co-Provincials were present, and his bearing when he died was that of a true religious. Father Crespí was seventy years and ten months old, he had been a religious for forty years less three days, and he had been a missionary devoted to converting the heathen for thirty years, in Sierra Gorda, [Lower] California, and Monterey. I, formerly his teacher and then his companion of many years, have signed the above for the record.

Fr. Junípero Serra [rubric]

[152]Ibid., 4:113 (Serra to Fr. Fermín de Lasuén, 31 March 1782); and Geiger, *The Life and Times of Fray Junípero Serra, O.F.M.,* 2:287.

[153]Tibesar, *Writings of Junípero Serra,* 4:141 (Serra to Fr. Fermín de Lasuén, 29 April 1782).

[154]Ibid., 4:153 (Serra to Fr. Francisco Pangua, 17 July 1782).

[155]Ibid., p. 165 (Serra to Fr. Fermín de Lasuén, 20 July 1782).

[156]Geiger, *The Life and Times of Fray Junípero Serra, O.F.M.*, 2:326.

[157]Geiger, *Palóu's Life of Fray Junípero Serra*, p. 237.

[158]Ibid.

[159]Tibesar, *Writings of Junípero Serra*, 4:193 (Serra to Fr. Juan Sancho, 27 October 1783).

[160]Ibid., p. 271 (Serra-Noriega Report on the Missions, 1 July 1784). Mission Carmel had cumulatively baptized 938 Indians by the end of 1783, with 175 baptized in that year alone. Little did Serra realize that this would be the mission's peak Baptism year for the entire 1770-1832 mission period.

[161]Ibid., 3:357 (Serra Report on the Missions, 15 August 1779).

[162]Ibid., 4:101, 103 (Serra to Fr. Fermín de Lasuén, 8 December 1781).

[163]Ibid., p. 275 (Serra-Noriega Report on the Missions, 1 July 1784).

[164]Crespí's remains were transferred here from the fourth church (the *Jacalón grande*), to the vault closest to the sanctuary wall. Serra was buried in the central vault (1784), and the present stone church (finished in 1797) was constructed to accomodate the vaults into its sanctuary floorplan.

[165]Tibesar, *Writings of Junípero Serra*, 4:275 (Serra-Noriega Report on the Missions, 1 July 1784).

[166]Ibid., p. 273.

[167]Ibid., p. 275.

[168]Ibid.

[169]Ibid., p. 223 (Serra to Fr. Fermín de Lasuén, 17 April 1784). When Serra performed Mission Carmel's 1,000th Baptism, he named the adult male Indian convert Millan Deogracias (after San Millan de Cogolla [Saint Emilian Cucullatus], sixth century Spanish hermit/abbot). Millan is very close to *millar*, Spanish for one thousand. When combined with *Deogracias*, the play on words creates "A thousand, thank God."

[170]Ibid., p. 223.

[171]Arthur D. Spearman, *The Five Franciscan Churches of Mission Santa Clara: 1777-1825* (Palo Alto: The National Press, 1963), p. 36.

[172]Ibid. Father José Murguía (1715-84), was born in Domayguia, Alava, Spain. He arrived in Mexico as a layman, joined San Fernando College (1736), was ordained (1744), and served in the Sierra Gorda missions (1748-67), most notably at Mission San Miguel de Concá where he built the mission's stone church during Serra's presidency. He traveled with Serra to Lower California (1767) and served at Mission Santiago de las Coras. He transferred to Upper California (1773), and was co-founder of Mission Santa Clara along with Father Tomás de la Peña in 1777. He is still buried "in the sanctuary at the Gospel side" of the third Mission Santa Clara Church, abandoned after earthquake damage in 1819. His unmarked grave is located under present Franklin Street near The Alameda (formerly Campbell Avenue) two blocks northeast of the present Mission Santa Clara.

[173]Geiger, *Palóu's Life of Fray Junípero Serra*, p. 241.

[174]Tibesar, *Writings of Junípero Serra*, 4:291 (Serra to Fr. Juan Sancho, 6 August 1784). Serra often commented on the letter writing aspect of his career. In 1775 he wrote: "half my life is passed at a writing desk" (Ibid., 2:321), and "how unfortunate for me that I am destined to be more of a writer than a missionary. Yet I am fully aware that I do not write as much as I should" (Ibid., p. 395). His desk was often makeshift when traveling, such as en route from San Diego to Monterey in 1770: "This letter I am writing sitting on the floor of my cabin, and it is no easy task, I assure you" (Ibid., 1:163), or after establishing the Santa Bárbara Presidio in 1782: "These, as this one and a great number of other items, are being written on my knees" (Ibid., 4:141).

[175]Geiger, *Palóu's Life of Fray Junípero Serra*, p. 243.

[176]Bolton, *Historical Memoirs of New California*, 3:355.

[177]Geiger, *Palóu's Life of Fray Junípero Serra*, p 244.

[178]Geiger, *The Life and Times of Junípero Serra, O.F.M.*, 2:381.

[179]Bolton, *Historical Memoirs of New California*, 4:356-57; and Geiger, *Palóu's Life of Fray Junípero Serra*, p. 245.

[180]Geiger, *Palóu's Life of Fray Junípero Serra*, p. 246.

[181]Bolton, *Historical Memoirs of New California*, 4:365-66.

[182]Ibid., p. 376. Most Rev. Rafael Verger, O.F.M. (1722-90), fellow Mallorcan of Palóu and Serra, Doctor of Philosophy from Llullian University, former San Fernando College guardian, and at that time Bishop of Nuevo León, Mexico.

[183]Geiger, *Representations of Father Junipero Serra in Painting and Woodcut*, p. 11.

[184]The painting bears a legend at its base (not shown in the photograph). As part of a Mexican research tour in December 1986, the author visited the National History Museum, Chapultepec Palace, Mexico City, to examine the painting and translate its legend. The painting was not on display, and none of the staff/administrators was able to locate it. They said it was either being restored, or in storage. Historian Henry R. Wagner offered the follwing translation in 1934:

> The Apostolic Father Preacher Fray Junípero Serra, native of the town of Petra in the Kingdom of Mallorca. He took the habit of the *observantes* [Observant Franciscans] in that province. Having professed and concluded his studies he read for three years the course of *artes*. On concluding this he obtained the hood and the chair of prime theology of S. D. Escoto [*sic*] [Duns Scotus chair *de prima* of Sacred Theology], in that royal and pontifical university. This chair he resigned after some years in order to come as a missionary to this province of San Fernando in Mexico, where he arrived April 2, 1750 [*sic*] [1 January 1750]. For three years he was master of novices and for another three a member of the council. He made several missionary excursions among the infidels in which he manifested the singular talent and ardent charity of his fervent soul. He acted in the capacity of president in the missions of Sierra Gorda and labored there with indefatigable zeal in the conversion of those Indians. From there he passed to the missions of Old California as president of them. From there he embarked on the discovery of the country of Monterey, where he founded nine missions, and confirmed in them more than 5,300 Indians [5,309 to be exact]. After fourteen years of his presidency in these and of many other labors and truly apostolic deeds, his soul adorned with virtues, he disposed himself for eternity. With a premonition which he without doubt had of his passing, as some days previously he had ordered a casket made in which to bury his body, he called his father confessor [Palóu] for his last Confession. He went to the church to receive the Holy Viaticum chanting at the same time that he received it with the greatest melody the *Eutrofa* [possibly referring to "trope," a type of liturgical chant] of the hymn *Tantum ergo Sacramentum*. On returning to his little cell, seated in a chair, he received with the greatest devotion the Sacrament of Extreme Unction [Anointing of the Sick], praying with the surrounding fathers the penitential Psalms. Afterwards with some perturbation of spirit he asked to commend his soul to God, and responded on his knees. This ceremony being over he exclaimed with joy and ecstasy "Thanks be to God, now there is no fear. I will rest a little." Reclining on his side on the boards he delivered his soul to his creator on the 28th of August of the year 1784. [Henry R. Wagner, "The Last Mass of Father Junipero Serra," *Westways* 26 (September 1934):9, 41]

[185]Geiger, *Palóu's Life of Fray Junípero Serra*, p. 247.

[186]Ibid.

[187]Ibid.

[188]Ibid.

[189]Ibid., p. 248.

[190]In his biography of Serra, Palóu mentions the now-lost crucifix (see page 57 for picture) in the context of Serra's 1749 transatlantic voyage. He writes: "During the entire voyage, he [Serra] never laid aside the crucifix which he wore on his breast even when he slept" (Geiger, *Palóu's Life of Fray Junípero Serra*, p. 15). He mentions it again at the time of Serra's death:

His bed [at Mission Carmel] consisted of some roughhewn boards, covered by a blanket serving more as a covering than as an aid to rest, for he never used even a sheepskin covering, such as was customary at our college. Along the road he used to do the same thing. He would stretch the blanket and a pillow on the ground, and would lie down on these to get his necessary rest. He always slept with a crucifix upon his breast, in the embrace of his hands. It was about a [Spanish] foot [11 inches] in length. He had carried it with him, together with the blanket and pillow. At his mission and whenever he stopped, as soon as he got up from bed he placed the crucifix upon the pillow. Thus he had it on this occasion when he did not wish to go to bed during the entire night or next morning, on the day when he was to deliver his soul to the Creator. [Ibid., p, 246]

[191]Ibid., pp. 248, 292. In Mission Carmel's *Libro de Difuntos*, Palóu wrote that Serra died "a little before four o'clock in the afternoon."

[192]Serra's prefatory Biblical inscription (2 Samuel 14:14) in Mission Carmel's *Libro de Difuntos*, written at Monterey-Carmel's 3 June 1770 founding.

IV. POST-MORTEM: 1784-1987

[1]Geiger, *Palóu's Life of Fray Junípero Serra*, p. 252.

[2]Ibid., p. 253. None of these personal effects is known to exist today. Serra's original eyeglasses survived however, and were displayed at Mission Carmel until stolen in the 1960s'.

[3]Ibid., p. 254.

[4]Translation:

381
Reverend Father Lector Fray Junípero Serra
President of the Missions

On 29 August 1784, I buried the Reverend Father Lector Fray Junípero Serra in the Church of the Mission of San Carlos de Monterey in the sanctuary, near the pulpit from which the Gospel is read, in front of the altar of Our Lady of Sorrows. The burial was preceded by a vigil and a High Requiem Mass which included all the liturgical prayers prescribed in the Constitution of our Order for the burial of members of religious communities. Among those attending were Dr. Cristóbal Díaz, Chaplain of the packetboat *San Carlos* anchored in the port, Father Preacher Buenaventura Sitjar, Minister of the Mission of San Antonio, and Father Preacher Matías de Santa Catalina, Minister of this Mission. Father Serra was the founder and President of the missions, as recorded on the first page of the Parish Book belonging to each. He was born in the holy province of Mallorca. He took his vows on 14 September 1730, when he was nineteen [*sic*] [seventeen] years, nine months and twenty-one days old, and he observed them thereafter with great competence and piety. He taught philosophy, and I had the good fortune of being one of his students. His course was very well received, and when it was over he was elected Professor *de prima* of Sacred Theology at the University of Mallorca. The faculty of the University honored him with the degree of Doctor, and he performed his professional duties to the entire satisfaction of both the University and the province. He was considered by all to be very learned, and likewise very capable in the pulpit. He was highly respected in both disciplines, and assigned to give the most important sermons. While at the height of everyone's esteem, after a great realization of truth behind which he sensed the will of God, Father Serra gave up all his past honors and those he might yet have received, to devote the talents bestowed upon him by God to the conversion of the Indian heathen. In 1749, having obtained the necessary licenses and letters of authorization, he joined the mission in Cádiz that was preparing to leave for the Apostolic College of San Fernando for the Propagation of the Faith, in Mexico City. He arrived at the College on 1 January 1750, and remained there until the beginning of June when he was sent to the missions of the Sierra Gorda, founded six years earlier. There he worked very zealously for nine years, always setting an example for everyone. He was then called by the Prelate to go to the mission at Río de San Sabá. This project was thwarted however by the death of the Viceroy, whose presence had encouraged the efforts of the conquest. Father Serra therefore stayed on at the College, continuing his missionary work among the faithful. He also carried out responsibilities for the Holy Office of the Inquisition, which had made him one of its Commissaries and was satisfied with his work. He was thus engaged when, in June 1767, the Reverend Guardian of the College appointed him President of the sixteen missionaries in charge of the fifteen missions in Lower California previously administered by the former Jesuit Fathers. He remained in Lower California for a year at the head Loreto mission, during which period he made several visits to the missions lying to the north and to the south. In April 1769, Father Serra left Loreto to accompany the land expedition that set out in search of the ports of Monterey and San Diego. Arriving at the Lower California border, he founded the mission of San Fernando de Velicatá. When he reached the port of San Diego, while the expedition continued its search for Monterey, he founded the San Diego mission. In 1770 he sailed with the expedition that found the Port of Monterey. He participated in the founding of this mission, and went on to found missions whenever possible until all those now recorded in the Parish books had been erected. Over a period of fourteen years Father Serra made several journeys, one as far as Mexico City, to obtain support for the efforts of the conquest and to visit the missions and inspire their subjects with his zeal and wisdom. His visitations became more frequent once he was empowered to confirm the faithful, after zealously applying for authority to do so. While his authority lasted, that is until it expired on 10 July last, he confirmed 5,307 [sic] [5,308] people. One month and a half after this date his Reverence died and gave up his soul to the Creator. At that time he was seventy years, nine months less four days old [sic] [nine months plus four days], had been a religious for fifty three years, eleven months and four days [sic] [fourteen days], and an apostolic missionary for thirty five years, four and a half months. Father Serra prepared to die by repeating the general Confession he had often pronounced. Then, on the 27th of this month, conscious of more discomfort in his chest and feeling that he was feverish, he prayed the Divine Office through Tierce, and walked to the church to receive the Holy Viaticum. He knelt down, setting an example for all the town and everyone who attended. I then gave him the Holy Viaticum with all the ceremony prescribed by the Roman and Franciscan rituals. As soon as the service started, Father Serra, who was on his knees, sang out in a loud voice as if nothing were wrong with him the lines *Tantum ergo*, etc., moving us all so that we were unable to accompany him. Thus did he receive the Viaticum with fervent devotion, and still in the same position he gave thanks to the Lord, after which he withdrew to his cell. That night he asked for the Last Rites, and prayed the penitential Psalms and the Litany with us. He spent the rest of the night giving thanks to God, at times on his knees and at others seated on the floor, without going to bed, dressed in his habit and mantle. At dawn he asked me to administer the Plenary Indulgence, for which he knelt down and prepared himself with a general Confession. On the morning of the 28th, the ship's Chaplain and its Captain, Don Jose Cañizares, came to visit him. He received them sitting up and thanked them for their visit, giving the Chaplain a warm embrace and saying to both, "I am thankful to God that now, after I have traveled over so much of the earth, you have come to throw a little of it over me." After a while he said he felt a bit afraid and asked to have the Commendation for a Departing Soul read aloud to him. I did this, and when I had finished the prayers, to which he responded as if he were well, he exclaimed in great joy, "I thank God that now I am without fear. There is no longer any need to worry. I feel better now and will have a bit of broth," for which he left the room and sat at the table. After he had taken the broth he desired to lie down, which he did without removing any clothing other than his mantle. Then, without making any sign, he went to his rest, delivering his soul to the Creator. This was shortly before four in the afternoon [In his biography of Serra, Palóu states that he died "a little before two in the afternoon" (Geiger, *Palóu's Life of Fray Junípero Serra*, p. 248)] on 28 August, feast of Saint Augustine, Doctor of the Church. When the bells began to toll all the people were afflicted, and the Indians cried over the death of their beloved Father, as did all rational beings, land dwellers and seamen alike. They asked for a small memento or some of the deceased Father's clothing, and even cut some pieces from the habit he had died in, in which he had been laid in the coffin without changing or removing anything (unbeknownst to us, he himself had arranged for his coffin, summoning the presido carpenter and asking him to make a box in which to bury his body). I promised them all that if they would be patient I would give them one of the deceased Father's tunics to make into scapulars, which they did. Even so, those watching over his body in the church cut off some of his fringe, moved by his reputation as a perfect and exemplary religious. Everyone living on land and aboard ship attended the deceased Father's funeral and did their best to honor him. The Captain of the ship ordered an artillery salute, giving him the honors of a general, and this was responded to in like manner from the Royal Presido. On 4 September there was a vigil and a High Memorial Mass. These ceremonies were also attended by all the people, including Father Preacher Antonio Paterna, Minister of the San Luís Mission, who had been unable to arrive in time for the burial service. The above has been set forth for the record and signed, by me, at this Mission, on 5 September 1784.

Fr. Francisco Palóu [rubric]

[5]Geiger, *The Life and Times of Fray Junípero Serra, O.F.M.*, 2:392.

[6]The expedition was lost at sea among the reefs north of New Hebrides in 1788, but La Pérouse's journals had already been forwarded to Paris, where they were published in 1797.

[7]Rudkin, *The First French Expedition to California*, p. 62.

[8]Finbar Kenneally, trans., *Writings of Fermín Francisco de Lasuén* (Washington, D.C.: Academy of American Franciscan History, 1965), 1:143.

[9]A few hundred copies were printed. The exact publication total, as well as the exact 1787 publication date, are unknown.

[10]Marguerite Eyer Wilber, ed., *Vancouver in California, 1792-1794* (Los Angeles: Glen Dawson, 1954), p. 65.

[11]Ibid.

[12]Ibid., p. 190. Vancouver did not visit Mission Carmel on his second tour of California. He presented the organ to Lasuén at San Diego. Lasuén wrote:

> Señor Vancouver made me a gift of an organ. I saw it in his cabin the previous year, and noted how much he esteemed it. I would not have parted with it for anything, and the thought of such a present never entered my mind. By merely turning a small handle you get the most beautiful sound. It plays thirty-four brief melodies (*tocadas*), and none is far removed from what is sacred. It is an instrument of beauty and a truly precious one. May God be his reward—for that was and can be the only price I can give in return. . . . Now I find I have the unavoidable problem of transporting it there [to Carmel]. The job will be a little risky, but not very difficult. It is now here in San Juan [Capistrano], and on Christmas Night [1793] and Christmas Day it was played to the indescribable delight and amazement of the Indians. [Kenneally, Writings of Fermín Francisco de Lasuén, 1:298]

Vancouver also named the northern and southern points of San Pedro Bay (Los Angeles County) after Lasuén. Today they are still known as Points Fermin and Lasuen.

[13]Kenneally, *Writings of Fermín Francisco de Lasuén*, 1:322. Vancouver's potatoes were descendents of the "perfectly sound" Chilean potatoes that La Pérouse had given the mission in 1786.

[14]"Report of the State of this Mission of San Carlos of Monterey on December 31st 1796," Mission Carmel Archives, Carmel, p. 2.

[15]Kenneally, *Writings of Fermín Francisco de Lasuén*, 2:329.

[16]F. W. Beechey, *An Account of a Visit to California, 1826-27* (San Francisco: Grabhorn Press, 1941), p. 71. The painting is also mentioned by Angustias de la Guerra Ord in her memoirs:

> A few months after my arrival in Monterey, [in 1833] he [Fr. Rafael de Jesús Moreno] gave my brother Juan a picture about a foot long which was in the parlor of the Mission . . . [which] portrayed the official reception given at the door of the Mission church for the Count de La Perousse [*sic*] [La Pérouse]. . . . This picture, when my brother Juan was prostrated by the illness of which he died, he gave me and I kept in a trunk until 1838 or 1839 when someone abstracted it and I was never again to see it, in spite of great efforts to find it. [Ord, *Occurrences in Hispanic California*, pp. 26-27]

[17]Zephyrin Engelhardt, *Mission San Carlos Borromeo* (Santa Barbara: Mission Santa Barbara, 1934), p. 214. Due to the instability of Mexican currency in 1834, it is very difficult to convert the *peso* into an equivalent U.S. dollar figure. As a reference point, of the total secularization amount for Mission Carmel (46,022 *pesos*), the church building accounted for 10,000 *pesos*. The church furniture, sacred vessels, vestments, etc., and the library were collectively assessed at 10,217 *pesos*, 7 *reales*, 4 *granos*. The Bucareli Monstrance was valued at 178 *pesos*, the *Glory of Heaven* painting at 20, and a copy of Palóu's *Relación histórica* Serra biography at 2 *pesos*.

[18]Richard Henry Dana, Jr., *Two Years Before the Mast* (New York: New American Library, 1964), pp. 219-20.

[19]Francis J. Weber, comp. and ed., *Father of the Missions: A Documentary History of San Carlos Borromeo* (Hong Kong: Libra Press Limited, 1984), pp. 54-55.

[20]Thomas Jefferson Farnham, *Travels in California* (Oakland: Biobooks, 1947), pp. 110, 112.

[21]William R. Garner, *Letters from California, 1846-1847* (Berkeley: University of California Press, 1970), p. 98.

[22]Bayard Taylor, *Eldorado, or, Adventures in the Path of Empire* (London: George Routledge and Co., 1850), pp. 117-18.

[23]Maynard Geiger, "Where is Serra Buried?," *Provincial Annals* 24 (April 1962):124.

[24]Ibid.

[25]Ibid.

[26]Ibid.

[27]Zephyrin Engelhardt, *Mission San Carlos Borromeo*, p. 217.

[28]Francis P. Farquhar, ed., *Up and Down California in 1860-1864: The Journal of William H. Brewer* (New Haven: Yale University Press, 1930), pp. 106-07.

[29]Marie C. Pagliarulo, "The Restoration of Mission San Carlos Borromeo, Carmel, California, 1931-1967," Mission Carmel Archives, Carmel, p. 14.

[30]Robert Louis Stevenson, *The Travels and Essays of Robert Louis Stevenson* (New York: Charles Scribner's Sons, 1895), pp. 167-68.

[31]Pagliarulo, "The Restoration of Mission San Carlos Borromeo," p. 14.

[32]"Father Serra's Grave," *Academy Scrapbook* 1 (October 1950):102-03. The stole must have faded, for although it does have somewhat of a violet hue, it is predominantly brown.

[33]Harry Downie to Eric O'Brien, O.F.M., Vice-Postulator, letter, 1 March 1945, Mission Carmel Archives, Carmel, p. 5.

[34]R. E. White, *Padre Junipero Serra and the Mission Church of San Carlos del Carmelo* (San Francisco: R. E. White, 1884), p. 22.

[35]Geiger, "Where is Serra Buried?," 24 (October 1962):231-32.

[36]White, *Padre Junipero Serra and the Mission Church of San Carlos del Carmelo*, p. 27.

[37]"At San Carlos. Padre Serra's Life Work Commemorated," *San Francisco Chronicle*, 29 August 1884, p. 1.

[38]Ibid.

[39]Ibid.

[40]"A Pioneer Padre. The 100th Anniversary of Junipero Serra's Death," *Daily Alta California*, 29 August 1884, p.1.

[41]"The Junipero Monument," *Pacific Grove Review*, 6 July 1891, p. 2.

[42]Ibid.

[43]Ibid. Before erecting her statue on U.S. government-owned Monterey Presidio property, Mrs. Stanford (wife of former California governor and U.S. Senator Leland Stanford) had been required to obtain permission from the War Department. In her letter of 17 May 1890 to Secretary of War Reofield Proctor, she wrote:

> While in California last year, I made a trip to Monterey and my attention was directed to a large white wooden cross, situated in an obscure spot. On questioning I learned that this cross was to mark the landing place of Father Junipero Serra who came to California to work among the Indians. During his lifetime he founded twelve [sic] [nine] different missions in California and was a successful worker for the Master. This cross marked the spot where the boat landed that brought him from the ship. I conceived the idea of erecting something more enduring and more instructive to his memory. The spot is at the base of an eminence, where still stand the ruins of the old fort, built at the time when General Fremont was stationed there. Only a little of the *adobe* still remains to mark the spot. I have now being made a large statue of the missionary representing him stepping from a small boat, an exact reproduction of that in which he landed. It rests on a granite foundation, depicting the land and water dashing against it. I really think when finished it will be a unique and beautiful monument. To carry out the idea of historical accuracy, I desire it should stand on the spot, where now are the ruins of the fort, and at the foot of this eminence, the wooden cross will remain. The land belongs to the United States government. I now ask of you the permission to com-

mence the foundations and granting the use of the site. With high esteem I remain Respectfully, Jane L. Stanford. [Jane Stanford to Secretary of War Reofield Proctor, 17 May 1890, U.S. Army Museum, Presidio of Monterey, Monterey]

Final approval was granted on 19 July 1890. The War Department document noted that

the monument to Father Junipero Serra on the site of the old fort at Monterey, California . . . can readily be so placed as not to interfere with any batteries which it may be found expedient to erect at that point at any future time. It will only be exposed to the remote chance of destruction in the improbable event of such batteries being subjected to the fire of an enemy. ["Document 12, Headquarters of the Army, Washington, July 9, 1890," U.S. Army Museum, Presidio of Monterey, Monterey]

[44]Ibid.

[45]"Historic Oak Tree is Dead," *Monterey New Era*, 6 July 1904, p. 3.

46"Historic Oak to be Preserved," *Monterey New Era*, 4 October 1905, p.1.

[47]"Monument Has Arrived," *Monterey Daily Cypress*, 24 March 1908, p. 1. None of the local newspapers carried the 3 June unveiling, if indeed there was one. Donor James Murray had spent nearly three years obtaining a monument that "suit[ed] him," and may have lost interest by 1908. The story began in August 1905, as recorded in the *Monterey New Era*:

A handsome cross of Vermont granite, twelve feet in height, set on a solid concrete base, will soon be reared. James H. Murray, the Montana millionare, who recently bought the Tevis hacienda in New Monterey, has obtained permission from the War Department to erect the proposed monument, and has arranged for the construction of its base. . . . Heretofore, this historic spot . . . has been marked merely by a simple cross of wood. It is but fitting that an enduring monument of stone should mark this landing place of [Serra,] the first and greatest of the pioneers. ["Monument for Serra's Landing Place," *Monterey New Era*, 30 August 1905, p. 1]

This first cross arrived in Monterey on 16 November 1906:

The new granite cross . . . has arrived. It will be unloaded from the car at the depot at the old Capital city in a few days. . . . The foundation for the cross was made several months ago and during the past few days workmen have been engaged in preparing for the reception of the cross. The cross is of granite and is ten [sic] [eight] feet in length. The base is also of granite and is four feet in heighth. The inscription on the base reads "Junipero Serra 1770." The letters are chiseled out in bold relief and are polished. Appropriate exercises will follow the unveiling of the cross and Mr. Murray will probably be asked to deliver the address on the occasion. The old wooden cross which marked the landing place of the Franciscan Fathers was removed several months ago. ["Monterey News Items," *Pacific Grove Daily Review*, 16 November 1906, p. 1]

However, Murray did not like the finished product, as reported five days later:

James Murray, the multi-millionare, has decided to purchase a cross in Ireland or Scotland to mark the landing place of Junipero Serra at Monterey. Mr. Murray had a granite cross constructed by a San Francisco firm, but it did not suit him and now he has decided to go across the pond and get one. He has evidently decided that American workmanship is inferior to that of our "cousins" across the sea. However, there are a good many Americans who think that as good a cross could be made in America as in Ireland, England, Scotland or Wales, and a native stone would be more appropriate to mark the landing place of Junipero Serra than an imported one. ["Monterey News Items," *Pacific Grove Daily Review*, 21 November 1906, p. 4]

The rejected cross (similar in "Celtic" design to the present one, but free-standing and not imbedded in a supporting shaft) was placed in San Carlos Cemetery, Monterey, where it still stands minus inscription (the cross measures 8′ 1″ tall on a 4′ pedestal base). Apparently Murray bowed to local pressure, for rather than "go[ing] across the pond" to commission a second cross, he once again chose a "native" firm to carve the present Vizcaíno-Serra landing site cross that arrived on 24 March 1908.

[48]"Junipero Serra Celebration at Carmel by the Sea," *Monterey Daily Cypress*, 25 November 1913, p. 1. The celebration was actually held one day early, on Sunday 23 November.

[49] Ibid.

[50]*Acceptance and Unveiling of the Statues of Junipero Serra and Thomas Starr King* (Washington, D.C.: United States Government Printing Office) p. 56.

[51]Harry Downie corrected the error when the cell was actually built and properly placed near the northeast corner of the mission quadrangle.

[52]Mora's artistic license permits the already deceased Crespí to attend Serra at his death, in an attempt to capture the conviviality of those who rest with Serra in death at the foot of Mission Carmel's altar. The cenotaph was originally intended for placement over Serra's grave, but as the scope of the project increased, the location was changed.

[53]Sydney Temple, *The Carmel Mission* (Fresno: Valley Publishers, 1980), p. 120.

[54]*Acceptance and Unveiling of the Statues of Junipero Serra and Thomas Starr King*, p. 21.

[55]Ibid., pp. 29-30. California had attempted to select Statuary Hall representatives on several occasions prior to 1931, but conflicting public opinion had stalled the process. On 1 January 1921, the *San Francisco Bulletin* ("Statuary Plebiscite at End," p. 2) conducted a poll, and out of "nearly a hundred" candidates, the leading contenders at that time were:

Mariano Vallejo (1808-90), military leader/politician . . . . 4,417 votes

Junípero Serra (1713-84), Catholic priest/missionary 3,341

Thomas Starr King (1824-64), Unitarian minister/orator 1,837

Francis Bret Harte (1836-1902), author/poet 1,174

Gaspar de Portolá ranked a distant fourteenth, with 119 votes. By March 1927, a number of prominent individuals and civic groups (especially the Native Sons of the Golden West, Native Daughters of the Golden West, and the California Federation of Women's Clubs) had organized enough support to pass state legislation providing for the following:

Thomas Starr King and Fra Junipero Serra have been selected as two California representatives in the Hall of Fame, Statuary Hall, at the National Capitol, Washington, D.C. This decision was reached today by the Senate Finance Committee, in approving a concurrent resolution and a companion bill to provide for statues of these early Californians. A commission composed of the State Librarian [Mabel Gillis] and four members selected by the Governor [Herbert Bolton, Chairman, Department of History, University of California, Berkeley; Hon. John Davis, Past Grand President, Native Sons of the Golden West; Mary Gibson, California Federation of Women's Clubs; and Grace Stoermer, Past Grand President, Native Daughters of the Golden West] will spend the next two years in examining models and selecting a sculptor to carve the statues. ["Two Clerics Chosen for Fame," *San Francisco Chronicle*, 30 March 1927, p. 1]

After the sculptors were chosen, the statues completed and transported to Washington, D.C., they were accepted by Act of Congress into Statuary Hall on 1 March 1931. The Act (Senate Concurrent Resolution 40, 72nd Congress, 1st Session) reads:

Resolved by the Senate (the House of Representatives concurring), that the statues of Junípero Serra and Thomas Starr King, presented by the State of California, to be placed in Statuary Hall, are accepted in the name of the United States, and that the thanks of Congress be tendered said State for the contribution of the statues of these eminent men, illustrious for their distinguished services as pioneer patriots of said State. [*Acceptance and Unveiling of the Statues of Junipero Serra and Thomas Starr King*, p. 61]

Thomas Starr King (17 December 1824—4 March 1864), was a Unitarian minister from Boston (1846-60) who accepted a call to the Unitarian parish of San Francisco (1860). He was an eloquent preacher and lecturer, and soon became the young state's moral arbiter, inspiring religion, culture, and a humanitarian search for "Yosemites of the soul." He ardently endorsed a pro-Union California during the Civil War, and as spokesman for the Sanitary Commission (American Red Cross predecessor), he helped raise over one million dollars for the Union Army. The state legislature adjourned for three days when he died of pneumonia, and 20,000 mourners lined the funeral route. He is buried in a white marble sarcophagus next to the Unitarian Church on Franklin Street between Starr King and Geary Streets, San Francisco. Paying tribute to both King and Serra, author Kevin Starr wrote:

> When the legislature selected statutes of Junípero Serra and Thomas Starr King to represent California in the National Hall of Fame, it showed how green the memory of King had remained. Serra stood for Spanish Catholic beginnings; King stood for the best possibilities of the American Protestant succession. [Starr, *Americans and the California Dream*, 1850-1915, p. 105]

Including Serra and Starr, sixteen religious leaders are represented in Statuary Hall (of which six are Catholics). Overall, Serra is one of thirteen Catholics represented in the Hall.

[56]"Serra's Death Remembered Here Sunday," *Monterey Peninsula Herald*, 26 August 1937, p. 9.

[57]Geiger, "Where is Serra Buried," 25 (April 1963):122.

[58]Ibid., 23 (October 1961):367.

[59]Ibid., 25 (October 1963):253-54.

[60]Ibid., 26 (January 1964):77.

[61]Ibid., 26 (April 1964):143.

[62]Ibid., 26 (January 1964):77.

[63]Ibid., 25 (July 1963):189, 191. The reliquary also contains a second-class relic of at least one other individual. The word *San* (Saint), is clearly discernable over one relic, which could not pertain to *Beato* (Blessed) Ramón Llull.

[64]Ibid., 26 (January 1964):77.

[65]"News Comments: A Day That Will Be Remembered," *Monterey Peninsula Herald*, 27 August 1956, p. 2.

[66]"President Visits Carmel Mission," *Monterey Peninsula Herald*, 27 August 1956, p. 1.

[67]*Exercises Commemorating and Honoring the Memory of Father Junipero Serra, O.F.M.* (Washington, D.C: United States Government Printing Office), p. iii.

[68]"Kennedy Denies Charges by Morse," *Monterey Peninsula Herald*, 30 May 1960, p. 1.

[69]In the following year (1962), Mission Carmel was again honored for its special historical significance when it was declared a U.S. National Historic Landmark. Mission Carmel is also registered California Historical Landmark number 135.

[70]Kieran McCarty, "Anniversary of Birth of Fray Junípero Serra," *The Americas* 20 (October 1963):206-07.

[71]Francis J. Weber, comp. and ed., *Some "Fugitive" Glimpses at Fray Junípero Serra* (Hong Kong: Libra Press Limited, 1983), p. 160.

[72]As the 250th anniversary of Serra's birth approached, supporters sought national recognition for the event. Rev. Noel Moholy, O.F.M., S.T.D., Serra Cause Vice-Postulator, discussed the possibilities in September 1963:

> Serra is . . . to be honored on the national scene. Approval continues to be sought from the Post Office Department for a commemorative postage stamp, marking the important anniversary. All the members of California's delegation to the Congress of the United States have introduced bills, authorizing the striking of an official commemorative medal by the Treasury Department. The bill, co-authored in the Senate by both Senators from California [the Hon. Thomas H. Kuchel and the Hon. Clair Engle], already has been passed. In the House of Representatives the parallel bill has been accepted by the Subcommittee on Consumer Affairs. Approval by the Committee on Banking and Currency and subsequent passage by the House of Representatives are anticipated in the near

future. [McCarty, "Anniversary of Birth of Fray Junípero Serra," *The Americas* 20 (October 1963), p. 206]

The stamp was not approved at this time, but all legislation necessary for the medal was passed. During discussions in the U.S. Senate, the Hon. Clair Engle noted:

It is significant that Father Serra labored in California in the same years during which men of politics labored on the eastern coast to establish the institutions and traditions that formed the basis of our democratic society. Father Serra's approach was somewhat different. His emphasis was on the cross and on the things of the spirit—but his labors were not restricted to this field. He knew as well or better than any man that, along with the things of the spirit, we must have economic, political, and social order. This diminutive man in body had the heart, mind, and spirit of a giant. Symbolically he represents the heart of California. We can do no less than to honor him by issuing the commemorative medal proposed in S. 743. [U.S. Congress, Senate, "Padre Junipero Serra 250th Anniversary Medal," 88th Cong., 1st sess., 24 June 1963, *Senate Reports: Miscellaneous Reports on Public Bills*, vol. 2, report no. 291, p 5.]

In the U.S. House of Representatives, the California delegation offered the following analogy:

Padre Junipero Serra represented in his life and in his works the spirit of our present-day Peace Corps, in that he voluntarily chose, instead of the quiet, comfortable life of a university professor or a city priest, the rugged, challenging assignment of bringing knowledge and assistance to peoples living in primitive, wilderness conditions. [U.S. Congress, House, "Padre Junipero Serra 250th Anniversary Medals," 88th Cong., 1st sess., 25 September 1963, *House Reports: Miscellaneous Reports on Public Bills*, vol. 4, report no. 768, pp. 2-3]

The Public Law that President Kennedy signed reads:

Public Law 88-143

Be it enacted by the Senate and House of Representatives of the United States of America in Congress assembled, that in the commemoration of the two hundred and fiftieth anniversary of the birth of Padre Junipero Serra, who was born in Mallorca, Spain, on November 24, 1713, and came to the west coast in 1769 where he founded the first ten [sic] [nine] missions, which became the nucleus of civilization in what is now California, the Secretary of the Treasury is authorized and directed to strike and furnish to the Padre Junipero Serra 250th Anniversary Association [a non-profit corporation formed by the Serra Cause to pay the full cost of minting the medal] not more than three hundred thousand medals with suitable emblems, devices and inscriptions to be determined by the Padre Junipero Serra 250th Anniversary Association subject to the approval of the Secretary of the Treasury. The medals shall be made and delivered at such time as may be required by the association in quantities of not less than two thousand, but no medals shall be made after December 31, 1964. The medals shall be considered to be national medals within the meaning of section 3551 of the Revised Statutes.
Sec. 2. The Secretary of the Treasury shall cause such medals to be struck and furnished at not less than the estimated cost of manufacture, including labor, material, dies, use of machinery, and overhead expenses; and security satisfactory to the Director of the Mint shall be furnished to indemnify the United States for the full payment of such cost.
Sec. 3. The medals authorized to be issued pursuant to this Act shall be of such size or sizes and of such metals as shall be determined by the Secretary of the Treasury in consultation with such association.
Approved October 16, 1963. [Public Law 88-143—October 16, 1963, *United States Statutes at Large* 77:251]

[73]Timothy Cardinal Manning, Homily, 28 August 1984, videotape transcript, Mission Carmel Archives, Carmel.

[74]Ronald Reagan to Most Rev. Thaddeus Shubsda, telegram, 19 August 1985, Mission Carmel Archives, Carmel.

[75]According to historian Francis J. Weber:

Efforts to have a postage stamp issued to honor Fray Junípero Serra are almost as old as his cause for canonization. Over the last thirty years innumerable people have joined forces to seek postal recognition for Serra. On at least one occasion [1963], the project got as far along as the Citizen's

Stamp Advisory Committee, but there was voted down. ["Serra Stamp to be Issued in San Diego," *The Tidings*, 16 August 1985, p. 3]

Appointed by the U.S. Postmaster General, the Citizen's Stamp Advisory Committee is an organization of private individuals with the authority to consider suggestions for new U.S. postage stamps. If they endorse a theme or individual, then the Postmaster General studies the proposal and makes the final decision. When the Serra Bicentennial Commission of the California Catholic Conference was established in 1983 to initiate and coordinate events during the 1984 bicentennial of Serra's death, one of its primary objectives was to promote issuance of a Serra postage stamp. The Commission suggested the idea to the Citizen's Stamp Advisory Committee, but it was rejected on grounds that the U.S. Postal Service never issues commemorative stamps to mark a person's death. Private and public support continued to grow however, including a letter of endorsement initiated by Hon. Leon E. Panetta, U.S. Representative, Sixteenth District, and signed by twenty-seven fellow California Congressman in March 1984. Congressman Panetta wrote in part:

> [This is] a very appropriate time to honor Father Serra and his contributions to our State and to Spanish culture in our country. . . . As one of the most important figures in California history, . . . [Serra] deserves the recognition that a commemorative stamp would provide. . . . I hope this strong bipartisan support . . . will convince the Postal Service to issue a stamp in Father Serra's honor. [Panetta, Rep. Leon E., "For Immediate Release—March 20, 1984: Panetta Leads Effort for Commemorative Stamp to Honor Father Serra," Mission Carmel Archives, Carmel]

After President Reagan's support was also gained, the proposal was finally accepted. In conjunction with his visit to Mallorca as a member of the official U.S. delegation commemorating the Serra bicentennial, U.S. Secretary of the Interior William P. Clark made the Serra stamp announcement on 13 October 1984. The stamp's design was announced at the fiftieth anniversary meeting of Serra International (a Catholic lay organization dedicated to promoting vocations to the priesthood), in New York City on 1 July 1985. The airmail format was chosen to reflect Serra's international appeal.

Of all the stamps issued to honor Serra, none is more a philatelic oddity than Mexico's eighty *centavo* stamp. Issued in 1969 to commemorate the bicentennial of California's founding, the stamp intended to portray Serra's face as reproduced from *Serra's Viaticum*. In fact, the inscription on the stamp does say "*Fray Junípero Serra, colonizador de las Californias*" (Fray Junípero Serra, colonizer of the Californias). However, the priest on the stamp is not Serra. The designer confused the identity of the two central characters in the painting, and excerpted the priest administering Communion (usually identified as Palóu), rather than the one receiving it!

[76]Imprimatur: Most Rev. Thaddeus Shubsda, Bishop of Monterey in California.

[77]Geiger, *The Life and Times of Fray Junípero Serra, O.F.M.*, 2:287.

Glossary

AGNUS DEI SACRAMENTAL: Sacramentals are

> sacred signs which bear a resemblance to the sacraments: they signifiy effects, particularly of a spiritual kind, which are obtained through the Church's intercession. By them, men are disposed to receive the chief effect of the sacraments, and various occasions in life are rendered holy. [*New Catholic Encyclopedia*, 12:790]

Examples of this "sign language" of the Catholic Church are rosaries, medals, holy water, ashes, and *Agnus Dei* sacramentals. An *Agnus Dei* is a small disc of wax blessed by the Pope. The tradition dates from the fourth century, and was associated with protection from pestilence, fire, flood, and calamity in general. The discs are customarily blessed on Holy Wednesday in the first and successive seventh year of each pontificate, and distributed on Holy Saturday. The obverse is impressed with the *Agnus Dei* (Lamb of God), referring to Christ in his sacrificial role, and bearing a cross or banner signifying the triumph of His Resurrection. The reverse bears the coat of arms of the Pope, figure of a saint, or in the case of the *Agnus Dei* in Serra's Indian reliquary, Our Lady of the Rosary and the Infant Jesus.

AGREDA, VENERABLE SOR MARÍA DE JESÚS DE (2 April 1602—24 May 1665): Born in Agreda, Burgos, Spain; baptized María Fernández Coronel; became Discalced Franciscan nun [also known as contemplative Poor Clares] (1620); served as Abbess of La Purísima Convent in Agreda (1627-65); adviser to and correspondent with Felipe IV of Spain (1643-65); wrote life of Blessed Virgin Mary on basis of alleged divine revelation, *Mística ciudad de Dios*, (*Mystical City of God*, pub. 1670, first English translation 1914). Known as the "Woman in Blue" or "Blue Lady of the Plains," Venerable Sister Mary allegedly possessed the divine gifts of bilocation and tongues. Numerous southwest U.S. missionary and Indian accounts tell of her miraculous evangelical visitations to various Indian tribes, and of preaching in native languages that paved the way for later Christian conversions. Although declared Venerable shortly after her death, her controversial book was condemned by the *Index Librorum Prohibitorum* (Catholic *Index of Prohibited Books*) in 1681 (ban lifted 1713), and the Sorbonne in 1696. The Spanish Inquisition pronounced in its favor, and Agreda's Spanish reputation remained intact. Several copies of *Mystical City* were always on hand at San Fernando College, and her life and writings influenced Serra and his contemporaries. In 1772, Serra wrote:

> In regard to the promise made by God in these modern times to Our Father Saint Francis—as our Seraphic Mother Mary of Jesus declares—that the gentiles, at the mere sight of his sons [the Franciscans], will be converted to our Holy Catholic Faith, it is my opinion that we are now seeing it with our eyes and touching it with our hands. [Tibesar, *Writings of Junípero Serra*, 1:267]

Palóu also linked Agreda to the California missions in 1773:

> These fathers [at Mission San Antonio] tell me that there was a very old heathen woman, who, according to her appearance, was more than a hundred years old [Serra called her the *puella centum annorum* (hundred-year-old girl) (Tibesar, *Writings of Junípero Serra*, 2:3, 5); Palóu gave her name as "Agueda," in another version (Geiger, *Palóu's Life of Fray Junípero Serra*, p. 112)]. She went to them to be baptized, telling the missionary fathers that the reason that moved her to do so was because when she was a girl she heard her father say that a priest who wore the same habit as we, had come to this land, not traveling on horseback or on foot, but flying; and that he preached to them the same as they

were now preaching, and that remembering this caused her to be a Christian. The fathers, surprised at the story of the happy old woman, happy because she succeeded at the end of so many years in obtaining holy Baptism, questioned the Indians who had already become Christians, and they told the same story, saying that they had heard their ancestors tell it, and that the story had passed from one to another. When the fathers told me about this occurrence, I recalled the letter which the Venerable María de Jesús de Agreda wrote to the missionaries of my holy Order employed in the conquest of New Mexico, in which she tells them that Our Father [Saint Francis of Assisi] took to these northern nations two friars of his Order to preach the faith of Jesus Christ, and that after converting many they died martyred. Comparing the time, it seems probable that one of them was the one which the old woman tells about. This being the case, we may hope for great conversions in this immense body of heathen. [Bolton, *Historical Memoirs of New California*, 3:227-28]

Mission Santa Cruz Indians also had a similar tradition, recounted by Fathers Marcelino Marquínez and Jayme Escudé in their 1814 reply to a Spanish government questionaire about Indian life and customs:

From their forefathers they preserve the tradition that in some former times a famous foreign missionary woman came to these regions. This seems to confirm the fact of the apostolic preaching of the Venerable María de Jesús de Agreda in California. [Geiger, *The Life and Times of Fray Junípero Serra, O.F.M.*, 1:295]

In another version of the story, the Santa Cruz Indians called Agreda

the *padre* of the "*mamas*" (the *padre* with the breasts) for, say they, she appeared to them dressed as a *padre* and had a "big bosom." They say she preached to them that within a short time there would come white men to show them the way to heaven. [Ibid., pp. 295-96]

ALCALDE: Mayor or magistrate. The policy of electing an Indian "mayor" at each California mission (along with *regidores* [counselors] to assist the *alcalde*) was initiated by Governor Neve in 1779. Envisioned as the first step toward Indian self-government, the plan drew sharp criticism from Serra, who felt that the Indians were not ready to assume such responsibility. The *alcalde* exercised jurisdiction over the treatment and discipline of fellow Indians, was exempt from physical punishment, and was given special regalia of office to wear. In August 1779 Serra wrote:

Touching on the matter of *alcaldes*, I have taxed my imagination. Never did I consider them as a mere formality. In a very short time I realized here that such was not the case. But in fact, this smashing up and breaking down simply wreaks havoc, and beyond repair, with the uniform organization of all the missions. Some, without thinking, were overjoyed, and reported that they were getting along splendidly with them. But the Father at San Luís, who was one of the most enthusiastic, now says that only the *regidor* is of any use. The alcalde took advantage of his office to indulge in numerous crimes. They had puffed them up so much, that they really thought they were *señores* [noble gentlemen]. The *alcalde* here [Baltasar, a native of the Ichxenta *Ranchería*, about forty-five years old, and a Christian for four years] has not yet come out of his strawberry-colored cotton drapes and knickers. [Tibesar, *Writings of Junípero Serra*, 3:364-65]

In January 1780, Serra discussed Baltasar's behavior in more detail:

Once aware of his privileges and exemption from correction by the Fathers, [he] began to do just as he pleased. He had a son by one of his relatives, and had a California Indian flogged because he carried out an order from the Father missionary. . . . There is no need to speak of his neglect of duty while in office. And now, everyone sees and knows in what circumstances he is living—deserter, adulterer, and inciting the people here, meeting personally those who leave here with permission, and thereby trying to swell the numbers of his band from the mountains by new desertions of the natives of this mission. [Ibid., p. 409]

Through confrontation and compromise, Neve's policy was slowly diluted until the posts of *alcalde* and *regidor* were largely ceremonial. Elections were held, Indians were chosen, but they were once again subordinate to the missionaries and subject to disciplinary action when recalcitrant.

ANZA, CAPTAIN JUAN BAUTISTA DE (1735—19 December 1788): Born at Fronteras Presidio, Sonora Province (present Arizona); commandant of Tubac Presidio, Sonora; authorized by Viceroy Bucareli to develop plan for opening land route from Sonora to the Pacific coast; reconnoitered (8 January—26 May 1774) through Colorado Desert to Mission San Gabriel, from there to Monterey and

back to Tubac; second expedition (29 September 1775—27 June 1776) from San Miguel de Horcasitas, Sonora, followed more southerly route, and successfully delivered 242 settlers to San Francisco for founding of presidio-mission (Anza was not present, having reversed course at Monterey to return to Mexico); served as governor of New Mexico (1777-88); buried in the former cathedral and now parish Church of Nuestra Señora de la Asunción, Arizpe, Sonora, Mexico. Anza's Sonora-California Trail was permanently abandoned after the Yuma Indians massacred a party of passing colonists on 17 July 1781 (near the confluence of the Colorado and Gila Rivers, where California, Arizona, and Mexico meet). Disappointed by unkept Spanish promises offering economic aid and a mission of their own, and infuriated by continued encroachments upon their territory, the Indians retaliated by killing expedition leader Captain Fernando de Rivera y Moncada, at least forty-six soldiers, four missionaries, taking women and children hostage, and destroying two missions. When Serra heard the news, he wrote:

> All we can do is to offer our sympathy for the sufferings of so many poor fellows who met their death there and bow before the inscrutable decrees of God. If they now kill the Indians, nothing more can be expected from the Colorado River which was so much talked about and the center of so many hopes. [Tibesar, *Writings of Junípero Serra*, 4:103]

Two months later the hostages were ransomed, and military reprisal, although planned, was never carried out. No further attempt was made to colonize or garrison the site, and California was thereafter accessible only by sea. The Yuma region remained isolated until American military intervention in the mid-to-late nineteenth century.

APOSTOLIC COLLEGE: First introduced into the New World by the Franciscans in 1683 with the establishment of Mexico's Santa Cruz de Querétaro College, an apostolic college was not an educational institution in the traditional sense, but rather a center for missionary recruitment, fieldwork training, and administration. In addition to Christianizing Indian territory, apostolic colleges also coordinated "missions" of preaching and prayer among the Christian populace. Mexico City's San Fernando College, autonomous daughter of Santa Cruz, was founded by royal decree on 15 October 1733. San Fernando served three mission fields between 1733 and 1853: the Sierra Gorda of Mexico (1744-1770); Lower California (1768-1773); and Upper California (1769-1853). Recruited mostly from Spain, San Fernando sent a total of 127 missionaries into Upper California between 1769 and 1833. Our Lady of Sorrows Apostolic College at Mission Santa Bárbara, daughter of San Fernando, was established in 1853, the forerunner of the modern Franciscan Santa Barbara Province, established in 1915 (Serra commented on this possibility in 1771: "We may not see it ourselves, but . . . some day our successors may see the holy Province of California. . . . Some may joke about such a plan. However it does not seem to me ludicrous at all." [Tibesar, *Writings of Junípero Serra*, 1:219]). San Fernando College was formally abolished in 1908, the last of its buildings demolished in 1935, and all that remains today of Serra's Mexico City home and college headquarters is the restored San Fernando Church, dedicated in 1755.

ASPERGES CEREMONY: From the Latin *Asperges me hyssopo et mundabor* (You will sprinkle me with hyssop [twigs from a Biblical plant used in certain Hebraic purificatory rites] and I shall be cleansed [Psalm 51:7]). A short rite, preceding a Mass or special ceremony, which consists of sprinkling the altar, congregation, etc., with holy water, i.e. water blessed by a priest and symbolic of spiritual cleansing. The holy water is drawn from a portable stoup/bucket, and is sprinkled by means of the "aspergill" or "aspergillum."

ASSISI, SAINT FRANCIS OF (c.1181—3 October 1226): Born in Assisi, Italy; baptized Giovanni (John) Bernardone, nicknamed Francesco (Francis) by his father; abandoned extravagant lifestyle after sickness, civil-war imprisonment, and vision which led to personal conversion through prayer and penance (1205); heard voice from crucifix at San Damiano Church near Assisi say: "Francis, repair my falling house" (1207); rebuilt churches, severed family relations, renounced possessions "to wed Lady Poverty" and "love the poor" (1207-09); formulated program based on observance of the Gospels after hearing the words of Matthew 10:6-16 during Mass (Francis was not a priest):

> Go . . . after the lost sheep . . . cure the sick, raise the dead, heal the leprous, expel demons. Provide yourselves with neither gold nor silver nor copper in your belts; no traveling bag, no change of shirt, no sandals, no walking staff. . . . What I am doing is sending you out like sheep among wolves. You must be clever as snakes and innocent as doves.

The force of Francis' personality, preaching, and sanctity initiated a strong penitential movement in Italy. With Santa María degli Angeli Chapel (also called the Portiuncula) near Assisi as headquarters, the first Franciscan "Rule" was verbally approved by Pope Innocent III (16 April 1209), whereby each follower received tonsure and a license to preach, subject to ecclesiastical jurisdiction (every Franciscan renews his/her vows annually on 16 April). Francis attempted a missionary journey to Syria (1212), but was shipwrecked in Dalmatia; attempted journey to Morocco (1213-14), but was taken ill in Spain; traveled to Middle East (1219), where he unsuccessfully tried to convert the Sultan of Egypt; returned to Italy (1220); Franciscan Rule revised and promulgated (1223); received the Stigmata (plural of Stigma, i.e. the supernatural gift of physically re-experiencing the five nail wounds of Jesus' Crucifixion) for the first time while praying on Mt. Alvernia in the Appenines (14 September 1224); suffered great pain/illness/blindness during the next two years until he welcomed "Sister Death." Francis was canonized in 1228, and is buried in the crypt of San Francesco Basilica, Assisi. His feast day is 4 October. Admiration and emulation of Saint Francis has been widespread and spontaneous among all Christians. In addition to the Franciscan Rule, his followers have been inspired by his writings, consisting of prayers, words of spiritual admonition, the *Office of the Passion, Testament*, and *Canticle of the Sun*. These works convey a man of tremendous spiritual insight and power, whose consuming love for Jesus Christ and redeemed creation found expression in everything he said and did. His inspiration came from the Gospels (and a special fondness for the teachings of Saint Paul) expressed in a practical following of Christ through fraternal charity and unpretentious poverty. To this task he brought simplicity, directness, single-mindedness, and a tempering of lyricism. Serra captured its essence when he wrote: "*Charitas Dei urget nos*" (The love of Christ is our driving force [2 Corinthians 5:14], Tibesar, *Writings of Junípero Serra*, 3:307).

ATOLE: *Nahuatl* (Mexican Aztec) word for a wheat or cornmeal mush/gruel.

BASILICA: From the Latin *basilicus* (royal), a Catholic title assigned to certain churches because of their antiquity, historical importance, dignity, or significance as centers of worship. There are two classes:
1) Major: reserved for the highest ranking churches in the world, such as Saint Peter's Basilica and Saint John Lateran Basilica, the Pope's cathedral. Major basilicas have a special Papal altar reserved exclusively for use by the Pope, and the Holy Door (opened only once every twenty-five years during the Holy Year, a tradition dating from 1300, during which pilgrims to Rome gain a special "jubilee" plenary indulgence [a pardon that remits the full temporal punishment incurred by a sinner]);
2) Minor: a church that enjoys certain Papally granted ceremonial privileges. In addition to historical importance, there are two other prerequisites: permanence of structure, and consecration of church/altar. Consecration involves placing relics of saints within the altar (Mission Carmel's altar was consecrated with the relics of Saint Innocent and Saint Candidus); anointing and affixing twelve small crosses to the inner walls of the nave; and carving two small crosses into the façade on either side of the main entrance (Mission Carmel was consecrated on 6-7 January 1960). There are four minor basilicas in California: Mission Dolores Parish Church adjoining Mission San Francisco, for its association with the old mission (Papal bull granting basilica status dated 8 February 1952); Mission Carmel (5 February 1960); Saint Joseph's Church, Alameda, for its artistic merit (21 January 1972); and Mission San Diego, successor to California's first church (17 November 1975). The clergy who serve in them enjoy a title of honor that gives them certain ceremonial rights, and within the church are displayed the following symbols of Papal recognition:

1) The *Tintinnabulum*: a small bell representing the medieval custom of Papal travel preceded by a bell to announce the Pope's passing. Mission Carmel Basilica's *Tintinnabulum* is inscribed *Basilica Sancti Caroli Borromaei* (Basilica [of] Saint Charles Borromeo).

2) The *Ombrellone*: a small canopy signifying the welcoming canopy that would greet the traveling Pope at the church door of his destination). Mission Carmel Basilica's *Ombrellone* was specially designed and embroidered with:

   a) Cardinal hat (Saint Charles Borromeo, patron of the mission and church).

   b) Lily and carpenter's square (Saint Joseph, titular patron of the church).

   c) Saw and blacksmith hammer (Serra is the Catalonian form of the Castilian *sierra*, or saw. His mother's maiden name, Ferrer, translates to *herrero* in Castilian, or ironworker/blacksmith). The Serra family did not have a coat of arms. These symbols were formulated specifically for Mission Carmel Basilica's *Ombrellone*.

d) Mountain with cross and three stars (Discalced Carmelite Order coat of arms, referring to basilica location. The mountain represents Palestine's Mount Carmel (meaning "orchard" in Hebrew), site of the Israelite prophet Elijah's altar and contest with the Canaanite god Baal (1 Kings 18: 19-46); the cross represents a return to primitive Carmelite rule instigated by Saint Teresa of Avila and Saint John of the Cross; the stars refer to the Old Testament, from which the Carmelites trace the origin of their Order back to Elijah).

BON ANY, NUESTRA SEÑORA DE: Our Lady of the Good Year, patroness of Petra, Mallorca. A sixteenth-century statue of the Blessed Virgin Mary is housed in a hilltop shrine above the town, completed in 1609. In that year of drought, a city-wide pilgrimage to the shrine brought rain and good crops. Hence, the title, and the following prayer of thanksgiving: "Give us a good year, O Lady, For key to a good year art thou" (Geiger, *The Life and Times of Fray Junípero Serra, O.F.M.*, 1: 11).

BONAVENTURE, SAINT (1221—15 July 1274): Born at Bagnoregio, near Viterbo, Italy; baptized Giovanni (John), name changed after grave illness, when, according to legend, Saint Francis of Assisi cured him and exclaimed "*O buona ventura*" (Oh good fortune); attended University of Paris and earned Master of Arts degree (1234); entered Franciscan Order (1243); earned Bachelor of Scripture degree, and taught theology and scripture (1248-53); earned doctorate in Theology along with classmate Thomas Aquinas (1257); elected Minister General of the Franciscan Order at age thirty-five (1257), and dubbed "second founder" of the Franciscans for effectively organizing, unifying, and reforming the Order; created cardinal, and appointed bishop of Albano (1273); advised Pope Gregory X and took active part in Second Council of Lyons, aimed at reuniting the Eastern Church with Rome; died suddenly while the council was in session, and buried in the Franciscan church at Lyons, France. Bonaventure was canonized in 1482, and declared a Doctor of the universal Catholic Church by the Franciscan Pope Sixtus V in 1588. His feast day is 15 July. Saint Bonaventure is known as *Doctor Seraphicus* (Seraphic Doctor) after Saint Francis, the "Seraph (Angel) of Assisi," and for his many biblical commentaries, sermons, and the "official" Franciscan biography of Saint Francis. He was responsible for crystalizing the loosely-defined threefold approach of Saint Francis (unity with God through prayer, imitation of Christ, and apostlic ministry) into a viable "new" Franciscan Rule that remained largely intact until Vatican Council II (1962-65). He formulated the most thorough exposition of Franciscan mystical theology (a spiritual discipline aimed at gaining knowledge of God through direct, intuitional experience known as "unifying love," as opposed to natural reason or divine revelation), and adopted many of Saint Augustine's theories to explain man's relationship to God. He concluded that natural, non-Christian knowledge is illusory, and that in order to attain true knowledge and wisdom, man must be led by Christ, the only true master. Bonaventure was also an influential scholastic thinker, and composed numerous theological and philosophical treatises.

BORROMEO, SAINT CHARLES (2 October 1538—3 November 1584): Born near Lake Maggiore, Lombardy, Italy, the second son of Count Giberto Borromeo and Margherita de Medici, sister of Pope Pius IV; studied law at University of Pavia and earned doctorate (1552-59); created Cardinal and appointed administrator of vacant See of Milan at age twenty-two (1560); appointed Vatican Secretary of State (1561); served as his uncle's most valued adviser during the reform-oriented Council of Trent (1562-63); ordained a priest and appointed archbishop of Milan (1563). Cardinal Borromeo spent the rest of his life applying the principles of the Council of Trent in his vast diocese, serving as a model of Catholic Counter-Reformation modernization and fighting for the suppression of Protestantism. In an era of lax discipline, his policies encountered opposition, and he was nearly assassinated on two occasions (1569). Borromeo established "Sunday schools," promoted a new catechism, opened seminaries, hospitals, orphanages, shelters for the homeless, and spent most of his fortune to aid the dying during the Great Plague of 1576. He was buried in the sanctuary of the Cathedral of Milan's main altar, and canonized in 1610. His feast day is 4 November.

BUCARELI Y URSÚA, VICEROY ANTONIO MARÍA. Full name with titles: The Most Excellent Lord Knight Commander Don Antonio Bucareli y Ursúa Henestrosa Laso de la Vega Villacís y Córdoba, Knight of the *Gran Cruz* and Knight Commander of the *Bóveda de Toro* in the Order of His Majesty with privilege of entrance, Lieutenant General of the Royal Army, Viceroy, Governor, and

 Captain General of New Spain, President of its Royal *Audiencia* (an administrative/judicial tribunal), Superintendent General of the Royal Treasury, President of its Board of Tobacco and Judge Conservator of this Branch, and Subdelegate General of Postal Revenues (24 January 1717—9 April 1779): Born in Seville, Spain, of noble lineage; fought in Italian and Portuguese military campaigns, achieved rank of lieutenant general; held various domestic administrative posts before leaving Spain; served as Governor and Captain General of Cuba (1766-71); served as the forty-sixth Viceroy of New Spain (22 September 1771—9 April 1779). With a population of nearly 5,000,000, the Viceroyalty of New Spain stretched from Guatemala in the south, to roughly Oregon and across to Louisiana in the north, a vast administrative network of kingdoms, provinces, colonies, presidencies, judicial divisions, and local governments. Bucareli wore many hats as viceroy, or "viceking" for Carlos III of Spain. As Superintendent of the *Real Hacienda* (Royal Treasury), he was responsible for the development, collection, and disbursement of Crown revenues (within the framework of the Gálvez *Visita* reforms). As Captain General of the Viceroyalty, he was supreme commander of all military personnel and attended to coastal defense, new territorial discovery, conquest, and settlement, as dictated by international politics. As the king's Vice-Patron, he monitored church-state relations based upon *Patronato Real* (Royal Patronage), whereby Rome had recognized the King of Spain as administrative head of the church in the Spanish Indies since the early sixteenth century, and which legitimized Carlos' 1767 expulsion of the Jesuits. Bucareli's New Spain was marked by great change, yet his viceregency capably and efficiently asssimilated them within the status quo. As for California, his policy took time to develop. In 1771 he wrote:

> Ask God to grant me strength to disentangle myself from the chaos of difficulties which enclose me in the confused management of these vast provinces, in which, to now, I walk in the shadows, because nothing is concluded. . . . Monte Rey, the Californias, and provinces of Sonora and Sinaloa neither have subsidies arranged, nor is it easily discovered how they are governed. [Bobb, *The Viceregency of Antonio María Bucareli in New Spain, 1771-1779*, p. 30]

After familiarizing himself with California's state of affairs, Bucareli devoted considerable attention to the province. Especially after Serra's visit (1773), he always managed to allocate sufficient funds to the enterprise, and constantly worked to improve the food supply link from San Blas to California. Also accomplished during his vice-regency: the Echeveste *Reglamento*, redefining all aspects of California provincial administration (drafted with input from Serra, about which Serra wrote: "In everything I was given a favorable hearing by His Excellency; he granted me all I asked for" [Tibesar, *Writings of Junípero Serra*, 1:391]) (1773); the first scientific expeditions to New Spain's northwest coast (1774 and 1775); and the Anza expedition, which opened the temporary California-Sonora overland trail and brought colonists to California (1776). With the creation of the *Provincias Internas* (1776), California passed from Bucareli's control, although he continued to administer the port of San Blas. He asked to retire at this time, and when the news reached California, Serra wrote:

> If this would be the last letter I am permitted to address to Your Excellency, because of these sad tidings, it is my duty to offer Your Excellency my most sincere thanks for the gracious favors you have deigned to show and dispense, during the successful and happy time of your government, to me, and to these new establishments, and through them to

our Apostolic College of San Fernando. . . . At the same time I ask you to pardon me and overlook, for the love of God, the importunity of my letters, many of them filled with indiscretions, with which I have burdened your attention throughout that time. My good intentions shall be my excuse. But, once more, I ask Your Excellency to pardon me. May Our Lord God keep Your Excellency, and grant you a most happy voyage, and long life, so that from Court, you may continue your good services in behalf of these new establishments. They have won for you great love, have cost you great troubles, and finally have merited for you a great crown of glory. [Tibesar, *Writings of Junípero Serra*, 2:413, 415]

Viceroy Bucareli did not retire, and remained in office until death. He is buried in the Old Basilica of Our Lady of Guadalupe, Mexico City.

CALIFORNIA, ORIGIN OF NAME: Word coined by Spanish author Garcí Ordóñez de Montalvo in his romantic narrative *Las sergas de Esplandián* (*The Exploits of Esplandián*, pub. 1510). The fictional character Esplandián visits a place

> at the right hand of the Indies . . . an island named California, very close to that part of the Terrestrial Paradise, which was inhabited by black women . . . liv[ing] in the manner of Amazons. . . . Their weapons were all made of gold. . . . There ruled over that island of California a queen of majestic proportions [Calafía]. [Wagner, *A History of California: The Spanish Period*, p. 58]

The first association between the book and the present State of California is uncertain. The name was originally applied to the Lower California Peninsula sometime shortly after its discovery (1533), possibly when pearls were found in peninsular waters. By the time of the Cabrillo-Ferrer expedition (1542), the link was common. The name remained restricted to the peninsula, appearing on maps as an island, with the present state vaguely known as Quivira, after another mythical kingdom. When Sir Francis Drake claimed northern California (New Albion) for England (1579), the Spanish began extending the name to the entire coast for purposes of preemptive sovereignty. The distinction between Upper (*Alta, Nueva* [New], or *Septentrional* [Northern]) and Lower (*Baja,* or *Antigua* [Old]) was introduced after Spanish colonization of the upper region (1769), to distinguish it from the older, already settled peninsular region. On 19 August 1773, Palóu set the first boundary between Lower California mission territory, newly ceded to the Dominicans, and Upper Califoria, retained by the Franciscans. He wrote:

> We came to the place which had been designated in the agreement [thirty miles south of the present border], approved by the royal council and confirmed by his Excellency [Viceroy Bucareli]. . . . We came provided with a cross made the preceding day from a large alder . . . bearing this inscription, "DIVIDING LINE BETWEEN THE MISSIONS OF OUR FATHER SANTO DOMINGO AND THOSE OF OUR FATHER SAN FRANCISCO, 1773." We planted it on a high rock . . . driving it into an opening in the rock itself, just as though it had been made for the purpose, and serving as a pedestal for the cross. . . . We sang with extraordinary joy the *Te Deum laudámus*, giving thanks to God our Lord for our arrival in the land of our destination. [Bolton, *Historical Memoirs of New California*, 1:300-01]

CANONICAL: Pertaining to, required by, or abiding by canon (ecclesiastical) law.

CANONIZATION: The act by which the Pope infallibly decrees that a member of the Catholic Church, a "servant of God" already declared "blessed," be inscribed in the *Roman Martyrology* ("Book of Saints"), and venerated in the universal Church with the full honors given to saints. The process involves several stages:
1) Introduction of the Cause: The canonization process is called a "Cause." The Postulator General of the Franciscan Order in Rome is responsible for advancing the Cause of Franciscan "Servants of God," i.e. those Franciscans who died with a reputation of sanctity. Since several Causes may be pending simultaneously, a deputy or "vice-postulator" is assigned to each one. His duty is to gather all required information to be presented and discussed before the cardinals of the Congregation for the Causes of Saints (formerly called the Sacred Congregation of Rites), a division of the Curia (Papal governing body) that handles all matters concerning beatification, canonization, and sacred relics. If the Cause is historical, as in Serra's case, then the process is even more rigorous, since there are no living witnesses, and all decisions must be based on historical evidence. Once all relevant documenta-

tion is forwarded to Rome, then the vice-postulator works with an advocate-procurator of the Congregation to prepare a "brief" aimed at proving the existence of true sanctity. A general promoter of the faith prepares counter arguments, and the case is analyzed before the Congregation in a court-of-law format. In barest terms, the candidate is presumed "guilty" (of unsaintly conduct), until proved "innocent" (holy). A summary is then written, called the *Positio* or *Summarium*, which is presented to the prelates (highest ranking members) of the Congregation. If they conclude that the candidate lived a life of "heroic" virtue (i.e. practicing extraordinary faith, hope, charity, prudence, justice, and temperance) and true sanctity, then they advance the Cause to the exclusive jurisdiction of the Apostolic See, i.e. the Pope. The Rev. Noel Moholy, O.F.M., S.T.D., Serra Cause Vice-Postulator, summed up this stage of the canonization process: "It is actually the most difficult step, from the viewpoint of human endeavor and scholarly diligence, in this entire complex procedure" ("Will Fray Junípero Serra be Declared a Saint," *Monterey Peninsula Herald Weekend Magazine*, 10 February 1973, p. 12).

2) Declaration of Venerable: The Pope, having been informed of the proceedings thus far, may solemnly decree that the servant of God is now declared "Venerable," from the Latin *venerari* (to regard with awe). This does not include public veneration or religious honor, but is simply a title allowed one whose Cause has been accepted for consideration of beatification. Serra was declared Venerable by His Holiness Pope John Paul II on 9 May 1985.

3) Beatification: This Apostolic process involves a complete review of all previous findings, and a search for unequivocal confirmation of God's approval of the candidate and his life, i.e. miracles ascribed to his or her intercession after death. In addition to historical, theological, and canonical issues, many scientific and medical questions must be addressed since miraculous medical recoveries are often alleged. One miracle must be proved at this stage. The candidate's life itself may provide the miracle, e.g. having spoken in tongues, or surmounted extraordinary hardshp. At his discretion, the Pope may dispense with the miracle requirement altogether, a process known as "equivalent canonization." If the miracle stage is favorably concluded, the Pope issues another solemn decree, and a date is selected for the "beatification" ceremony, from the Latin *beatificato* (the state of being blessed). Held either in Saint Peter's Basilica or "in the field," the ceremony begins with promulgation of the Apostolic brief by which the Pope grants the venerable servant of God the title "Blessed," from the Latin *beatus* (happy). A Pontifical Mass is celebrated as the first act of veneration toward the blessed, and the Pope is the first to pray before the remains/grave. The public cultus (from the Latin *colere*, to honor), i.e. the veneration of the blessed, is limited in nature, and restricted to a city, diocese, region, or religious Order.

4) Canonization: If, following beatification, another miracle is alleged, then the Cause is resumed, and if a final favorable decision is rendered, then the Pope may proceed to the ceremony of solemn canonization. He issues a bull of canonization, which extends veneration to the universal Church. An elaborate ceremony and Pontifical Mass are held in Saint Peter's Basilica, and the blessed is henceforth a "saint," from the Latin *sanctus* (holy or sacred). Historian Maynard Geiger discussed this honor with regard to Serra:

> Serra . . . will always be the Serra of the history books and the Serra of household phrase. But once he is given the honor of the altar, he would be officially called . . . Saint Junípero. Then he will be privileged to have not only monuments—mere civic tributes—to his memory in parks and along the "Camino Real," but also statues with a halo on a thousand Catholic altars in the form of ecclesiastical recognition. And no doubt, should that event occur, all will recall what Serra uttered in reference to the long time it took to canonize Saint Bonaventure as well as to found Mission San Buenaventura: "The longer it took, the more solemnly did we celebrate it." [Geiger, *The Long Road: Padre Serra's March to Saintly Honors*, pp 31-32]

CARLOS: A Christian Indian of the Cuiamac *Ranchería*, and alleged organizer/leader of the 5 November 1776 Mission San Diego attack and murders. He voluntarily returned to the mission on 26 March 1776, appealed to Father Vicente Fuster, and took asylum in the presidio church until finally turned over to Captain-Commander Rivera y Moncada on 18 May. Serra appealed to Viceroy Bucareli, seeking amnesty for Carlos and others implicated in the killings:

> I am most sincerely grateful, knowing how little I deserve it, for the kindness with which Your Excellency listened to my pleas, and looked with mercy on the pitiful criminals from San Diego by sending a new order to the Governor [Neve] that he should not punish them as their sacrilegious crime deserved, but that because of the Christian piety with which they are treated, they should be brought to a realization of their duty to love those who love them. [Tibesar, *Writings of Junípero Serra*, 3:143]

Serra's plea succeeded, and he later wrote:

Great was our joy when we secured a general amnesty for those who had set fire to the Mission of San Diego and had most cruelly murdered its principal minister, the Reverend Father Professor Luís Jayme. They are now all living in the said mission; they are held in high esteem, and receive every attention from the religious there. [Tibesar, *Writings of Junípero Serra*, 3:253]

Carlos was involved in another raid in 1779, uniting with a large number of "gentiles" to attack the inland Jaló *Ranchería*. At least twelve of its members were killed. Serra wrote to Lasuén at Mission San Diego:

I am grieved exceedingly at Carlos' and Bernardino's [a co-conspirator's] continued bad conduct. I have a particular affection for them, and long for the salvation of their souls. With that end in view, I would not feel sorry no matter what punishment they [the civil authorities] gave them, if they would commute it to prison for life, or in the stocks every day since then it would be easier for them to die well. Do you think it possible that if they kept them prisoners for some time, and by means of interpreters explained to them about the life to come and its eternal duration, and if we prayed to God for them—might not we persuade them to repent and win them over to a better life? You could impress on them that the only reason they are still alive is because of our affection for them, and the trouble we took to save their lives. Whereas they, because of their criminal conduct, have deserved punishment and death. But, because of our love for God, we set them free, so that they might lead better lives, etc. But all of this, and much more, Your Reverence must have told them . . . so I will not delay on the subject, except to ask you to give them my warmest greetings, since they are members of my own family. [Tibesar, *Writings of Junípero Serra*, 3:423, 425]

Banishment was considered as punishment, which distressed Serra because

over and above the punishment inflicted and the many promises that had been made to them, they should have to die away from their native land and be without Confession because no one would be able to understand their language. [Ibid., 4:139]

Bernardino was eventually released. Despite Serra's appeals, Carlos was banished to Loreto, Lower California. Lasuén obtained his release six years later in 1785.

CARLOS III: Charles III of Spain (1716—1788): son of Philip V and Isabella of Parma; great-grandson of Louis XIV of France; became King of Spain (1759-88) on death of half-brother Ferdinand VI, and strengthened the empire by reforming finances, aiding agriculture and commerce; signed Family Compact with France against England (1761); suffered losses in Seven Year's War (1756-63); firmly established Crown's authority over Catholic Church, especially in the colonies; expelled Society of Jesus from the Spanish empire (1767); issued order (1767) to "reconnoiter the coasts of . . . the Californias and make a landing there . . . to take efficacious measures for its security . . . and arrange for an expedition by sea to said port [of Monterey] (Bobb, *The Viceregency of Antonio María Bucareli in New Spain, 1771-79*, p. 158), (1767); allied with France against England in its war with American colonies (1779). In March 1780, Carlos decreed that "his vassals of America contribute for one time a donation of one *peso* per Indian and other castes and two for each Spaniard and noble to sustain the present war" (Archibald, *The Economic Aspects of the California Missions*, p. 88). Serra explained how the money was raised in California:

The Indians never have had a *peso*, nor have they such *pesos* now. . . . But the Governor found a way out. His method worked smoothly and the result has been that the Indians, without their realizing it, have paid throughout the missions the *pesos* required of them. . . . The money was realized from the offering of Masses, which a number of soldiers had owed, and from other debts of the same for some things which they received from the missions to satisfy their hunger, for which the Governor did not allow them to run up a bill at the storehouse. But now, to help him realize the levy he has thrown open its door. And so, thanks to this change in policy, the Govenor will secure the cash. [Tibesar, *Writings of Junípero Serra*, 4:147]

CASANOVA, VERY REVEREND ANGELO D. (1833—11 March 1893): Born in the Canton of Ticino, Switzerland; educated at the College of Propaganda Fide in Genoa; member of Genoa Foreign Mission Society; arrived in Los Angeles and joined Diocese of Monterey-Los Angeles (1860); served at Mission San Juan Bautista, and at parishes in Watsonville and Santa Cruz; appointed by Bishop Amat to pastorate of Royal Presidio Chapel (San Carlos Church), Monterey, and Mission Carmel dependency (1863); re-roofed Mission Carmel sacristy, and began holding annual "San Carlos Day" Mass there on 4 November feast of church namesake (1877); stimulated interest in preservation of Mission Carmel, located Serra's grave with help of caretaker Christiano Machado, and orchestrated public viewing of Serra's remains (1882); raised money for first-phase restoration of Mission Carmel (1882-84), most notably a new roof which, even though high pitched and shingled, halted further interior decay; appointed Vicar Forane (diocesan assistant to the bishop) of the Diocese of Monterey-Los Angeles (1883); buried in the Pacheco crypt, San Carlos Cathedral (Royal Presidio Chapel), Monterey.

CATEDRÁTICO DE PRIMA: A *catedrático* is a professor, or in Franciscan terminology, a lector. *De prima* refers to the highest ranking professor, who taught in the morning, after *Prima* (Prime, one of the canonical hours in the Divine Office). When Serra was *catedrático de prima* at Llullian University, he was the highest ranking professor of theology at the university. The secondary professor taught in the afternoon, after Vespers, and was called *catedrático de vísperas*.

CHASING: Metalworking design that is indented or grooved, by use of a chisel or punch.

CHRISM: A mixture of olive oil and balsam, consecrated by a bishop, and used for anointing in various church Sacraments, such as Baptism and Confirmation.

CHURRIGUERESQUE: Of or relating to a style of baroque architecture of Spain and its Latin American colonies, characterized by elaborate and extravagant decoration. After Spanish architect José Churriguera (1650-1723).

CONFESSOR: 1) A priest qualified to hear Confession and grant sacramental absolution. A confessor is also empowered to grant certain dispensations and absolve from censures, according to the provisions of ecclesiastical law; 2) Any male saint not a martyr is called a confessor, in reference to one who bears witness to the Christian faith through word and deed.

CONVENTO: A monastic house, which often includes a school administered by its members.

COUNSELOR: An elected adviser to the guardian of an apostolic college.

CRESPÍ, O.F.M., REVEREND JUAN (1 March 1721—2 January 1782): Born in Palma, Mallorca, Spain; entered Franciscan Order (1738); solemn profession into the Order (9 January 1739); Serra's philosophy student for three years, folowed by three years of theology (1740-46); ordained (probably 1746); departed Palma for Mexican missions (1749), described at that time as "short of stature, [with] sallow skin but somewhat florid complexion, blue eyes, and dark hair" (Geiger, *The Life and Times of Fray Junípero Serra, O.F.M.*, 1:58), (there is no known authentic portrait of Crespí; arrived at San Fernando College (April 1750); served at Mission San Francisco de Tilaco, easternmost Sierra Gorda mission (1752-67); served at Mission Purísima Concepción, Lower California (1768-69); volunteered for Upper California conquest and served as chaplain/diarist with Rivera y Moncada land contingent to San Diego Bay, and as such was "the first missionary to tread" into Upper California (Bolton, *Historical Memoirs of New California*, 4:194), (arrived 14 May 1769); chaplain/diarist of Portolá expedition to locate Monterey Bay/Harbor (14 July 1769—24 January 1770), performing Upper California's second recorded Baptism en route (22 July); accompanied second successful Monterey search party (17

April—24 May 1770); served at Monterey Presidio/Mission Carmel (1770-1772); chaplain/diarist of Fages reconnaissance of greater San Francisco Bay area, reaching Sacramento Delta at present Antioch, and discovering San Joaquin River/Valley (20 March—5 April 1772); served at Mission San Diego (1772), and returned to Mission Carmel in the same year, where he served for the rest of his life; chaplain/diarist of Pérez maritime expedition, first Spanish scientific Pacific coastal survey, reaching present British Columbia at fifty-fifth parallel (1774); buried next to Serra in Mission Carmel sanctuary, where epitaph reads: "Compañero de Serra" (Serra's Friend). Historian Herbert Bolton described Crespí as a "gentle character, devout Christian, zealous missionary, faithful companion, . . . [and] great diarist . . . in the New World, . . . participat[ing] in all the major path-breaking expeditions" (Bolton, *Fray Juan Crespi: Missionary Explorer on the Pacific Coast, 1769-1774*, pp. xv-xvi). Serra offered his opinion in 1771:

> On a number of occasions while he was busily engaged with his writing, I tried to take the matter in hand—suggesting that he go light on the minutiae and superlatives. Putting on a big frown, he would say: "then you do not want me to tell things just as they are, or as I saw them?" And so I let him have his way. [Tibesar, *Writings of Junípero Serra*, 1:213, 215]

Serra noted Crespí's "childish changeableness" (Geiger, *The Life and Times of Fray Junípero Serra, O.F.M.*, 1:285) when he transferred from Mission Carmel to Mission San Diego because of the cold weather in 1772, and then begged to be reinstated at Carmel because of San Diego's hot weather, but added: "The truth of the matter is, . . . as regards explorations, [he] has accomplished more than all of us put together" (Tibesar, *Writings of Junípero Serra*, 1:253). Palóu wrote of his lifelong friend in 1787:

> He was adorned with merits and exercised in the virtues which he had practiced from his youth. . . . I always knew him to be extremely exemplary. Among his companions he was always known by the name of [*Beato* (Blessed)]. He persevered in this manner for the rest of his life, with a dovelike simplicity. He was possessed of a most profound humility. He was so humble, in fact, that when he was a student cleric, if at any time he thought he had irked any of his fellow students, he would go to his cell, fall on his knees and ask for his pardon. Since he had a poor memory and could not learn by heart or recite from memory the doctrinal sermons at Mass on Sundays and holydays, he used to take along a book, and after the Gospel of the Mass for the people he would read one of the doctrinal sermons. By this means he instructed the people and edified all with his humility. . . . All of us who knew him and had dealings with him piously believe that he went directly to enjoy God. . . . The cries [of those at his funeral] demonstrated the love they had for him as a father. [Geiger, *Palóu's Life of Fray Junípero Serra*, pp. 214-15]

Crespí was buried in Mission Carmel's fourth church in 1782 (the *Jacalón grande*), transferred to the fifth church when it was completed in 1783 (the "Serra *adobe*"), in which Serra was also buried in 1784. The present stone church incorporated their burial vaults into its sanctuary.

CROIX, VICEROY CARLOS FRANCISCO DE. MARQUES DE CROIX (b.1710): Born in Lille, France, of Flemish extraction; served as military governor of Galicia, Spain; served as forty-fifth viceroy of New Spain (1766-71). Under Croix's administration, the Jesuits were expelled from New Spain (1767); California was occupied (1769); and Monterey was founded as New Spain's northernmost frontier settlement (3 June 1770). News of Monterey's founding reached Mexico City on 10 August, and Croix issued a public proclamation recounting the details on 16 August, in which he noted Serra's involvement:

> The Reverend Father President of those missions, who is destined to serve at Monterey, states in a very detailed way and with particular joy that the Indians are affable. They have already promised him to bring him their children to be instructed in the mysteries of our holy Catholic religion. That exemplary and zealous missionary also gave a detailed account of the solemn Masses which had been celebrated from the arrival of both expeditions until the departure of the packet-boat *San Antonio*. [Geiger, *Palóu's Life of Fray Junípero Serra*, pp. 99-100]

Vicery Croix transferred the viceregal baton to Antonio María Bucareli on 22 September 1771, and then returned to Europe for the remainder of his life.

C.Ss.R.: Congregation of the Most Holy Redeemer, designating a member of the Redemptorist Order.

D.D.: Doctor of Divinity.

DISCALCED: From the Latin *discalceātus* (not shod), i.e. barefoot or in sandals. A measure of austerity practiced by certain orders of monks.

DIVINE OFFICE: Catholic prayers and hymns, formulated for recitation or chant at specific times each day. Also known as the Canonical Hours or the Liturgy of the Hours, and formerly divided into Matins, Lauds, Prime, Tierce, Sext, None, Vespers and Compline (revised and renamed after Vatican Council II). Every priest is obliged to say the full daily office, contained in a special book called a breviary.

DOCTOR OF THE CHURCH: Title given since the Middle Ages to certain saints for outstanding writing or preaching that has influenced and guided the universal (worldwide) Catholic Church's course of development. The Western Fathers of the Church (Saints Ambrose, Augustine of Hippo, Gregory the Great and Jerome), are considered the original Doctors, but many others have been added, e.g. Saint Anthony of Padua, Saint Bonaventure, and recently the first two women: Saint Teresa of Avila and Saint Catherine of Siena, declared Doctors by Pope Paul VI in 1970.

DOWNIE, K.S.G., SIR HENRY (Harry) J. (25 April 1903—10 March 1980): Born in San Francisco; cabinet-maker by profession; temporary job repairing Mission Carmel statuary evolved into lifetime position as restorer/curator (arrived 28 August 1931). Restoration chronology: restored first two rooms of "*padres*' living quarters," at NW corner of north quadrangle wing, next to Serra Cenotaph

room (1932); coordinated staging of *The Apostle of California* at the mission, which raised $12,000 for restoration (1934); formed "The Carmel Mission Restoration Committee" (1935); replaced high-pitched 1884 roof with tile roof and vaulted interior ceiling, as per original (1936); restored Serra cell at NE corner of north wing, leaving gap in wing (1937); completed restoration of north wing with addition of central section, and converted entire wing into mission museum (1941); constructed rectory at SE corner of south wing, leaving gap in wing (1942); exhumed Serra's remains as part of official canonization process, lowered sanctuary floor to original level, and designed/installed new markers over the sanctuary graves (1943); restored south wing as Junípero Serra School, grades K-8 (1945); completed restoration of east wing with addition of central section as the Blessed Sacrament Chapel (1947); moved Crespí Hall out of path of west wing to present site at NW corner of mission property (1951); restored west wing as expansion of Junípero Serra School (1953-55); designed/constructed/installed new church *reredos* altarpiece, and installed new travertine-marble altar (1956); renovated church sacristy (1963). Downie was also responsible for the reclamation, restoration, and permanent display of Mission Carmel's original furnishings, such as the return of California's most historic statue (Our Lady of Bethlehem) to Mission Carmel in 1945; the gathering and cataloging of "California's first library" and the identification and return of many of Serra's original possessions over a period of years. In his words: "We now [1964] have at Carmel all the things Serra used at the altar . . . his . . . monstrance, the silver candlesticks and other appurtenances. Gradually we have been able to reclaim the pictures and statues the good people of Monterey presumed were their own. Everything we have is well documented" (Weber, *Father of the Missions: A Documentary History of San Carlos Borromeo*, pp. 203-04). Downie, buried in Mission Carmel cemetery next to his wife Mabel (1913-1981), was eulogized by Hon. Leon E. Panetta, U.S. Representative, Sixteenth District, on the floor of the U.S. House of Representatives:

> Mr. Speaker, it is with great pride that I bring to the attention of my colleagues the accomplishments of a friend and a remarkable man who resided in my district and who died recently. California is known for the Spanish missions that dot its coastline. These missions exist today largely because of the dedication and work of Harry Downie. He was a man who used his great skills and knowledge to bring history to life. For some fifty

years, Harry dedicated his considerable energy to the restoration of Spanish missions and other historical sites around the state of California. Beginning in 1926 with the restoration of Mission Santa Clara, Harry was either a participant in or responsible for the restoration of most of our beautiful historical sites. This list illustrates his extensive influence: Mission Santa Clara, Carmel Mission, Mission San Luis Obispo, Mission San Antonio de Padua, Royal Presidio Chapel, Mission San Juan Bautista, Mission San Buenaventura, Mission Soledad. In addition to these sites, Harry served as a consultant on a variety of other historical preservation projects, including the following: Mission Santa Cruz, Mission La Purisima, Mission Sonoma, Mission Santa Inez, Mission San Gabriel, the Plaza Church, Los Angeles. I would also like to mention that Harry was a consultant on the restoration of the Fremont House and Colton Hall in Monterey and several other historical sites in Salinas and San Juan Bautista in my district. As any traveler around the State of California can readily see, Harry Downie made an incredible imprint on our culture and history. Without his work, many of the missions and other sites I have mentioned might have been left to decay and simply forgotten. But because of his dedication, we have a living connnection to our past. Harry Downie's work did not go unrecognized. He received numerous awards during his lifetime, from the Knight of St. Gregory [K.S.G.] conferred by Pope Pius XII [1954], to the Monterey Peninsula Chamber of Commerce's Man of the Year Award [1968], from the California Historical Society's Award of Merit [1968] and award for Historical Preservation [1980] to the Knight of Castle Belvere [sic] [Bellver] given by King Juan Carlos of Spain [1976]. Not only his fellow citizens but also kings and popes recognized Harry's accomplishments. Mr. Speaker, I first came to know Harry Downie as a young boy attending Junipero Serra School at Carmel Mission. His presence was everywhere, working in the garden, repairing a door, designing an addition, researching history, helping the children or the nuns. On Sundays, he was usually at the rear of the mission making sure all went well. I am proud to have known Harry Downie, and I know that the communities in which he worked and lived are grateful to him for his life's work. He is no longer with us, but the history he brought to life for us will always keep him alive in our memories. [U.S. Congress, House, "Harry Downie: Bringing History to Life," 96th Cong., 2nd sess., 1 July 1980, *Congressional Record* 126:18040-41]

DUNS SCOTUS, JOHN (1266?—1308): Born in Scotland, joined Franciscan Order; studied at Oxford and Paris; ordained priest (1291); earned Master's in Theology, University of Paris (1305); professor at Cologne (1307-08); buried in Franciscan church in Cologne. Duns Scotus was the founder of Scotism, a form of scholasticism (the central phase of Western Latin medieval thought). Scotism argued that faith, upon which theology rests, is not speculative but an act of will. It also upheld the separability and independence of the rational soul from the body, provoking a long controversy between Scotists and Thomists (followers of Saint Thomas Aquinas). Historically revered by the Franciscans, especially for perfecting and defending the doctrines of Primacy of Christ and Immaculate Conception, he was given the scholastic nickname *Doctor Subtilis* (Subtle Doctor. He is not a universal Doctor of the Catholic Church). In addition to the Duns Scotus Chair of Sacred Theology at Serra's Llullian University, the Franciscan chair of theology at the University of Paris was posthumously renamed in his honor.

EL CAMINO REAL: The Royal or King's Highway, in essence a public road. Any series of major arteries that linked travel and supply routes within the Spanish empire. Upper California's twenty-one missions were separated by roughly one day's journey on its El Camino, although in Serra's day there were not as many "steppingstones." As Serra wrote in 1774, they were spaced "so that every third day one might sleep in a village . . . and passage through all of the country [was] made easy" (Tibesar, *Writings of Junípero Serra*, 2:143). In 1906 the Camino Real Association marked the route with 450 cast-iron mission bell replicas, as "distinctive, emblematic and appropriate guidepost[s]" (A.S.C. Forbes, *Califoria Missions and Landmarks*, p. 361).

ENCARNACIÓN: The process of applying several layers of extremely thin gesso (a preparation of plaster of paris and glue used as a surface for painting or as a base for low-relief), to achieve a porcelain-like sheen that resembles flesh tone.

ENGELHARDT, O.F.M., REVEREND ZEPHYRIN (13 November 1851—27 April 1934): Mission Santa Bárbara archivist/historian (1900-34); author of numerous California mission history books; major four volume work *Missions and Missionaries of California* (pub. 1908-15) remains an important primary source of information, though marked by special pleading.

ENRAMADA: An arbor or bower, constructed of branches and brush.

ESTOFADO: An extension of polychromy (the art of employing many colors in decorating statuary). The first step consists of applying several layers of gold or silver leaf on carved wood or gesso (a fine plaster of paris), followed by either painting, which produces a lustrous effect, or stenciling, which allows the gold/silver to shine through in pattern form.

EXCOMMUNICATION: Ecclesiastical censure which cuts one off from the rites, privileges, or fellowship of church membership.

FRANCISCAN: A member of a religious mendicant Order (depending upon alms for a living, i.e. corporate poverty), founded by Saint Francis of Assisi in 1209. The original sincerity of such a dependence is demonstrated by the fact that members were not allowed to receive or handle money. All funds, including those destined for the missions, were entrusted to an intermediary layman called an apostolic syndic. The Franciscan Order is now divided into three autonomous branches: 1) Order of Friars Minor (O.F.M.), from the Latin *fratres minores* (lesser bretheren): no private/corporate ownership of property allowed. In Serra's day the Order was subdivided into Observant, Discalced, Alcantarin, Recollect and Reformed groups, each with separate customs, but all governed by one Minister General. Serra's Province of Mallorca belonged to the Observant family; 2) Conventual: corporate ownership allowed; 3) Capuchin: poverty and austerity strictly emphasized. In addition to these, the Second Order Franciscan (Poor Clares, after Saint Clare of Assisi) is also part of the Franciscan network, along with the Third Order Franciscan, for those involved in apostolic work, but under simple vows. Third Order Secular, popularly called Tertiary, is an order for the laity who wish to follow the Franciscan Rule (Juan Evangelista was a Tertiary). Pope Paul VI approved a new Rule for the entire Third Order in 1978, and changed the name to Franciscan Secular Order.

FRANCISCAN SPIRITUALITY: Also called "Seraphic" spirituality after its founder Saint Francis of Assisi, the "Seraph" (Angel) of Assisi. The philosophy consists of three major tenets embodied in the Franciscan Rule (a "general plan" for living a religious way of life as a Franciscan, as opposed to a religious constitution, which contains specific rules and regulations) formulated by Saint Francis and refined by his followers, most notably Saint Bonaventure, and to a lesser degree Saint Anthony of Padua and John Duns Scotus: 1) To be united with God: This ideal is attained through prayer, contemplation of the Gospels, and as Serra said, by "put[ting] our confidence in God; He is our Father; He knows what we need, and that is enough" (Tibesar, *Writings of Junípero Serra*, 3:387). Also, since God is Father to every creature, each must be shown love and reverence, especially mankind, who bears the image of the Father through His Incarnate Son; 2) To be an apostle of the Church and win for God the souls that Jesus suffered and died for: Francis' call to "repair God's house" quickly evolved into an international missionary apostolate that has produced more than 150 Franciscan saints and beatified wordwide. Serra felt that "the dignity of Apostolic Preacher, especially when united with the actual duty, is the highest vocation" (Ibid., 1:3), and he was "ready to do what is required of me, and may God assist me in all my endeavors. He, without doubt, will bring to pass all that is best for us" (Ibid., 2:439); 3) To imitate literally the life of Jesus: because God has become Man, Jesus Christ is the center and meaning of man's destiny, and his words and deeds should be revered and imitated (and his Virgin Mother Mary especially honored). Francis' disciples imitate Christ's suffering through practical detachment from "self" (the Franciscan concept of "littleness," which traditionally included self-mortification as a means of identifying with the "poor and crucified Christ"), and actual detachment from "creatures" (the concepts of chastity and poverty). In this manner the Franciscan is completely free to "re-present" Christ to contemporaries. Also, since God has become Man, our present state of being is sanctified; there is no need to wait for the Last Judgment. This promotes reverence for all created things, and engenders cultivation of temporal as well as spiritual reality. For example, Franciscans started many of the Church's most popular "graphic" devotions, such as the Crèche (Saint Francis of Assisi); the Sacred Heart (Saint Bonaventure); and the Stations of the Cross (Saint Leonard of Port Maurice). All of this had a great impact on Serra. His Franciscan education and training (beginning at age six) provided the perfect philosphical base for channeling his natural vitality and intense spirituality into a dynamic "hands on" missionary ministry. Serra may have lived with spiritual eyes raised upward to Heaven, but he knew that his primary goal of glorifying God through the conversion of souls could not be attained without temporal feet planted firmly on Earth. He never complained of personal illness, lack of food, or even "tunics falling to pieces," but when it came to the "harvesting of souls," or matters concerning his "tender [mission] plants," he was zealously concerned and "always on fire with a longing to see the spiritual conquests, in which we are engaged, show signs of progress" (Ibid., 2:413). He incessantly strove for more "missions, my Lord, missions—that is what this country needs" (Ibid., Serra to Commandant General Teodoro de Croix 3:255), and optimistically envisioned using ships to establish missions north of San Francisco Bay. Returning full circle, Serra never forgot that God was the ascribed source of, and reason for everything he achieved as he "work[ed] with a . . . fervor in tilling the vineyard of the Lord" (Ibid., 2:83). He shared his philosophy with his nephew in Mallorca when he too became a Franciscan:

> I wish to congratulate you a thousand times on the reception of the holy habit and on your solemn profession into so holy an Order [in 1758]. Be always grateful to God for so great a favor—the greatest we can imagine. Do the best you can, with the grace of God, to become a true and perfect Friars Minor, and when you appear to have attained that ideal state, if you are ever privileged to come so far, then say in the sincerity of your heart: *servi inutiles sumus* [We are useless servants]. [Tibesar, *Writings of Junípero Serra*, 1:25, 27]

For a complete understanding of Serra's philosophy, one must also study the lives and writings of Saint Bonaventure, John Duns Scotus, Blessed Ramón Llull, Saint Francis Solano, and Venerable Mary of Agreda (all in turn influenced by the life and Gospel-inspired teachings of Saint Francis of Assisi).

FRAY: Fra, or Brother. Title given to a friar. Short form of Italian *frate* (brother), from the Latin *frater*. A friar is distinct from a monk. Friars combine active ministries with monasticism, whereas monks lead an entirely monastic life.

GÁLVEZ, JOSÉ DE. MARQUÉS DE LA SONORA (2 January 1720—17 June 1787): Born in Macharavialla, Andalusia, Spain; studied law at University of Salamanca; served as crown attorney; appointed secretary to Spanish Minister of State; appointed civil and criminal magistrate (1764); appointed *Visitador General de Nueva España* by King Carlos III (Visitor or Inspector General, a direct

 agent of the king, with authority equal to a viceroy, sent to a particular viceroyalty for a *visita* tour of general inspection or investigation into a specific problem therein), and given honorary membership in the Council of the Indies (the governing body of Spain's American and Philippine colonies), (20 February 1765); arrived in Mexico to begin his *visita* (18 July 1765); overhauled internal colonial administration and developed new sources of royal revenue (1765-78); implemented royal decree expelling Jesuits from New Spain (June 1767); traveled to western Mexican coastal port of San Blas to inspect new naval base and shipyard he had initiated (May 1768); convened the military *junta* (council) at San Blas which issued the specific directive for exploration and colonization of Upper California as per instructions of Carlos III (16 May 1768); arrived in Lower California, appointed Gaspar de Portolá as military commander of Upper California expedition, and accepted Junípero Serra's offer to join as religious leader (July 1768); supervised assemblage of soldiers, sailors, missionaries, muleteers, Indian personnel, equipment, food, and animals destined for Upper California (August-December 1768), and when met with Serra for first time he praised the Franciscans for "not depart[ing] one iota from their holy institute of poverty. They love the Indians with great charity and tenderness nor do they lose sight of the public interest of the crown and its vassals" (Geiger, *The Life and Times of Fray Junípero Serra, O.F.M.*, 1:204); witnessed departure of *San Carlos* and *San Antonio* for San Diego Bay (6 January, 15 February 1769, respectively); suffered from *accidente* (mental illness), hampering return to Mexico City (February 1769—May 1770); recovery in Mexico City, and request granted to return to Spain (August 1769); arrived in Spain (May 1772); appointed Minister-General of the Indies (1776); initiated *Provincias Internas* plan to streamline administration of New Spain, whereby the northern frontier provinces (including California) were severed from the viceroyalty and consolidated into an independent military/political government under a Commandant-General of the Internal Provinces (1776); admitted to Spanish Council of State (1780); given title of Marqués de la Sonora and Viscondé de Sinaloa (1785); initiated *intendencia* system within New Spain, whereby antiquated system of local government was supplanted by centralized form of administration (1786); suffered from recurring mental illness until death.

GEIGER, O.F.M., Ph. D., REVEREND MAYNARD J. (24 August 1901—13 May 1977): Born in Lancaster, Pennsylvania, baptized Joseph; invested with Franciscan habit at Saint Anthony's Preparatory Seminary, Santa Barbara, and assumed religious name Maynard (15 July 1923); ordained at Mission Santa Bárbara (15 June 1929); received doctorate in history, Catholic University of America,

Washington, D.C., doctoral thesis *The Franciscan Conquest of Florida* (1937); appointed Mission Santa Bárbara Archivist and Historian for the Franciscan Province of Santa Barbara (1937), a post held for life; founding member and editor of the Franciscan *Provincial Annals* (1938-53); appointed to the Diocesan Historical Commission for the Canonization Cause of Junípero Serra, and assisted at the canonical exhumation of Serra's remains (December 1943); traveled over 100,000 miles in the U.S., Mexico, and Spain, collected thousands of documents for the Serra Cause, and traced every step of Serra's life (1943-58); founding member of the Academy of American Franciscan History, and its scholarly journal *The Americas* (1944); awarded the Hispanic Institute of Florida Cervantes Medal (1947); edited *Palóu's Life of Fray Junípero Serra*, the best translation of Palóu's 1787 biography of Serra, with 188 pages of annotation (pub. 1955); wrote the definitive modern biography of Serra, *The Life and Times of Fray Junípero Serra, O.F.M.* (2 vols., pub. 1959); awarded the Spanish government's Cross of Isabella for overall contribution to the interpretation of Spain's cultural role in the New World (1959); awarded the John Gilmary Shea Award from the American Catholic Historical Association, and the Henry R. Wagner Award from the California Historical Society (1960); elected a Fellow of the California Historical Society (1961); completed organization and expansion of Santa Bárbara Mission Archive-Library (tripling its holdings), and dedicated a new archival center (11 October 1970), "one of the nation's most precious depositories for Hispanic-American materials" (Weber and Nunis, *Maynard J. Geiger, O.F.M.: Franciscan and Historian*, p. 5). Commenting on his life as a research historian, Geiger wrote:

> Aside from any other consideration, and simply as a historian, I may say that my life has been immeasurably enriched by my long association with Junípero. To have gone over his many trails, to have met the people who are descendents of those with whom Serra dealt, to have treated with the custodians of his documents, to have participated in retrospect in his eighteenth-century life and in his twentieth-century fame, are indeed, a consummate satisfaction. Junípero . . . was so vital in life. [Geiger, *The Long Road: Padre Serra's March to Saintly Honors*, p 32]

Geiger's own vitality left a remarkable legacy (13 books and nearly 200 scholarly articles on Serra and all aspects of mission history), which have secured not only Serra's place in California history, but his own as well. In the opinion of historian Francis J. Weber:

> The works of Maynard J. Geiger are now and will long remain among the truly significant contributions to the field of American ecclesiastical history. The subtitle of his Serra biography, *The Man Who Never Turned Back*, also characterizes the energetic friar who spent the long hours of seven days a week, for thirty years, in a bare-walled Santa Barbara cell, slowly but ever so accurately grinding out the story of the Franciscan spiritual conquest along the New World's Pacific Slope. [Weber and Nunis, *Maynard J. Geiger, O.F.M.: Franciscan and Historian*, p. 18]

Geiger is buried in the Franciscan friars vault, Mission Santa Bárbara.

GENTILE: A missionary term used to describe a non-Christian (usually an Indian). Also called a "pagan" or "heathen," as opposed to a "neophyte," i.e a newly baptized Christian.

GILT: Gilded. Having the appearance of gold. Traditionally, the principal method of applying gold to metal is by fire gilding. An amalgam of gold and mercury is brushed on the surface of the metal, the mercury is then volatilized by heat, and the remaining gold is then polished.

GOVERNOR: Gaspar de Portolá was technically Upper California's first *gobernante* (governing official), but he left the province as soon as Monterey was established. Lieutenant Pedro Fages served as first military commandant at the Monterey Presidio (June 1770—May 1774), and as such was the *gobernante*. The position was expanded to commandant-general (1774), second in rank only to the *gobernador* (governor) of Both Californias, who resided in Loreto, Lower California. Fages frequently clashed with fellow officers, alienated his troops to the point of desertion, and sharply differed with the missionaries. Serra successfully lobbied before Viceroy Bucareli for his removal (1773), at which time he wrote:

> If I were called upon to tell, not of the annoyances he has caused me, and the rest of the religious—a story that shall remain untold—but of the damage his conduct has continually done to the missions, it would be a long story. [Tibesar, *Writings of Junípero Serra*, 1:301]

Former Lower California governor (under the Jesuits, before Upper California was settled, from 1750-67) Captain Fernando de Rivera y Moncada was chosen as replacement captain-commander (May 1774—February 1777). Rivera y Moncada was an anxious, overly cautious administrator, and his delay in executing superior orders, combined with an inability to cooperate with associates (most notably Serra and Anza), resulted in temporary excommunication from the Church, and removal from office. Writing to the San Fernando College guardian in July 1774, Serra expressed his opinion of Rivera y Moncada:

> Now, and for some time to come, you will see if I had good reason for my lack of enthusiasm concerning this man. I am no wizard, but with what experience I have had of men of his sort, I was not inclined to expect much from him anyway. [Tibesar, *Writings of Junípero Serra*, 2:110-11]

The capital of the Californias was transferred to Montery (1777), and from that point the Monterey *gobernante* and California *gobernador* were one and the same. Lieutenant Colonel Felipe de Neve, already governor of Both Californias (since March 1775), arrived in the new capital on 3 February 1777. He was capable but aloof, and did little to heal the rift with the missionaries. He was not removed from office however, and implemented a number of changes in California civil law, codified in the 1779 *Reglamento*, which superseded the 1773 *Reglamento*. After Neve's promotion to commandant-inspector of the *Provincias Internas*, a seasoned, more mature Lieutenant Colonel Pedro Fages returned to Monterey to serve as governor (September 1782—April 1791) during Serra's final years.

GUARDIAN: The elected superior of an apostolic college and its territorial jurisdiction, usually serving for three years.

HABIT, FRANCISCAN: Pursuant to an 1897 "letter" of Pope Leo XIII, all Franciscans now wear brown habits. However, in Serra's day there was a choice, and he wore a gray habit in conformity with the approved custom of his apostolic college. Woven from black and white wool, without any dye permitted, the habit had a cowl (hood), and was held in place by the cincture (rope cord/belt girdle). The three knots in the cincture signified the Franciscan vows of obedience, poverty, and chastity, inspired by biblical references ("Let your belts be fastened around your waists and your lamps be burning ready" Luke 12:35; "Stand fast, with the truth as the belt around your waist" Ephesians 6:14). An inner tunic (loose-fitting garment extending to the knees, made of cotton or light wool) was worn under the habit. A mantle (loose, sleeveless wool coat) was worn over the habit in cold weather. Footwear consisted of simple leather or hempen sandals. Serra was buried wearing his habit, and Palóu offered two slightly different versions of the details:

> He remained in the shroud in which he died, that is, the habit, cowl and the cord, but no inner tunic, for the two which he had for use on his journeys he had sent out to be washed six days before, together with a change of underclothing, which he did not care to use, for he wanted to die wearing only the habit, cowl and cord. [Geiger, *Palóu's Life of Fray Junípero Serra*, p. 249]
> Shortly before dying he ordered it [his clothing] washed and set aside, having only his habit, cowl, cord and some underclothing; and these served him as his burial shroud. [Ibid., p. 283]

HAIRSHIRT: A coarse garment worn next to the skin by religious ascetics to mortify the flesh, often fitted with horsehair, wire bristles or hooks.

HIGH MASS: A sung Mass celebrated by a priest. A Pontifical High Mass is one sung by a bishop in his own diocese.

IHS: The first three letters of Ihsus, the Greek word for Jesus.

INDIANS, TREATMENT OF: Serra and his missionaries did not come to California to study Indian culture. They came to change it. Their perspective is embodied in the final lines of the Gospel according to Matthew:

> Jesus came forward and addressed them [the Apostles] in these words: Full authority has been given to me both in heaven and on earth; go, therefore, and make disciples of all the nations. Baptize them in the name of the Father, and of the Son, and of the Holy Spirit. Teach them to carry out everything I have commanded you. And know that I am with you always, until the end of the world! [Matthew 28:18-20]

In conjunction with the teachings of Saint Francis of Assisi, the Franciscans interpreted this as a solemn mandate to Christianize and Hispanicize the Indians. Segregation of Christian Indians from their non-Christian brethren in the "wild" ensured effective religious instruction, moral training, avoidance of the occasion of sin, and education in the arts of Western civilization. In Palóu's words:

> They [the Indians] can be conquered first only by their interest in being fed and clothed, and afterwards they gradually acquire a knowledge of what is spiritually good and evil. If the missionaries had nothing to give them, they could not win them over. If the Indians did not live in a town within hearing of the mission bell, but rather in their villages after the fashion of their pagan days . . . the missionaries would not be able to get them to leave off their vicious pagan practices. Nor could they be civilized, as His Majesty so greatly enjoins on the missionaries laboring in these new missions, according to the clear evidence of his Laws of the Indies. [Geiger, *Palóu's Life of Fray Junípero Serra*, p 232]

Eighteenth-century Spanish Franciscan methods of aboriginal evangelization and acculturation must not be judged by twentieth-century standards. European scholars had no scientific means of measuring intelligence, hence the Indians were thought of as "adult children." Under Spanish law they were legally classified as *personas miserables* (unfortunate persons) along with the poor, blind, leprous, etc. The missionaries acted as legal guardians *in loco parentis* (in the place of a parent), and used corporal punishment as a means of discipline. Serra offered the following defense:

> In reference to the care we take of our converts . . . they are our children; for none except us has engendered them in Christ. The result is we look upon them as a father looks upon his family. We shower all our love and care upon them. . . . That spiritual fathers should punish their sons, the Indians, with blows appears to be as old as the conquest of these kingdoms; so general, in fact, that the saints do not seem to be any exception to the rule. Undoubtedly, the first to evangelize these shores followed the practice, and they surely were saints. In the life of Saint Francis Solano, . . . we read that, while he had a special gift from God to soften the ferocity of the most barbarous by the sweetness of his presence and his words, nevertheless, in the running of his mission in the Province of Tucumán . . . we are told in his biography, . . . [that] when they failed to carry out his orders, he gave directions for his Indians to be whipped. . . . The whole world is aware of the fact that when the famous . . . [Hernán] Cortés permitted himself or, to speak more accurately, saw to it that he should be flogged by the Fathers, in full sight of the Indians, he took this course of action . . . to set an example to all. [Tibesar, *Writings of Junípero Serra*, 3:253, 413]

There is absolutely no documentary evidence to indicate that Serra ever mistreated anyone, either personally or indirectly. On the contrary, he was harshest on himself, seeking to transcend his perceived faults through privation and self-mortification. The California missions and missionaries have always had their detractors, and probably always will. Fueled by emotion rather than persuaded by fact, the allegations tend to generalize and blame Serra for every excess and abuse that occurred during the entire 1769-1834 mission period. Analogously, is George Washington personally responsible for American slavery, or for events that took place fifty years after his death? The mission system's greatest "sin" was not individual shortcoming, but inculpable eighteenth-century ignorance. Unable to solve complex medical, social, and environmental problems, the Indian population was drastically reduced, especially through disease. However, the worst was yet to come. When the American flood of "Manifest Destiny" swept into California seeking hides, pelts, gold, and statehood, the decline was catastrophic. California's estimated pre-1769 Indian population of 300,000 dropped to approximately 225,000 by the end of the mission period in 1834, but between 1848-1900 it fell to an alarming low of 20,000 (Cook, *The Population of the California Indians*, p. 199). Whether Spanish, English, Russian, or even if no settlers had preceded the Americans, the result would have been the same. At least the Spanish sought to incorporate the Indians into their economic and social structure (including through miscegenation), rather than rigidly excluding and exterminating them.

INFORME: A "Report on the Missions" or "State-of-the-Mission" report, consisting of a written summary of each mission's material/spiritual status and progress, filed intermittently until 1783, then required annually by law. The data was reviewed by the Father-President and the appropriate government officials, and provided a comparative profile of the relative success of each mission, as well as the entire chain.

INQUISITION, HOLY OFFICE OF THE: A former tribunal in the Catholic Church directed at the suppression of heresy. Serra was appointed Commissary of the Holy Office of the Spanish Inquisition (deputy in charge of faith and morals within a given territory, but not including jurisdiction over Indians, who were exempt from inquisitorial procedure and prosecution) for the Sierra Gorda district in 1752. If he visited an area that lacked a commissary, then his authority extended there as well. Palóu states that Serra "had to labor in many parts and to travel many leagues, fulfilling his duties to the satisfaction of the officials of the Inquisition" (Geiger, *Palóu's Life of Fray Junípero Serra*, p. 43), but Mexican archival documents illustrate only one trial that Serra was directly involved in. María Pasquala de Nava, a mulatto and native of Valle de Maíz in the Sierra Gorda, was accused of sorcery in 1766. Serra prepared the initial documents for the hearing at Mission Nuestra Señora de la Luz de Tancoyol, but was called back to San Fernando College before the proceedings were completed. A substitute was called in, and Maria was judged a true *maléfica* (sorceress). She died shortly thereafter, although the cause of death is not clear.

JACAL: A crude mission structure that usually preceded a more permanent *adobe* brick building, "until such time as a skilled master [could] be obtained to build . . . as the country requires (Bolton, *Historical Memoirs of New California*, 3:230). Constructed of palisades (poles/logs) set upright in the ground, spaced three to four feet apart, interwoven with brush, and stones at the base. Both sides were plastered with mud, and the interior was usually whitewashed with lime. A larger, more elaborate *jacal* (called a *jacalón*), might substitute wood planks for brush. Roofed with simple tule (reeds), beams plastered with mud, or a combination of the two. Earthen roofs minimized risk of fire, but as Serra wrote: "No matter what we did they always leaked like a sieve and between that and the humidity everything would rot" (Tibesar, *Writings of Junípero Serra*, 4:273).

J.C.D.: Doctor of Canon Law.

JESUITS, EXPULSION OF: Jesuit devotion to the Papacy elicited opposition from nationalistic, reform-oriented, eighteenth-century European monarchies. Jesuit zeal for ecclesiastical reform antagonized the clergy. These two factors, combined with jealousy, political intrigue, and unsubstantiated accusations leveled at the Order, resulted in the expulsion of the Society of Jesus from Portugal and its colonies, along with seizure of all its properties (1759); a declaration of suppression in France and its colonies, without exile (1764); and total expulsion (5,100 priests), and seizure of all properties/revenues in Spain and its colonies (order signed by Carlos III on 27 February 1767, promulgated 25 June). Under pressure from the "enlightened" Bourbon monarchs of Europe, Pope Clement XIV finally issued a brief of suppression against the entire Order (1773). The ban contained no condemnation of the Jesuit constitutions, Jesuit teaching, or individual Jesuits, and the expelled priests were offered asylum in the Papal States. Pockets of support kept the Society alive, such as in Russia where Catherine II refused to enforce the ban. Pope Pius VII revoked the brief and restored the Society on a worldwide basis in 1814, at which time there were 600 Jesuits remaining. Not until 1932 did the Order reach pre-suppression membership.

LASUÉN, O.F.M., REVEREND FERMÍN FRANCISCO DE (9 July 1736—26 June 1803): Born in Vitoria, in the Spanish Basque province of Alava; entered Franciscan Order (1751); solemn profession into the Order, retaining baptismal name (1752); ordained deacon (1758); departed Spain for Mexican missions (1759), described at that time as "of medium height, with a swarthy complexion, light beard and black hair" (Guest, *Fermín Francisco de Lasuén*, p. 11), (there is no known authentic portrait of Lasuén); arrived at San Fernando College (1759); ordained (probably 1761); served in the Sierra Gorda district (1762-67); served in Lower California at Mission San Francisco de Borja (1768-73); made land journey (along with Palóu) from Lower California to San Diego (arrived 30 August 1773); served at Mission San Gabriel (October 1773—June 1775); served as Monterey Presidio chaplain (June—August 1775); founded Mission San Juan Capistrano (30 October 1775), but mission aborted due to Indian destruction of Mission San Diego ("refounded" by Serra on 1 November 1776); served at Mission San Diego (1775-1785); served briefly at Mission San Luís Obispo (1777); received news of appointment to presidency of Upper California missions (11 October 1785); arrived at Mission Carmel to assume presidency (12 January 1786); founded Mission Santa Bárbara (4 December 1786); founded Mission La Purísima Concepción (8 December 1787); received patent to administer Confirmation (26 May 1790), but only valid for five more years due to same church-state delays that Serra had experienced (he was still able to confirm more than 1,000 persons during his term); founded Mission Santa Cruz (28 August 1791); founded Mission Nuestra Señora de la Soledad (9 October 1791); appointed Commissary of the Holy Office of the Inquisition (1795); granted full power to delegate faculties to missionaries (preaching/Confession, granted by the Bishop of Sonora, in whose diocese California belonged), and appointed Vicar Forane (special diocesan assistant to the bishop), and ecclesiastical judge for California (1796); founded four missions in summer 1797: San José (11 June), San Juan Bautista (24 June), San Miguel Arcángel (25 July), San Fernando Rey (8 September); founded Mission San Luís Rey (13 June 1798). Although forceful, assertive Serra defined basic mission policy and laid the foundation for future prosperity, credit must go to patient, flexible, diplomatic Lasuén for nurturing the missions to successful maturity. During his eighteen-year presidency, the number of missions rose from nine to eighteen; missionaries from eighteen to forty; resident mission Indians from 5,123 to 15,562; and Baptisms from 6,736 to 37,976. Stock raising and agriculture firmly took root, with cattle increasing during the same period from 6,813 to 67,782; sheep from 6,813 to 107,172; and overall production of wheat from 9,624 *fanegas* in 1785 to 45,701 in 1802. Lasuén was also a sound planner, builder, and administrator, and his importation of Mexican craftsmen and artisans introduced contemporary manufacturing, building trades, and the decorative arts into California. Serra described Lasuén as "invaluable for the work here, and . . . his example as a religious is outstanding" (Tibesar, *Writings of Junípero Serra*, 2:123). After Serra's death, Lasuén became something of an international figure. Frenchman Jean François de Galaup, Comte de La Pérouse wrote: "La Suen [sic] is one of the most estimable men, and most deserving of respect, that I have ever met. His gentleness, his charity, his love for the Indians are inexpressible" (Rudkin, *The First French Expedition to California*, p. 68). Englishman George Vancouver commented that Lasuén's "gentle manners, united to a most venerable and placid countenance, indicated the tranquilized state of mind, that fitted him in an eminent degree for presiding over so benevolent an institution" (Guest, *Fermín Francisco de Lasuén*, p. 270). Lasuén was buried on 27 June 1803, "in the sanctuary of Mission Carmel on the Gospel side and in the stone vault nearest the high altar" (Kenneally, *Writings of Fermín Francisco de Lasuén*, 2:329).

LITURGICAL VESTMENTS: Any of the garments worn by clergymen or altar boys; especially a garment worn during the celebration of the Mass. The following are mentioned in the text:

1) Alb: A full-length white linen tunic secured with a cincture, worn under the chasuble during Mass. Symbolic of the tunic Herod made Jesus wear ("Herod and his guards . . . put a magnificent robe on him and sent him back to Pilate" Luke 23:11).

2) Chasuble: A full-length sleeveless outer garment worn over the alb, made of silk, wool, or cotton; the outer vestment. Symbolic of the "yoke of Christ" that Pilate's soldiers made Jesus wear ("The soldiers then wove a crown of thorns and fixed it on his head, throwing around his shoulders a cloak of royal purple" John 19:2).

3) Cope: A mantle-like outer garment or "cape" of varying length, open in front and fastened at the neck, and usually made of silk. Worn during Benediction, festal ceremonies/processions, and occasionally when administering the Sacraments.

4) Dalmatic: A wide-sleeved, ornate outer garment worn over the alb, used in place of the chasuble, and usually made of silk. Reserved for special Masses and festal ceremonies/processions, and usually worn only by bishops and prelates. A simpler version of the dalmatic is used by subdeacons/deacons as the outer vestment, in place of the chasuble.

5) Humeral veil: An oblong vestment worn around the neck and shoulders, over the chasuble or dalmatic, and usually made of silk. The veil is used to cover a priest's hands when he raises the monstrance during Benediction.

6) Stole: A long, band-like scarf worn around the neck and falling to about the knees, made of silk, wool, or cotton. Symbolic of the rope used to lead Jesus to Calvary ("They bound Jesus, led him away, and handed him over to Pilate" Mark 15:1).

7) Surplice: A wide-sleeved, half-length outer garment made of linen or cotton, derived from the alb. Often embroidered at the hem and sleeves, it is worn by all clergy in choir, during festal ceremonies/processions, and when administering the Sacraments.

LLULL, BLESSED RÁMON (Raymond Lull or Lully in English) (1235—1315): Born in Palma, Mallorca; experienced mystical visions (c. 1263); abandoned former self-indulgent lifestyle, became member of Franciscan Secular Order, and devoted balance of life to philosophy, theology, and missionary work; traveled throughout Asia Minor and North Africa attempting to convert Muslims, and according to legend, was stoned to death in Bougie, Algeria; buried in Basilica of San Francisco, Palma; beatified in 1858. Llull's major work, *Ars generalis ultima* (*Highest General Knowledge*, c. 1308), was a theosophical attempt to encompass all knowledge into a Neoplatonic schema that resolved all religious differences and established a tranquil world. He also composed religious poetry, mystical literature, an encyclopedia of medieval thought, and approximately 240 philosophical and theological Latin treatises, most notably addressing the cult of the Blessed Virgin Mary. Along with the writings of John Duns Scotus, this paved the way for the modern Catholic doctrines of Immaculate Conception, Assumption, and Intercession. Historically revered by the Franciscans, Llull was given the scholastic nickname *Doctor Illuminatus* (Illuminated Doctor. He is not a universal Doctor of the Catholic Church). Palma's university was founded in his honor in 1483 (first known as Estudio General Lluliano [Llulian General Study]); granted university status by Charles I in 1526 (renamed Imperial and Royal University); granted Papal approbation in 1673 (name lengthened to Pontifical, Imperial, Royal and Literary University of Mallorca); operated at peak in Serra's day, with schools of theology, jurisprudence, and medicine; ceased functioning in 1832.

MACHADO, CHRISTIANO: (14 July 1838—28 June 1924): Born in the Azores Islands, Portugal; seaman by profession; arrived in Monterey (1864); married Mary Dutra, member of early Monterey

pioneer family; worked at Carmel Whaling Company, Point Lobos (1865-70); hired as caretaker of abandoned Mission Carmel by Father Casanova (1870), and lived in the *"adobe orchard"* house one hundred yards east of the mission until his family grew too large (fourteen children), at which time he constructed a new two-story redwood house (which still stands, fronting present Rio Road). Machado spent thirty-seven years as Mission Carmel caretaker. He cleaned, repaired, and maintainted the mission and grounds, which included rediscovering the location of Serra's forgotten grave in 1882, and helping Casanova with his restoration program of 1882-84. He retired in 1907, and moved to Monterey where he lived until death.

MATUTE, LIEUTENANT JUAN BAUTISTA: Arrived at San Blas naval department (1789); frequent commander of San Blas supply vessels to California; commanding the *Aránzazu*, led an unsuccessful expedition to establish a colony at Bodega Bay, California (1793); donated silver crown to Mission Carmel's Our Lady of Bethlehem statue after safe return from perilous voyage to the Philippines, most likely as commander of the *Concepción*, a Manila galleon escort (1798); killed during the naval Battle of Trafalgar (21 October 1805, in which England won a decisive Napoleonic War battle over the combined Spanish/French navies off the southwest coast of Spain).

MESTRES, RIGHT REVEREND MONSIGNOR RÁMON M. (19 October 1865—5 August 1930): Born in Barcelona, Spain; arrived in California as a seminarian, joined Diocese of Monterey-Los Angeles;

ordained (1888); served in Los Angeles, San Luis Obispo, Santa Cruz and San Diego; appointed to pastorate of Royal Presidio Chapel (San Carlos Church), Monterey, and Mission Carmel dependency (7 April 1893); founded San Carlos School, Monterey (1898); performed marriage of local public school teacher, Lou Henry, to Herbert Hoover at outdoor ceremony in Royal Presidio Chapel garden (10 February 1899), (both were Quakers, but in the absence of a Quaker meeting house, Mestres was asked to officiate as civil magistrate. Thus, Hoover became the first U.S. President to be married by a Catholic priest); installed Vizcaíno-Serra oak tree trunk at rear of Royal Presidio Chapel (1905); formed Mission Restoration League and began soliciting private and political support for restoration of Mission Carmel (1910); awarded membership in Royal Order of Isabella by King Alfonso XIII for contribution to preservation of Spain's cultural heritage in the New World (1915); proposed grand plan to restore entire Mission Carmel compound at an estimated cost of $100,000, and enlisted San Francisco architect Bernard Maybeck to draw plans (1919); built small rectory at Mission Carmel (not a restoration, although built on site of the mission's original physician quarters—the present Harry Downie Museum), in order to hold regular services (1919); performed Serra cell groundbreaking in the wrong location (1919); performed Serra Cenotaph room groundbreaking (1921); commissioned local sculptor/painter/muralist Joseph Mora to design Serra Cenotaph (1921); unveiled Serra Cenotaph (12 October 1924); appointed domestic prelate with the title Right Reverend Monsignor (an honorary rank without corresponding ecclesiastical jurisdiction) by Pope Pius XI, in recognition of service to the Church (1925); appointed Vicar General (highest ranking diocesan assistant to the bishop) of the Diocese of Monterey-Fresno (1925); buried in Los Angeles despite wish to be buried at Mission Carmel; reinterred in Mission Carmel cemetery (20 March 1984).

MISSION: 1) A religious foundation in non-Christian territory, comprising a church, living quarters, cemetery, fields, etc., or as termed by Serra, "tender plants in the garden of Christianity" (Tibesar, *Writings of Junípero Serra*, 3:75). California's missions were organized around the typical Spanish colonial *reducción* (reduction) or *congregación* (congregation) model, whereby Indians in sparsely settled areas were "reduced" from a "free, undisciplined" state into productive, civilized "congregations"; 2) A group of missionaries traveling from town to town, giving a "mission" of prayer/preaching/inspiration for the Christian populace.

MISSION REGISTERS: Each mission had separate "spiritual result" registers, as described by Serra in 1771: "Each mission received from me . . . two blank registers, well bound and lined in reddish sheepskin for the registration of Baptisms and burials—the two things that are first likely to occur" (Tibesar, *Writings of Junípero Serra*, 1:222-23). In addition to the *Libro de Bautismos* (Book of Baptisms) and *Libro de Difuntos* (Book of Deaths), each mission eventually received a *Libro de Casamientos* (Book of Marriages), and a *Libro de Confirmaciones* (Book of Confirmations).

MISSIONS, LOWER CALIFORNIA: Serra was president of the following missions from April 1768 to April 1769 (all founded by the Jesuits):
1) Nuestra Señora de Loreto (founded 1697)
2) San Francisco Xavier (1699)
3) Santa Rosalía de Mulegé (1705)
4) San José de Comondú (1708)
5) La Purísima Concepción de María Cadegomó (1720)
6) Nuestra Señora de Guadalupe (1720)
7) Santiago de las Coras (1721)
8) Nuestra Señora de los Dolores (1721)
9) San Ignacio (1728)
10) San José del Cabo (1730)
11) Todos Santos (1733)
12) San Luís Gonzaga (1737)
13) Santa Gertrudis (1752)
14) San Francisco de Borja (1762)
15) Santa María de Los Angeles (1767)

En route to settle Upper California, Serra founded his very first mission at San Fernando de Velicatá on 14 May 1769, Lower California's sixteenth, and the only Franciscan mission in the former Jesuit peninsular-province. Before leaving Father Miguel de la Campa behind to begin the actual task of building the mission, Serra supplied him with

> one-fifth of the cattleherd that was brought together for the [Upper California] expedition, . . . four loads of biscuits, an allotment of flour and soap . . . some chocolate, raisins and figs, and more than forty *fanegas* of maize. Thus he would be able to live, and, in addition, entertain the Indians for some time, until he should receive more help. [Tibesar, *Writings of Junípero Serra*, 1:61]

The mission soon grew to include an *adobe* church, *adobe* "mission house," storehouse, corral, and crops irrigated by a small earthenwork dam. Between 1769 and 1773, Campa and two other priests baptized 445 Indians, performed 167 weddings, and buried only one person, a baby. The Franciscans transferred the Lower California missions to the Dominicans in 1773 so that they could concentrate on Upper California. During the Dominican period (1773-1821), 2,572 Baptisms, 592 marriages, and

2,156 burials were recorded. The mission was abandoned in 1821, for as an important supply link in the overland trail from Loreto to San Diego, it had been exposed to the vicissitudes of epidemic, which slowly decimated the Indian population. Velicatá, about 350 miles south of San Diego, is today an abandoned mound of earth, save for a few *adobe* mounds.

MISSIONS, SIERRA GORDA: Serra served in the Mexican Sierra Gorda mission district from May 1750 to September 1758, and as president of its missions from May 1751 to November 1755. The area was home to the Pame Indians, belonging to the Chichimeca ethnic group, and the Otomi linguistic group. Dominicans and Augustinians first evangelized among the Pames in the early seventeenth century, but because of the Pames nomadic lifestyle and rugged mountain homeland, permanent missionary activity was not possible until military resettlement of the Indians in 1743. The San Fernando College Franciscans were entrusted with the region in 1744, and founded five missions in April and May of that year: Santiago de Jalpan; San Miguel de Concá; La Purísima de Landa; San Francisco de Tilaco; and Nuestra Señora de la Luz de Tancoyol. The missions were spaced approximately fifteen miles apart, and at his residence/headquarters in centrally located Jalpan, Serra built Santiago de Jalpan Church. Palóu, also a resident, described it as a

> church of stonework, sufficient to hold th[e] large number of people. He [Serra] proposed his devout plan to all those Indians, who gladly agreed to do it, offering themselves to haul the stone (which was at hand) and all the sand, to make the lime and mortar, and to serve as helpers in carying it to the masons. This work was begun and was carried on during the entire dry season and when the Indians were not needed for work in the fields. In a period of seven years a church was built, fifty-three yards [sic] [*varas*] long and eleven wide, with its corresponding transept and dome, and adjacent to it the sacristy (which was also vaulted); and also a chapel dedicated to the Holy Sepulcher [Jesus' tomb], which he adorned with statues and the stations of our Savior's Passion in order to draw the affections more closely to the devout ceremonies of Holy Week. The church was likewise adorned with *reredoses*, altars and side *reredoses*, all gilded. An organ was installed in the choir, and he sought a teacher to instruct the Indians how to play it for use at High Mass. . . . In imitation [of Serra] . . . the missionaries of the other four missions acted in the same way, building their chuches in the same manner . . . according to the number of people at the missions. [Geiger, *Palóu's Life of Fray Junípero Serra*, p. 33]

Palóu described Serra's actual participation in the construction:

> He did not disdain to perform the most menial and humble chores, working as a day laborer or as a helper to the artisan in carrying stones to build the church, making mortar with the boys as if he were one of them, and with the adults carrying lumber for the structure. He also joined in with the masons to fill the crevices between the stones with rubble to strengthen the walls. All this he did in the most humble sort of clothing, wearing a habit which had become tattered, wrapping around himself a piece of old mantle, despite the fact that the land is very hot. . . . One day [Serra was] among a group of Indians, more than twenty in number, who were carrying a large beam, and he was helping them to carry it. Since he was shorter than the others, he inserted a piece of his mantle between his shoulder and the beam to equalize it. Edified at what he saw, Father Pumeda [a visiting priest] hurriedly called me [Palóu] so I might see him, thinking it something new for me also. And he said to me: "Look at your professor, and see how he is making the Way of the Cross, and in what garments!" But I answered him: "This happens every day." [Geiger, *Palóu's Life of Fray Junípero Serra*, pp. 265-66]

Palóu mentions an artisan. This indicates utilization of skilled labor, most likely working from the plans of a master stonemason. All five churches are similar in design, possibly the work of the same designer. They are generally smaller than the California missions, but appear larger with their high domes, and are certainly more ornate with their churrigueresque façades. Palóu mentions that construction took seven years, implying that it was finished before Serra left the Sierra Gorda in 1758. A plaque within Santiago de Jalpan Church begs to differ, which reads: "completed in 1768, restored in 1895."

MISSIONS, UPPER CALIFORNIA: Serra was responsible for the founding of California's first nine missions (asterisk indicates Serra not present at founding):
1) San Diego de Alcalá . . . . 16 July 1769
2) San Carlos Borromeo . . . . 3 June 1770
3) San Antonio de Padua . . . . 14 July 1771

4)   San Gabriel Arcángel . . . . 8 September 1771*
5)   San Luís Obispo de Tolosa . . . . 1 September 1772
6)   San Francisco de Asís . . . . 9 October 1776*
7)   San Juan Capistrano . . . . 1 November 1776
8)   Santa Clara de Asís . . . . 12 January 1777*
9)   San Buenaventura . . . . 31 March 1782
        Lasuén founded the next nine, and was present on each occasion:
10) Santa Bárbara . . . . 4 December 1786
11) La Purísima Concepción . . . . 8 December 1787
12) Santa Cruz . . . . 28 August 1791
13) Nuestra Señora de la Soledad . . . . . 9 October 1791
14) San José . . . . 11 June 1797
15) San Juan Bautista . . . . 24 June 1797
16) San Miguel Arcángel . . . . 25 July 1797
17) San Fernando Rey . . . . 8 September 1797
18) San Luís Rey . . . . 13 June 1798
        The last three were founded by three different individuals:
19) Santa Inés . . . . 17 December 1804
        (Founded by Father Estevan Tapis, Lasuén's successor president.)
20) San Rafael Arcángel . . . . 14 December 1817
        (Founded by Father Vicente de Sarría, first commissary prefect of the missions [a post
        created in 1812 to relieve the president of certain responsibilities, e.g. government matters
        and supervision of priests, however the president still outranked the commissary prefect].)
21) San Francisco Solano . . . . .4 July 1823
        (Founded by Father José Altimira, a Mission San Francisco priest. He acted without official
        authorization, but the new mission was legitimized nine months later, the only one
        founded under Mexican rule.)

MONTEREY, EXPEDITIONS TO: Juan Rodríguez Cabrillo (born c.1498, probably in Seville, Spain, and not in Portugal as commonly assumed), was the first European to explore Upper California's coast, and as such can be considered discoverer of Monterey. After participating with Hernán Cortés in the conquest of Aztec Mexico (1519-21), he was commissioned by Viceroy Antonio Mendoza to explore Mexico's northwest coast (1542-43). Only fifty years after Columbus, the search for golden cities and the Strait of Anian (Northwest Passage) to the Far East still merited serious attention. The *San Salvador* and *Victoria* reached as far north as Cape Mendocino (March 1543). However, the expedition returned to Mexico without Cabrillo. While wintering on San Miguel Island in the Santa Barbara Channel, he had slipped and broken his leg and/or arm. He died from the resulting infection on 3 January 1543, and was most likely buried on the same island. Although arriving at its Mexican home port of Navidad Bay without solving any riddles, the Cabrillo-Ferrer expedition (chief pilot Bartolomé Ferrer assumed command after Cabrillo's death) did chart the coast for the first time, and discover the present bays of San Diego and Monterey. Cabrillo called San Diego "San Miguel" and Monterey "Bahía de los Piños" (Bay of the Pines). The surviving record of the expedition (actually a sixteenth-century summary of now lost original diaries narrated in the third person) describes Cabrillo's 16 November 1542 discovery of Monterey Bay:

> Thursday, November 16, at break of day they arrived off a large *ensenada* [Monterey Bay], which came up from behind. As it seemed to have a port and a river, they went beating [tacking] about all that day and night and the following Friday until they saw there was no river nor any haven [they may have seen the Carmel and/or Salinas Rivers, but they did not meet the specifications of the legendary "Río de Nuestra Señora" that they were looking for, a great "arm of the sea" supposedly leading far inland to the mythical riches of Quivira]. In order to take possession they cast anchor in forty-five fathoms [somewhere off Point Piños], but did not dare go ashore on account of the great surf. This *ensenada* is in full thirty-nine degrees; all of it is full of pines down to the sea, and they named it "Bahía de los Piños." [Wagner, *Spanish Voyages to the Northwest Coast of America in the Sixteenth Century*, pp. 89-90]

During the next fifty years, New Spain's viceroys sponsored several explorations of coastal California in search of a sheltered port for repair/defense of trans-Pacific Manila galleons on the last leg of their return voyage to Acapulco. Francisco Gali may have passed Monterey Bay in 1584, and Sebastián Cermeño visited it on a return trip from the Philippines in December 1595 (taken from a 1596 abstract of his original narrative):

He made sail [heading south] with favorable weather and discovered a very large *ensenada* which bore to the east and southeast, all a bold coast [Monterey Bay, which Cermeño states in his narrative he named "San Pedro," and that it was fifteen leagues across from Point Cypress at its south to Point Año Nuevo at its north]. This day he observed the sun at midday at thirty-seven degrees [his exact location when the sun broke is uncertain, but it appears to be in the middle of the bay]. From the mouth of the *ensenada* the land bore to the south. From morning he sailed seven leagues and anchored behind a point [probably Point Cypress] in order not to run before the wind. Monday, at dawn, the eleventh of the month, he made sail and traveled twenty leagues. All the coast trends northwest-southeast, is bold and high, and of bare ranges all of a kind, without any point or place of shelter where one could stop [the Big Sur coast]. [Ibid., pp. 160-61]

These explorations were capped by the voyage of Sebastián Vizcaíno (1548?-1623), a Spanish merchant-adventurer granted concessions to set up a pearl-fishing enterprise in Lower California, on condition that he explore and chart the entire California coastline as far north as Cape Mendocino. Departing from Acapulco on 5 May 1602, Vizcaíno commanded the flagship *San Diego*, the *Santo Tomás*, and the *Tres Reyes*. He located and entered Monterey Bay on 16 December 1602, and subsequently "re-named" the bay, discovered the harbor he also called Monterey, and became the first European on record to step ashore at Monterey. After resting and exploring inland, he departed on 4 January 1603. The expedition reached Cape Mendocino, headed back to Acapulco without stopping at Monterey, and arrived on 21 March. While at Monterey, Vizcaíno wrote the following to King Felipe III on 28 December 1602:

> This harbor of Monterey is . . . well situated in point of latitude for what His Majesty intends to do for the protection and security of ships coming from the Philippines. In it may be repaired the damages which they may have sustained, for there is a great extent of pine forest from which to obtain masts and yards, even though the vessel be of a thousand tons burthen [burden], live oaks and white oaks for shipbuilding, and this close to the seaside in great number. And the harbor is very secure against all winds. The land is thickly peopled by Indians and is very fertile, in its climate and the quality of the soil resembling Castile, and any seed sown there will give fruit, and there are extensive lands fit for pasturage, and many kinds of animals and birds. [Vizcaíno, *The Voyage of Sebastián Vizcaíno*, pp. 47-48]

Three Carmelite priests served as Vizcaíno expedition chaplains: Fathers Andrés de la Asumpción, Tomás de Aquino, and Antonio de la Ascención. Father de la Ascención recorded his impressions of Monterey:

> December 16 when the fleet entered the Puerto de Monterey, it was already night. The following day the General [Vizcaíno] ordered the necessary things to be taken ashore, so that Father Andrés and Father Antonio could say Mass every day while they had to remain. This was done, and a large capacious tent was set up under the shade of a very large live-oak to serve as a church [A companion diary, probably Vizcaíno's, describes it as "a great oak near the shore, where he made the hut and arbor to say Mass" (Bolton, *Spanish Exploration in the Southwest, 1542-1706*, p. 91)]. At twenty paces from this there was an *arroyo* or ravine in which were some holes of good water, into which trickled all that was necessary for the men in the fleet. The friars said the Mass of the Holy Ghost, so that the General and those of his council might have the wisdom to order and provide what was most agreeable to the service of Our Lord, Jesus Christ, and of the King. . . . It [Monterey] is a very good port and well protected from all winds. There is much wood and water in it and an immense number of great pine trees, smooth and straight, suitable for the masts and yards of ships; many were very large live-oaks with which to build ships; great white oaks, and forests of scarlet oaks. There are rock-roses, broom, roses of Castile, brambles, willows, alders, poplars, and other trees like those of Castile. There are springs of good water; beautiful large lakes, which were covered with ducks and many other birds; most fertile pastures; good meadows for cattle, and fertile fields for growing crops. There are many different kinds of animals, and large ones such as bears, so large that their feet are a good third of a yard [sic] [*vara*] long and a hand wide. There are other animals which have hoofs like mules [buffalo], . . . of which there must be a great number, as the fields were full of their tracks. There are others [elk] as large as three-year old bulls, resembling stags in their build. Their neck was long, and on the head they had very large branching horns like those of a stag. Their tail must have been a yard [sic] [*vara*] in length and half a one wide, and their hoofs were cleft like those of an ox. . . . There are many of these animals, and besides them there are large deer, stags, jackrabbits, and rabbits, and wild-cats as large as kids. There is an abundance of ducks of all kinds, geese, doves, thrushes, spar-

rows, linnets, cardinals, quails, partridges, magpies, cranes, and buzzards, all like those of Castile. There are some other birds of the shape of turkeys, the largest I saw on this voyage. From the point of one wing to that of the other it was found to measure seventeen spans [equivalent to eight feet, and most likely a California condor]. . . . There are . . . gulls, crows and many other seabirds which live on the fish they catch. In this port there are a good many fish in the sea, and among the rocks there are many *lapas* [shellfish] and mussels, and at depth attached to the rocks are some very large shells of fine mother-of-pearl, very beautiful and of a very fine color [abalone]. There are oysters, lobsters, crabs . . . and many large seals, or seacalves, and whales. One very large one recently dead had gone ashore on the coast in this port and the bears came by night to dine on it. The port is all surrounded by settlements of affable Indians of good disposition and well built, very willing to give what they have. They brought us some of the skins of bears, lions, and deers. They use bows and arrows and have their form of government. They are naked. They would have much pleasure in seeing us make a settlement in their country. [Wagner, *Spanish Voyages to the Northwest Coast of America in the Sixteenth Century*, pp. 244, 246-47]

A companion diary mentions the winter weather, and an excursion to Carmel Bay and River:

Making our preparations necessary for our voyage to Cape Mendocino, [t]he men worked under great difficulties in taking on wood and water because of the extreme cold, which was so intense that Wednesday, New Year's Day of 1603, dawned and with all the mountains covered with snow and resembling the volcano of Mexico, and that the hole from which we were taking water was frozen over more than a palm in thickness, and the bottles, which had been left full over night, were all frozen so that even when turned upside down—not a drop ran out. . . . By Friday night, the third of the said month, we were all ready. This day the general, with the commissary and ten arquebusiers [soldiers], went inland, toward the southeast, . . . He proceeded some three leagues when he discovered another good port [Carmel Bay], into which entered a copious river [Carmel River] descending from some high, snow-covered mountains with large pines, white and black poplars, and willows. It had an extended river bottom, and in it were many cattle [elk] as large as cows . . . an effort was made to kill some of them but they did not wait long enough. No people were found because, on account of the great cold, they were living in the interior. [Bolton, *Spanish Exploration in the Southwest, 1542-1706*, pp. 93-94]

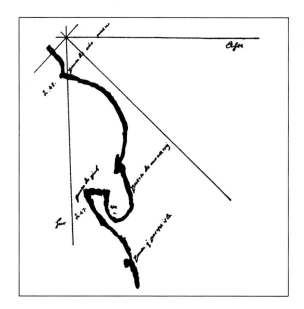

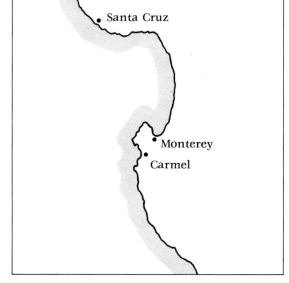

Vizcaíno expedition map of Monterey Bay and harbor, 1602.

Monterey Bay and harbor.

The favorable Vizcaíno expedition diaries and official reports left an indelible imprint on the Spanish psyche for 167 years. When Upper California was finally settled in 1769 as a buffer against Russian and British encroachment on the northern frontier, there was never any doubt as to where the principal settlement should be: Monterey. The only problem was finding it. The 1769 Portolá land expedition in search of Monterey Harbor traveled north from San Diego with Vizcaíno's descriptions and Admiral José Cabrera Bueno's *Navegación especulativa, y práctica* (*Speculative Navigation and Practice*, pub. 1734), the best compilation of all knowledge pertaining to the west coast of New Spain. Cabrera Bueno described Monterey in part as follows:

> From the point [Año Nuevo] the coast runs more to the east, making a large bay until it comes out from a point of low land, very heavily forested to the very sea, to which was given the name of Punta de Piños, . . . near the southern point [it forms] a maze of *barrancas* [gorges], which is a sign by which to recognize it. On the northeast the Punta de Piños forms a famous harbor, and by steering straight one may enter it and run close to the land in six fathoms. All this point and roadstead is rocky, but steering to the southeast and east until all the rocks are passed one comes to a famous beach. Before reaching it there is a good anchorage, clear and sheltered from all winds except from the northwest. In this port which they call Monte Rey there are many pines good for masts and lateen yards. Right close to the sea and the beach there is a salty estuary into which in spring tide the sea enters. To the southeast of this estuary at the distance of a musket shot from the beach, and close to the estuary, is a very moist plain, where, by digging just a little, fresh, abundant, and very good water flows. . . . This harbor is in thirty-seven degrees [Monterey Harbor is actually at thirty-six degrees, thirty-seven minutes], and it is a good port in which to succor the China ships, because the land is the first they see when they come to New Spain. Following the coast from the Punta de Piños toward the south-southeast there is another fine harbor [Carmel Bay] running from north to south. It is sheltered from all winds and has a river [Carmel River] of very good water and of slight depth, whose banks are well grown with black poplars very high and smooth, and other trees native of Spain. It comes down from very high, white mountains, and is called Río de Carmelo, because the friars of this Order discovered it. [Bolton, *Fray Juan Crespi: Missionary Explorer on the Pacific Coast, 1769-1774*, p. 236]

The Portolá expedition hugged the coast as much as possible to take maximum advantage of Cabrera Bueno's instructions (which diarist Crespí referred to as their "road map"), and also, of course, because they were searching for a harbor. When they arrived at the Salinas River mouth (which empties directly into Monterey Bay) on the afternoon of 1 October, they seemed to recognize their location. Crespí wrote:

> Soon after our arrival the commander [Portolá], the engineer [Miguel Costansó], and I, accompanied by five soldiers, went to examine the beach. Ascending a small hill which is not far from it, from the top we saw a great bay, which we conjectured to be the one which Cabrera Bueno places between Point Año Nuevo and the Point of Pines of Monterey, for we saw this point covered with tall pines, and it must be that the port of Monterey is near it. The river which we have been following for so many days empties into this great bay, which forms an estuary that penetrates the land about two leagues and causes the river to rise and fall [near Elkhorn Slough, one mile north of present Moss Landing. This was the terminus of the Salinas River until it diverted course between 1908-10. It now empties into the bay 4.5 miles south of Moss Landing, immediately south of a shoreline-knoll called Mulligan Hill]. Near the beach it is now very full and of great depth, so that it cannot be forded; the mouth is narrow, perhaps twelve *varas* wide, and near the sea it resembles a very deep pond. The plain is very large, and extends for many leagues until it reaches the other point, which we conjectured to be Año Nuevo. [Ibid., pp. 203-04]

Camp was made near the river. Captain Rivera y Moncada and eight scouts ventured south toward the "tall pines" on 2 October, and returned the next day with a problem:

> Both the captain and the soldiers said they had seen no harbor, either to the north or to the south of the point, but they did see that the point was covered with pines, and after passing it they saw a small bay formed between this Point of Pines and another somewhat farther south [Carmel Bay], with an *arroyo* of water which came down from the mountains [Carmel River], well forested with trees, and an estuary into which the *arroyo* empties, near some small lagoons of little consequence. Farther on [Carmel Highlands/Big Sur,] the precipitous coast ran south by southwest, and its ruggedness compelled them to

retreat. . . . This report heard, the commander decided that the following day a council of the officers should be held to determine what was to be done. [Ibid., pp. 204-05]

The *junta* (council) was held on 4 October, and Portolá

told them [the officers] about the shortage of provisions in which we found ourselves, and the number of sick on hand (there were seventeen men who were half crippled and of no use for labor); he called attention to the fact that the season was now far advanced, and to the great hardships of the men still in good health from the excessive labor in watching the animals at night, in guarding the camp, and in the constant sallies to explore and reconnoiter. In view of this and . . . considering that the time we have been on the road has not only been sufficient but longer than necessary to reach that destination [Monterey]; and considering that, according to the indications which Cabrera Bueno gives in his account, it was inevitable that we should find it; [now] having examined [the country], expecting every moment [to come upon] the port, we have only found, as Captain Rivera y Moncada who went to explore declares, that what should be the Carmelo River is merely a gully, and that what should be a port [Carmel Bay] is a small inlet, that what were [described] as great lakes [of fresh water] are mere ponds, and that what should be a port [Monterey] is only a bay; [I am, therefore,] now disturbed in the hope of finding the port, seeing so great a stretch of level ground as lies before us, and [considering] that—if we are to believe the account [of Cabrera Bueno]—in order to reach the port it is necessary that we first come to the Sierra de Santa Lucía [Mountains], a journey for which, I recognize, much time is required. . . . Having heard the commander's proposal the officers voted unanimously to continue the journey, as it seemed to be the only thing to do, in the hope of finding, through the favor of God, the desired harbor of Monterey. [Ibid., pp. 205-06; and Academy of Pacific Coast History, *Publications: Volume I*, p. 83]

The expedition continued north, accidently discovered San Francisco Bay, returned past Monterey, once again failed o recognize it, and arrived at San Diego on 24 January 1770. What had gone wrong? Several factors coalesced: Vizcaíno had oversold Monterey as "very secure against all winds," and portrayed it as a well-defined and substantially protected harbor on his map, when in fact it is not (a breakwater built in 1934 finally made Monterey "secure"); Vizcaíno described Monterey at the height of winter, when Carmel River was a "copious river." Portolá arrived at the end of the dry season, when this important reference point was an "*arroyo* [stream] of water;" Portolá's latitude did not agree exactly with Cabrera Bueno's, leading to the "false notion . . . that the port had been obliterated . . . [by] the great banks of sand in the place where it [Monterey] ought to have been" (Tibesar, *Writings of Junípero Serra*, 1:159, 167), and to speculation that the Salinas River was the Carmel River, therefore placing Monterey further north; they were on land, rather than at sea where they could fully appreciate Cabrera Bueno's navigational reference points and make soundings; the men were exhausted and ill from eighty days of walking (with only fourteen rest days), combined with the fatigue of the immediately preceding land/sea journey from Lower California to San Diego; and 167 years of psychological expectation had created a legendary Monterey "mystique" that was not easily shattered by the reality of the harbor's humble proportions. Portolá later commented:

I . . . went on by land to Monterey with that small company of persons, or rather say skeletons, who had been spared by scurvy, hunger, and thirst [from the Lower California to San Diego trek]. We reached Monterey after struggling thirty-eight days against the greatest hardships and difficulties . . . without food and . . . not know[ing] where we were. For, although the signs whereby we were to recognize the port were the same as those set down by General Sebastián Vizcaíno in his log, the fact is that, without being able to guess the reason, we were all under hallucination, and no one dared assert openly that the port was indeed Monterey. [Chapman, *A History of California: The Spanish Period*, p. 226]

Portolá finally recognized the simple, unassuming anchorage after a second expedition to Monterey Harbor, arriving 24 May 1770:

As the day was clear they [Portolá, Fages, and Crespí] saw the great bay which is formed by the Point of Pines and the other point, which projects much farther into the sea, and which was still thought to be Point Año Nuevo. They observed that the sea in the whole immense bay was so calm that it resembled a large lake. In it were swimming and barking innumerable sea wolves, and near the shore there were two large whale cubs, not farther than five yards [sic] [*varas*] from the land, a clear indication that there was good depth. They traveled a short distance along the same [Monterey] beach and soon perceived that the bay resembled a round lake like an "O." Upon seeing this the three broke out with one voice: "This is the port of Monterey that we were seeking, for this is the letter described by Sebastián Viczaíno and Cabrera Bueno." The father [Crespí] immediately took out the needle, in order to observe the direction of the mouth, to be more certain, and he found that it is open to the north-northwest, and in that direction the mouth and entrance is open to that great bay, in which they believed, without doubt, was the harbor of Monterey. [Bolton, *Historical Memoirs of New California*, 2:284-85]

MONTEREY, ORIGIN OF NAME: The bay and harbor of Monterey were named in 1602 by Sebastián Vizcaíno, in honor of the incumbent Viceroy of New Spain, Gaspar de Zúñiga y Acevedo, Condé de Monterrey (Monterrey was spelled correctly in the earliest accounts, but was altered to Monte-Rey and Monterey during the mission period). He also named Carmel Bay/River, in honor of Our Lady of Mount Carmel, patroness of the expedition's three Carmelite Order chaplains. In 1768, Inspector General Gálvez selected the name San Carlos Borromeo (Saint Charles Borromeo) for the new Monterey Bay mission, in honor of the patron saint of both King Carlos III of Spain, and Carlos Francisco de Croix, Viceroy of New Spain. As reiterated by Serra:

> It is called "San Carlos de Monte-Rey," as arranged by the Most Illustrious Inspector General in honor of our Catholic Monarch and of the Most Excellent Lord, the present Viceroy—both of them Carlos by name. [Tibesar, *Writings of Junípero Serra*, 1:170-71]

When Serra detached the mission from the Monterey Presidio and moved it near the shore of Carmel River in 1771, it alternately became known as Misión San Carlos de Monterey, or Misión San Carlos Borromeo del Río Carmelo (Mission Saint Charles Borromeo of the Carmel River). Today it is familiarly known as "Mission Carmel Basilica," or simply "Mission Carmel." The original San Carlos Borromeo Church at the Monterey Presidio became known as La Capilla del Presidio de San Carlos de Monterey (The Royal Presidio Chapel of Saint Charles of Monterey), or simply La Capilla Real. Alternately called San Carlos Church since the advent of the American period, today the Royal Presidio Chapel's formal title is San Carlos Cathedral, mother church of the Diocese of Monterey in California.

MONTEREY IN CALIFORNIA, ROMAN CATHOLIC DIOCESE OF: Descended from original Franciscan missionary territory under ecclesiastical jurisdiction of Diocese of Sonora, Mexico; Diocese of Both Californias established, including most of Nevada and Utah (1840); area restricted to southern half of American California, title changed to Monterey, See (from the Latin *sēdes*, the official "seat") at Monterey, Royal Presidio Chapel named diocesan cathedral (1849); See moved to Los Angeles, title changed to Monterey-Los Angeles (1859); area restricted to central California, title altered to Monterey-Fresno, See at Fresno (1922); area further restricted to counties of Monterey, San Benito, San Luis Obispo and Santa Cruz, original title restored (Diocese of Monterey in California, as distinguished from the Diocese of Monterrey in Mexico), See at Monterey, Royal Presidio Chapel named diocesan San Carlos Cathedral, Most Rev. Harry A. Clinch, D.D. named first bishop (1967), (or technically third if the two bishops who served when the diocese was originally called Monterey are included: Most Rev. Joseph Alemany, O.P. [Order of Preachers, a member of the Dominican Order] 1850-53; and Most Rev. Thaddeus Amat, C.M. [Congregation of the Mission, a member of the Vincentian Order] 1854-59); ceremony establishing Diocese of Monterey in California and installing Bishop Clinch held at Mission Carmel Basilica, installing prelates Most Rev. Luigi Raimondi, D.D., Apostolic Delegate to the U.S., and His Eminence James Cardinal McIntyre, Archbishop of Los Angeles (14 December 1967); Bishop Clinch retires (18 January 1982); ceremony installing Most Rev. Thaddeus Shubsda, D.D., as fourth Bishop of Monterey in California held at Mission Carmel Basilica, installing prelate and homilist His Eminence Timothy Cardinal Manning, D.D., J.C.D., Archbishop of Los Angeles (1 July 1982). In his homily, Cardinal Manning said:

> The dust in the ground beneath our feet here is unquestionably the holiest of all of California because here lie the mortal remains of Father Junípero Serra, and side by side with him, his dearest companions Father Fermín Lasuén and Father Juan Crespí. All of the sanctities, all of the church history, all of the glory of our California church and state are interred in this holy soil. It is fitting that we should begin this ceremony, this episcopal installation in this place. [Weber, *Father of the Missions: A Documentary History of San Carlos Borromeo*, pp. 220-21]

MORGADO, MARTIN J. (30 September 1956—): Born in Los Angeles, California; raised in San Jose and Carmel; earned Associate in Arts Degree from Orange Coast College (1976); earned Bachelor of Arts Degree (Summa Cum Laude) in International Policy Studies (an interdisciplinary major combining political science, economics and foreign language) from the Monterey Institute of International Studies (1983); earned Master of Arts Degree (With Distinction) in International Policy Studies (and a specialization in Latin American Studies) from the Monterey Institute of International Studies (1984); currently attending Santa Clara University Law School. A lifelong interest in California history (particularly the Spanish period) has led to a position as Mission Carmel Archivist since 1984, and involvement in a number of mission research and restoration projects.

NOVENA: A recitation of prayers for nine consecutive days, with some special intention or occasion. Symbolic of the nine days that Mary and the Twelve Apostles spent together in prayer between Ascension Thursday and Pentecost Sunday.

ORDINATION: The ceremony during which a person is admitted to the ministry of a church. Serra's Franciscan path to the priesthood consisted of the following chronological steps:
1) Solemn profession into the Franciscan Order: ceremony and assumption of "religious" name.
2) Tonsure: shaving the hair from the top of the head, symbolic of Jesus' crown of thorns, rejection of temporal things, and a reminder of striving for spiritual perfection.
3) Four minor orders: acolyte, reader/lector, exorcist, and doorkeeper.
4) Sub-deacon: assistant to the deacon at Mass.
5) Deacon: assistant to the priest in various functions, such as preaching, conferral of Baptisms, etc.
6) Priest: having authority to pronounce absolution and administer all Sacraments save that of ordination, which is reserved to bishops.

ORLE: A heraldic design similar to a *bordure* (border around a shield), but not reaching to the edge of the shield.

PACKETBOAT: A large, two-masted sailing vessel (*paquebote* in Spanish) that carried passengers, freight, and mail. Inspector General Gálvez originally assigned three packetboats to supply Upper California, the *San Carlos* (alias *El Toisón de Oro* [*The Golden Fleece*], since each vessel had a secular or "popular" name as well as a "Christian" name); the *San Antonio* (*El Príncipe*, [*The Prince*]); and the *San José* (*El Descubridor* [*The Discoverer*]). Commissioned by Gálvez at the new San Blas shipyard in 1768, the *San José* was built especially for California service. She sailed from Loreto on 16 June 1769, but wandered aimlessly in the Gulf of California for three months as the result of a broken foremast suffered in a storm. After being refitted, the *San José* once again sailed for San Diego, leaving the port of Cabo San Lucas on 6 July 1770. The *San José* was never seen again, and no trace of wreckage was ever found. The Upper California enterprise did not recover from this unexpected and costly setback until 1774-76, when the supply fleet finally matured. Forty-five men were aboard the *San José*, along with food, supplies, tools, church furnishings, and three tower bells.

PAEZ, JOSÉ DE (1715—c. 1790): Prolific Mexican painter, although little is known about his life. Active throughout the second half of the eighteenth century, he is represented by extant works in Mexico, Guatemala, Peru, Venezuela, and the U.S. In addition to the *Glory of Heaven* at Mission Carmel, other California mission period works include: *San Antonio*, signed (presently at Mission San Miguel, but originally at Mission San Antonio as per Serra's 1774 delivery); *San Juan Capistrano*, unsigned (at Mission San Juan Capistrano); *San Luís Obispo*, unsigned (at Mission San Luís Obispo, which may be the painting the mission fathers rejected in 1774, prompting Serra to take it to Mission Carmel). Serra took note of Paez's talent when he ordered *San Juan Capistrano* in August 1775:

> May I ask . . . that it should not be painted by any kind of painter, of the *alcayseria* [common marketplace] . . . but they should find a good engraving and have Paez paint it, or some other good artist. . . . The saint should have a handsome, resolute and devout appearance. . . . His habit should not be blue, as in other pictures which have come here. [Tibesar, *Writings of Junípero Serra*, 2:319]

PALÓU, O.F.M., REVEREND FRANCISCO (26 January 1723—6 April 1789): Born in Palma, Mallorca, Spain; entered Franciscan Order (1739); solemn profession into the Order (1740); Serra's philosophy student for three years, followed by three years of theology (1740-46); ordained (1743); successfully competed for Lectorate in Philosophy (1749), although never taught the course; departed Palma with

Serra, bound for the Mexican missions (13 April 1749), described at that time as "of medium height, swarthy, [with] dark eyes and hair" (Geiger, *The Life and Times of Fray Junípero Serra, O.F.M.*, 1:58); arrived at Vera Cruz, Mexico (7 December 1749); made horseback journey to San Fernando College without Serra, who walked (December 1749); volunteered for Sierra Gorda missions, walked to Jalpan with Serra, and served at Mission Santiago de Jalpan (June 1750-1758); served as home missionary at San Fernando College (1758-67), acting as college vicar, counselor, Commissary of the Holy Office of the Inquisition; served at Mission San Francisco Xavier, Lower California (1768-69); appointed president of the Lower California missions after Serra departed for Upper California, serving at Mission Nuestra Señora de Loreto headquarters (1769-73); volunteered for Upper California service when Lower California missions transferred to Dominican Order (beginning April 1772); arrived at San Diego after sea/land journey (30 August 1773), having set first Lower/Upper California boundary en route; served as acting president of Upper California missions until Serra returned from Mexico City, residing at Mission Carmel headquarters (14 November 1773—13 March 1774), where reunited with Crespí after almost five year separation, about which he wrote: "The pleasure that I felt on seeing him was great, for we grew up together as children and studied almost from our A-B-C's until we finished theology" (Bolton, *Historical Memoirs of New California*, 1:312); welcomed Serra home from Mexico, ending five year separation (11 May 1774); served as diarist for two exploratory expeditions to San Francisco, and selected site for future mission (23 November—4 December 1774, and 4 September—1 October 1775); founded San Francisco Presidio (17 September 1776); founded Mission San Francisco de Asís (9 October 1776); served at Mission San Francisco (1776-85); assisted Serra at his death, buried him, wrote a lengthy obituary in Mission Carmel's *Libro de Difuntos*, and commissioned his portrait (August—September 1784); served as acting president of the missions, residing at Mission San Francisco, where he wrote all but the last chapter of his Serra biography, the first book written in California (mid-September 1784—13 November 1785); arrived at San Fernando College after request granted to return to Mexico City (21 February 1786); finished writing Serra biography, *Relación histórica de la vida y apostolicas tareas del Venerable Padre Fray Junípero Serra* (*Historical Account of the Life and Apostolic Labors of the Venerable Father Fray Junípero Serra*, pub. 1787, first English translation 1884), so that "he [Serra] shall be forever in the memory of all" (Geiger, *Palóu's Life of Fray Junípero Serra*, p. 257), and of their relationship he wrote:

> He [Serra] was serious from childhood, which seriousness he retained all through his life, so that exteriorly he appeared to be austere and almost unapproachable. But as soon as one talked and dealt with him, one had to change his opinion and consider him gentle, amiable and attractive, for he won the hearts of all. . . . From the year 1740, when he received me as one of his students, until the year 1784, when death separated us, I was the object of his very special affection, an affection we always mutually shared, more than if we had been brothers in the flesh. [Ibid., pp. xxv, 279]

Palóu was elected guardian of San Fernando College (summer 1786), and served until death while on visitation at Santa Cruz de Querétaro College; buried in unmarked grave at Santa Cruz de Querétaro College, Querétaro. Palóu's posthumously published *Noticias de la Antigua y Nueva California* (*Historical Memoirs of Old and New California*, pub. 1857 in Mexico City, first English translation 1926), along with the *Relación histórica*, form the "basic text[s] employed by writers in producing the books, articles, brochures, pageants and orations about Serra that in almost endless succession have appeared down to our day" (Ibid., p. iv). In the words of historian Hubert Bancroft:

> I have sometimes been tempted to entertain a selfish regret that Palóu wrote, or that his writings were ever printed, yet all the same he must be regarded as the best original authority. . . . There was no man so well qualified by opportunities and ability to write the early history of California. [Bancroft, *History of California*, 1:418, 420]

PIOUS FUND OF THE CALIFORNIAS: A fund of charitable contributions donated for the express purpose of evangelizing the Indians, inaugurated by the Lower California Jesuits in 1733. With the capital placed in trust, and the interest used to support the missions, the Fund was administered on behalf of the Jesuits until they were expelled from New Spain in 1767. The government assumed control of the Fund at this point, which was worth nearly 2 million *pesos* and generated an annual interest income of 50,000 *pesos* (in comparison, a mission soldier earned 325 *pesos* annually at this time). The Fund continued to contribute 1,000 *pesos* to each new mission established in Lower and Upper

California, maintained the existing missions, and gave an annual 400-*peso sínodo* (alms stipend) to each missionary in the field. The money was not sent directly to the missionaries, but to San Fernando College, where the college's apostolic syndic used it to buy additional supplies for the missions. After Mexican independence, the Fund's assets were sold, the capital co-minlged with the national treasury's, and only after a century of negotiation and litigation on behalf of California and southwest U.S. bishops to gain compensation as successors in interest to the trust (including international arbitration before the Hague Tribunal in 1902), was a final settlement reached in 1964. The Mexican government agreed to settle all past overdue and future annuities for $719,546.00 (Mexico had already paid nearly one million dollars between 1877-1912). The 1964 award was donated to the Seminario Nacional Pontificio in Montezuma, New Mexico, to endow scholarships for seminarians training to serve in Mexico.

PORTOLÁ Y ROVIRA, COLONEL GASPAR DE (1717—10 October 1786): Born in Balaguer, Catalonia, Spain; participated in Italian campaigns of War of Austrian Succession, and Spain's invasion of Portugal during Seven Years' War (1743-62); appointed

Captain in newly created Regiment of Dragoons of Spain, created for service in New Spain (1764); arrived in Vera Cruz, Mexico (31 July 1764); served as Governor of Lower California (30 November 1767—9 March 1769), and as Commissioner of Expulsion of the Jesuits from Lower California (30 November 1767—3 February 1768); welcomed Serra to Loreto as new president of the Lower California missions (1 April 1768); appointed military commander of the Upper California colonizing expedition (July 1768); departed Loreto to begin northward march (9 March 1769); successfully reached San Diego (1 July 1769), with Serra accompanying his party from Mission Santa María de los Angeles, Lower California; led unsuccessful first expedition to locate Monterey Bay/Harbor (14 July 1769—24 January 1770), but discovered San Francisco Bay (Sergeant José Ortega's scouting party actually discovered the bay on 2 November, first viewing it from Sweeney Ridge near Pacifica in San Mateo County); led successful second expedition to Monterey Harbor (17 April—24 May 1770), (thirty-six days marching and two resting, as opposed to the first trip, which took sixty-six days marching and fourteen resting to reach Monterey, due to unfamiliarity with the terrain); officiated at founding of Monterey's Presidio-Mission San Carlos Borromeo (3 June 1770), and recorded it as follows:

> Since it is among the articles of the orders which I am to execute immediately on my arrival at the cited port of Monterey, that I am to take possession in the name of His Catholic Majesty—I ordered the officials of sea and land to assemble, and I begged the Reverend Fathers to be pleased to assist in obeying the said order, directing the troops to place themselves under arms, after notifying them that it had been so ordered, and after these preparations had been made I proceeded to take possession in the name of His Majesty under the circumstances that the decree provides, performing the ceremony of throwing earth and stones to the four winds, and proclaiming possession in the royal name of His Catholic Majesty, Don Carlos III, whom God preserve, and whose possession of the said port of Monterey and other territories that rightfully ought and must be included, must be recognized. After planting the triumphant standard of the holy cross, primary cause of the Catholic, Christian, and pious zeal of His Majesty, which is manifested by the superior orders and perceived in the extent with which his royal exchequer is opened for the purpose of gathering the evangelical seed which is procured to the benefit of the numerous heathen dwelling in it, in order that it may appear at all times I sign [this document] and the gentlemen officials sign it as witnesses. [Treutlein, "The Portolá Expedition of 1769-1770," *The California Historical Society Quarterly* 47 (December 1968):307]

Portolá technically served as Upper California's first *gobernante* (military governor) (9 March—9 July 1770); departed Monterey aboard the *Santiago* (9 July 1770); served in Mexico, and promoted to lieutenant colonel in Regiment of Dragoons of Spain (1770-73); on leave of absence in Spain (1773-76?); promoted to colonel (1777); served as Governor of Puebla, New Spain (1777-85); returned to Spain (1785); appointed colonel in Regiment of Dragoons of Numancia (1785); appointed honorary *Teniente de Rey de la Plaza y Castillos de la Ciudad de Lérida* (King's Lieutenant of the Town and Castles of the City of Lérida) (1786); buried in Lérida, Catalonia, Spain.

POZOLE: *Nahuatl* (Mexican Aztec) word for a stew made with meat, corn, and other assorted vegetables such as cabbage, beans, lentils and peas.

PRESIDENT: The chief religious official of a mission territory, appointed by the ruling body of his apostolic college. Serra was "field commander" of the five Sierra Gorda Missions (1751-54); the fifteen Lower California Missions (1768-69); and the nine Upper California Missions he founded (1769-84).

PRESIDIO: A military post and fortification, from the Latin *praesidium* (garrison). There were five presidios in the present western U.S., one at San Ignacio de Tubac, Arizona (est. 1752), and four in California, the latter all designed by Military Engineer Miguel Costansó (1741-1814): San Diego (16 July 1769); Monterey (3 June 1770); San Francisco (17 September 1776); and Santa Bárbara (21 April 1782). Serra lived at Monterey's Presidio-Mission San Carlos Borromeo for fourteen months before transferring the mission to Carmel. Within the enclosed stockade of pine logs and earth, his first church was one room in a three-room *jacal*, the other two serving as priest quarters and warehouse. The compound was expanded to conform to Costansó's plan (1771-78), which consisted of a fifty *vara* square plaza enclosed by *adobe* walls and a solid bank of one-story buildings. These included a chapel and sacristy (c. 1775), several workshops, warehouses, and military/priest living quarters. Four ravelins, or triangular gun platforms, were erected at each corner and mounted with small cannons. Work on the present Santa Lucía sandstone church began in 1792, under the direction of master stone-mason Manuel Ruíz, who also supervised construction of Mission Carmel's stone church. Since the building was constructed at government expense, plans were drawn by the San Carlos Academy of Fine Arts in Mexico City, where they are still on file in the Archivo General de la Nación, Mexico City (along with plans for Mission Santa Clara, these are the only known extant California mission blueprints). Lasuén dedicated the new church on 25 January 1795, and it served the military/government and their families throughout the Spanish and Mexican periods, staffed by priests from Mission Carmel. After the mission was secularized, the chapel became a parish church, and as such, was never abandoned. Monterey's Royal Presidio Chapel, California's only remaining original presidio chapel, was declared a National Historic Landmark in 1961, and is registered California Historical Landmark number 105. Each presidio also had a separate naval artillery fortification. Monterey's El Castillo (The Castle/Fortress), was located on the site of a former Indian *ranchería* approximately 8/10ths of a mile from the actual presidio. This gentle rise overlooking the Vizcaíno-Serra landing cove and Monterey Harbor is now part of the U.S. Army Presidio of Monterey. Beginning as an open V-shaped structure with about eleven guns in 1792, El Castillo was strengthened and enlarged over the years, and served as the principal fort during Monterey's Spanish and Mexican periods. After the American takeover in 1846, it was replaced by the U.S. Army's larger Fort Mervine, located farther up the hill. Archaeological excavations revealed El Castillo's foundation in 1967, subsequently reburied for preservation. Eugene Duflot de Mofras, French attaché of a Mexican delegation sent to inspect California and Oregon in 1841-42, assessed Monterey's military defenses:

> The presidio of Monterey, at one time the most important fort in the province, is not entirely demolished, [for a] few traces of the foundations [are] remaining. Although strategically situated with guns commanding all ships entering the port, . . . it was built of such inferior materials and was so poorly equipped that it would have been unable to resist any serious attack. In 1819 [*sic*] [1818] a pirate [Hippolyte Bouchard], flying the colors of insurgents from Buenos Ayres [*sic*] [Aires], fired on the presidio and, going ashore, seized some cattle needed aboard his vessel. During the wave of revolutions that swept over Monterey, the presidio was pillaged by inhabitants who used the material for building houses. Plans, however, have been made to reconstruct the church, which, although in a weakened condition, is still standing. The edifice on the whole is devoid of interesting features. A small barbette battery known as El Castillo, stands on the west side of the anchorage. . . . On the sea approach, its sole support is a small earthen embankment, four feet high. In the vicinity are a crumbling building inhabited by five soldiers and a small shack used as a powder magazine. The battery has neither moat nor counter-guard, and can be readily approached on all sides since it is on a level with the surrounding land. In conjunction with the presidio its situation is strategic, for El Castillo properly built and equipped could sweep with its guns any ship that approached moorings. [Wilbur, *Duflot de Mofras: Travels on the Pacific Coast*, 1: 211-12]

Plaza del Presidio de Monte-Rey. *Pen and ink sketch by artist José Cardero of the 1791 Malaspina expedition. View shows* adobe *church shortly before commencement of present stone church, and after bell tower had collapsed due to fire in 1789 (note* adobe *rubble next to bells).*

The Royal Presidio Chapel, c. 1875, and Rev. Angelo Casanova, Pastor. Sandstone figure of Our Lady of Guadalupe in apex of façade considered California's oldest indigenous sculpture. Inscription at base reads: Ano D. *[anno Domini (in the year of Our Lord)]* 1794.

PUEBLO: A town with a civil government. Three *pueblos* were established in Spanish California: San José de Guadalupe 1777); Nuestra Señora de Los Angeles (1781); and Branciforte (present Santa Cruz), (1791). Governor Neve's 1779 *Reglamento* provided the blueprint for California's *pueblos*, designed to attract *pobladores* (settlers) from Mexico by granting them land and supplies. Each *pueblo* was governed by an elected *alcalde* (mayor), and *regidores* (councilmen). According to the *Recopilación de leyes de los reynos de las Indias* (*Compilation of the Laws of the Kingdoms of the Indies,* a nine-volume code of 6,400 laws for governing the Spanish colonies, first promulgated in 1680), a *pueblo* should consist of (as excerpted by Maynard Geiger in *The Life and Times of Fray Junípero Serra, O.F.M.*)

> a central plaza or square . . . [around which] *solares* [homesites] were to be measured off, each family being given a plot on which to build a house. The plot and house were inalienable. Beyond the *solares* were the *suertes,* or agricultural plots. These too were marked off, a separate plot being given to each settler. . . . Half of the town area . . . was to be retained by the town government. . . . All about it the *pueblo* was to have *ejidos,* or common land . . . there the townspeople could recreate and graze a few animals. . . . Sufficient pasture lands . . . were to be set aside adjoining the *ejidos.* All *pueblos* were to cover four square leagues of land in square or oblong shape. . . . It had to be in an unoccupied place and its locale not prejudicial to the Indians. . . . In founding towns high places were to be avoided because of winds and inacessibility; low places because they were considered unhealthy. If a river was near, the sun was to strike the town before it hit the river. No swamps or estuaries were to be near the town. The church was to face the plaza and to be separate from other buildings, so as to give it perspective from all angles. In cold climates the streets were to be wide, in warm ones, narrow. . . . The fields were to be sown first, then the houses built. All houses were to be in the same style and ornamented in accord with their size and the means of the people. . . . For purposes of defense the town was to form a physical unit. . . . The colonists were to receive pay of ten *pesos* a month and ordinary rations for five years. Each family was to receive two cows, two oxen, two mares, two beeves, one mule, two sheep, two goats, and farm implements. Eventually they had to reimburse they royal treasury for everything except the pay and rations. [2:192-94]

RANCHERÍA: An Indian village/group homesite. Mission Carmel's nearest original *rancherías* were Achista (called San Carlos by the missionaries, and located in Carmel proper), and Ichxenta (called San José, and located on the coast between San Jose Creek and Point Lobos). The *rancherías* formed part of the Rumsen ethnic group, and the Costanoan (from the Spanish "Costaños," [Coast People]) linguistic group.

REGLAMENTO: *Regulation;* a codified set of ordinances, a civil constitution. Two *Reglamentos* were promulgated during Serra's California tenure. The first, in 1773, was the "Provisional Regulation and Instruction for the Aid and Conservation of the New and Old Establishments of the Californias, and for the Department of San Blas." It was the product of the following efforts: 1) Serra's *Representación* (*Petition*), presented to Viceroy Bucareli when he visited Mexico City; 2) the supplementary opinion of a *junta* (government council), regarding Serra's proposals; 3) a series of recommendations by Juan José Echeveste, former government purchasing agent for the Californias in Mexico City; 4) and Bucareli's decree adopting Serra's ideas, with the changes proposed by the *junta,* and reflecting most of Echeveste's recommendations. The 1779 *Reglamento,* entitled "Regulation for the Government of the Californias Province," was drafted to remedy several defects in the 1773 *Reglamento,* and completely superseded it on 1 January 1781. Largely the work of California Governor Felipe de Neve, the new *Reglamento* attempted to resolve economic problems relating to financing the California province; sought to promote internal development and settlement, including formulation of the first land title system of ownership; and generally favored secular over mission rights, contracting gains won by Serra in the 1773 *Reglamento.* Some of the harsher measures were eventually diluted, such as a plan to reduce the number of priests at each mission from two to one. However, the 1779 *Reglamento* remained largely intact as California's fundamental civil code throughout the balance of the Spanish period.

RELIC: An object connected with a canonized saint, from the Latin *reliquiae* (remains). There are three grades:
1) First class: A saint's body (small bone fragments are usually distributed after canonization), or a penitential object used by a saint, e.g., Serra's "discipline" if he were a canonized saint.
2) Second class: Anything a saint used during his or her life, e.g. clothing, possessions, etc.

3) Third class: Any object that has been touched to a first-class relic, e.g., a piece of cloth touched to the saint's grave.

RELIGIOUS SELF-MORTIFICATION: Striving to improve one's relationship with God by renouncing the comforts of society and leading a life of austere self-discipline does not easily harmonize with late twentieth-century man's notion of self, nor the nature of his relationship to God. Man's perfection is now found in acceptance of what is most deeply human, the organic interdependence of body and spirit, rather than in its denial. However, this was not always so. In the Gospels, asceticism is presented under the theme of following the historical Christ, sharing his hardship and suffering, and completely renouncing one's identity to become a "disciple" ("If a man wishes to come after me, he must deny his very self, take up his cross, and follow in my steps. Whoever would preserve his life will lose it, but whoever loses his life for my sake and the gospel's will preserve it" Mark 8:34-35). Martyrdom became the ultimate sacrifice, but for those who fell short, severe penance and mortification served as substitute supererogation, offering a "daily death" of the flesh in mystic union with Christ, and as a literal imitation of His suffering in the form of flagellation ("Pilate, who wished to satisfy the crowd, . . . had Jesus scourged" Mark 15:15). Other motives were: expiation of personal sin/sins of others, impetration of divine grace and favor, self-discipline, and the medieval belief that the body was an "enemy" of the soul. European monks were the first to adopt scourging as a systematic ascetic exercise, and the practice spread to the clergy and laity, becoming common throughout the Middle Ages. Provisions for flagellation have been found in practically all religious "Rules" composed or revived until the late eighteenth century, whereby the practice was prescribed and regulated for certain days, especially during the penitential season of Lent. Use of the "discipline" was the most common method of self-flagellation, ranging in form from rope bound together and knotted at the ends, to thorny branches, leather/iron straps tipped with metal/bone, etc., and iron chains. Palóu offers the best elaboration of Serra's ascetic and devotional practices:

> He was not content with the ordinary exercise of the college [San Fernando] in regard to acts of discipline, vigils and fasts, but he privately scourged his flesh with rough hair shirts, made either of bristles or with points of metal wire, with which he covered his body. He also took the discipline unto blood during the most silent part of the night, when he would betake himself to one of the tribunes [screened-off seating area] of the choir. Although the place was so remote and the hour so quiet, there were friars who heard the cruel strokes. Nor were there lacking the curious who, desiring to learn the friar's identity, took the trouble to satisfy their curiosity; and they were edified. [Geiger, *Palóu's Life of Fray Junípero Serra*, p. 279]

Following the custom of former ascetics, Serra also performed public acts of self-mortification:

> He struck his breast with the stone, in imitation of St. Jerome; in imitation of his St. Francis Solanus [Solano], to whom he was devoted, he used the chain to scourge himself; he used the burning torch [candle], applying it to his uncovered chest, burning his flesh in imitation of St. John Capistran and various other saints. All this he did with the purpose not only of punishing himself, but also of moving his hearers to penance for their own sins. [Ibid., p. 280]

As San Fernando College's *Método de misionar* (*Missionary Methods*, pub. 1780) handbook indicates, self-mortification (at least publicly), was on the wane by the late eighteenth century:

> Some missionaries have the custom of taking out a chain and, uncovering their shoulders, scourging themselves with it while they ask the Lord for mercy. . . . Although this is a most efficacious means to move and to break hard hearts, great modesty, prudence and judgment are needed to use it. And although St. Francis Solanus used this means, and other illustrious missionaries have done likewise, it was only on rare occasions; so our missionaries must not make it ordinary and commonplace. [Ibid., p. 356]

RELIQUARY: A receptacle, such as a coffer or shrine, for keeping or displaying relics.

REPOUSSÉ: A metalworking technique that combines embossing (from the inside), and chasing (from the outside) to create three-dimensional relief.

REREDOS, MISION CARMEL BASILICA: An altarpiece, also called a *retablo* (retable), from the Latin *retrōtabulum* (structure at the back of an altar). Mission Carmel Basilica's present *reredos* (32' tall x 26' 6" wide) is an approximate reproduction of the original imported Mexican *reredos* installed in 1807, and destroyed after the roof collapsed and the mission was abandoned in 1852. The statues were taken to the Royal Presidio Chapel, Monterey, where they were used or stored in the rectory's attic until returned and restored by Harry Downie beginning in the 1930s.' Since there are no known renderings of the original *reredos*, Downie used mission records and early visitor descriptions to assist in designing the 1956 version. Mission Carmel's secularization inventories describe a "main altar . . . ten and one-half *varas* [tall] . . . of wood, painted and gilded" ("Inventory and Evaluation of the Chattels of the Town of San Carlos, 10 December 1834," p. 16; and "General Inventory of Existing Things in the Church, Sacristy, Chapel, Baptistry, and House of the Father Ministers of the Mission of San Carlos of Monterey, 22 June 1842," p. 3). Bayard Taylor, a visitor in 1849, wrote: "the [altar] shrine [is] a faded mass of gilding and paint, with some monkish portraits of saints" (Taylor, *Eldorado, or, Adventures in the Path of Empire*, p. 117). Mission San Francisco's *reredos* also served as a guide since it dates from the same period as Mission Carmel's, and was designed/carved in Mexico as well.

Key

1) Dove representing the Holy Spirit (modern).
2) Saint Charles Borromeo (acquired for Mission Carmel from Mexico in 1792) wearing bishop's mitre; holding crozier (modern).
3) Saint Peter with keys (a sixteenth-century Italian carving acquired for the 1956 *reredos*).
4) Saint Paul (also acquired for the 1956 *reredos*) with open book (his epistles); sword (with which he was beheaded).
5) Saint Michael the Archangel (acquired for Mission Carmel from Mexico in 1809); holding sword (modern).
6) Saint Anthony of Padua (acquired for Mission Carmel from Mexico in 1809) holding Infant Jesus (modern); lily-staff (modern).
7) Ave María Purísima (acquired for the Royal Presidio Chapel, Monterey, by Father Casanova in the late nineteenth century, possibly from Mission Soledad, and transferred to Mission Carmel, c. 1940).
8) Crucifix (acquired for Mission Carmel from Mexico in 1791) with original corpus and its articulated, leather-socketed arms intact; reproduction cross made c. 1884 by Casanova.
9) Our Lady of Sorrows and Saint John (both acquired for Mission Carmel from Mexico, date unknown) with Our Lady wearing silver aureole; Saint John wearing silver halo. (The Crucifix, Our Lady of Sorrows and Saint John were originally in the side mortuary chapel. Our Lady of Bethlehem occupied the central *reredos* niche during the mission period. Downie did not discover this until after he had finished the *reredos* and had already installed Our Lady of Bethlehem in the side chapel).
10) Saint Bonaventure (acquired for Mission Carmel from Mexico in 1824) wearing cardinal's biretta; holding open book (theologian/teacher).
11) Set of six late-eighteenth-century bronze (silver-plated) candlesticks (24" tall), (originally from Mission San Antonio, acquired for the Royal Presidio Chapel by Casanova in the late nineteenth century, and transferred to Mission Carmel, c. 1940).

RUBRIC: 1) *rubrica* in Spanish, from *rubricar* (to sign and seal). Traditionally, a distinguishing flourish at the end of a Spanish male signature, a legal requirement comparable to a seal or official stamp; 2) from the Latin *rubrīca terra* (red earth or ocher). In accordance with liturgical rubrics, i.e. rules or codes, traditionally printed in red; 3) first-class relics of saints are "rubrically sealed" via the process of affixing a cord under red-wax seal to the back of the relic case, embossed with an official episcopal seal as authorized by the Congregation for the Causes of Saints. An official certificate of authenticity usually accompanies the relic

SACRAMENT: Any of seven rites of the historical Christian Church considered to have been instituted or observed by Jesus Christ as a testament to inner grace or as a channel that mediates grace. In the Catholic Church, these rites are:

1) Baptism: By the use of water and the recital of words, the recipient is cleansed of Original Sin (the sin committed by Adam [Genesis 3] and passed on to his progeny, i.e. the human race) and admitted into the Church. Serra performed more than 6,000 Baptisms during his career. He administered his first Upper California baptism to Bernardino de Jesús at Mission Carmel on 26 December 1770. California's first recorded Baptism was performed by Father Francisco Gómez on 22 July 1769, while he was accompanying the 1769-70 Portolá expedition in search of Monterey Bay/Harbor. On the same day, fellow expedition chaplain Father Juan Crespí performed the second Baptism, and recorded the event as follows:

> The explorers informed us that on the preceding day they saw in the village two sick little girls. After asking the commander for some soldiers to go with us to visit them we went, and we found one which the mother had at her breast apparently dying. We asked for it, saying that we wished to see it, but it was impossible to get it from its mother. So we said to her by signs that we would not do it any harm, but wished to sprinkle its head, so that if it died it might go to heaven. She consented to this, and my companion, Fray Francisco Gómez, baptized it, giving it the name María Magdalena. We went then to the other, also small, who had been burned and was apparently about to die. In the same way I baptized it, giving it the name of Margarita. We did not doubt that both would die and go to heaven. With this, the only success that we have obtained, we fathers consider well worth while the long journey and the hardships that are being suffered in it and are still await-ing us. May it all be for the greater glory of God and the salvation of souls. For this reason this place is known to the soldiers as [Los Cristianitos (The Christians), presently known as Cristianitos Canyon, Camp Pendleton, San Diego County]; I named it San Apolinario [St. Apollinarius, whose feast day was 23 July]; others called it [Cañada de los Bautismos (Ravine of the Baptisms)]. [Bolton, *Fray Juan Crespi: Missionary Explorer on the Pacific Coast, 1769-1774*, p. 135]

2) Confirmation: By the authorized "laying on of hands," anointing with chrism, and prayer, a bap-tized person is admitted to full membership in the Church. Serra administered Upper California's first Confirmation to Junípero Bucareli at Mission Carmel on 29 June 1778. By the date of his last Con-firmation on 6 July 1784 (ten days before the patent expired), Serra had confirmed 5,308 persons, with a total of 5,309 personally listed in his *Libro de Confirmaciones*. Juan Evangelista accounts for the dif-ference, because although listed as number one, he was actually confirmed by Mexico City's archbishop in 1773. Palóu recorded one less: "When his Paternity saw his faculty expire, he had con-firmed 5,307 persons" (Geiger, *Palóu's Life of Fray Junípero Serra*, p. 241). Possibly he examined every entry and found that Serra had erred by one.

3) Eucharist: A commemoration of Jesus Christ's Last Supper, in which His true Body and Blood is really and substantially present in the consecrated elements of bread and wine, i.e. Holy Communion. Upper California's first recorded Mass (and the state's first Christian service) was performed by Car-melite Fathers Asumpción, Aquino, and Ascención of the Vizcaíno expedition, on the shores of San Diego Bay, 12 November 1602. Serra's first California Mass was also performed at San Diego, on Sun-day 2 July 1769, a solemn High Mass of Thanksgiving for his expedition's safe arrival the day before. There is only one California church building still standing where Serra may have said Mass, since all the early mission churches were superseded by later structures: the Serra Chapel at Mission San Juan Capistrano, built in 1777. In the words of historian Zephyrin Engelhardt:

> We may confidently assert that Fr. Serra officiated at Confirmations in 1778 and 1783 in the still existing chapel, which was the rear half of the present structure; and that, there-fore, this chapel may glory in the distinction of being the only chapel or church in Califor-nia in which the founder of the California Missions celebrated holy Mass and ad-ministered the Sacraments. [Engelhardt, *San Juan Capistrano Mission*, p. 18]

4) Matrimony: The act or state of being married. Upper California's first marriage was performed at Mission San Antonio on 16 May 1773. Juan María Ruíz, 25, a native of El Fuerte, Sonora, Mexico, was married to Margarita de Cortona, 22, a Christian mission Indian. Serra performed his first Upper California marriage (and the state's first Caucasian wedding) at Mission San Gabriel on 19 April 1774, while on his way home from Mexico City. He married José Lorenzó de Esparza, carpenter, native of Aguascalientes, Mexico, and María Josefa Dávila, of Guadalajara, Mexico. The couple had come from Mexico with Serra as part of the first group of families and artisans enlisted to relocate in California.

5) Holy Orders: The rite of ordination into the priesthood.

6) Penance (Confession): The rite of contrition, confession to a priest, acceptance of punishment, and absolution.

7) Anointing of the Sick (Extreme Unction): The rite of anointing and praying for one in danger of death. Explorer Juan Rodríguez Cabrillo was the first Christian buried in Upper California, on 3 January 1543, in a presently undiscovered grave on the Santa Barbara Channel Island of San Miguel. The first mainland Christian burials were performed in July 1769, when at least thirty Portolá-Serra

expeditions sailors died of scurvy, and were buried by Serra and fellow priests in presently undiscovered graves near the original presidio-mission.

SACRED VESSELS AND LINENS: Of the many items required for the celebration of the Mass and various other ceremonies, those mentioned in the text are:
1) Burse: A square, stiff, flat pocket, open at one end, in which the folded corporal is placed when carried to and from the altar.
2) Chalice: A cup for the consecrated wine of the Eucharist. The chalice and paten (plate) are the vessels in which wine and bread, respectively, are offered, consecrated, and consumed by the priest during Mass.
3) Ciborium: Similar to a chalice, but larger and with a cover. Used for holding the hosts for distribution to the faithful, and for the reservation of hosts in the tabernacle.
4) Corporal: A square piece of white cloth spread on the altar cloth, on which the vessels holding the Sacred Species (the consecrated Host(s) and wine) are placed during the Eucharisitic Liturgy. The corporal is similarly used whenever the Blessed Sacrament is removed from the tabernacle; e.g. during Benediction the monstrance rests on a corporal.
5) Monstrance: A vessel used for holding the consecrated Host (the Blessed Sacrament, i.e. the Eucharist) when it is carried in procession or exposed on the altar during Benediction (a short service of prayer, hymn, and the blessing of the congregation with the Host, also known as Exposition of the Blessed Sacrament if extended over a period of time). The ritual dates from c. 1300, and by c. 1700 the monstrance assumed its typical form of a sun radiating light. Symbolically, at the moment of exposure, the congregation is flooded by the life-force of the sun, akin to God's presence. Known as a *custodia* in Spanish, and alternatively as an ostensorium in English (monstrance is derived from the Latin *mōnstrāre* [to show]). The lunette (*luna* in Spanish) is the small crescent-shaped receptacle that holds the Host in an upright position in the monstrance.

SACRISTY: A room in the church housing the sacred vessels and vestments; a vestry.

SAN BLAS DE NAYARIT, PORT OF: Former Mexican west coast port of supply for the California missions, shipbuilding center, naval reconnaisance base, and missionary embarkation point located between Mazatlán and Bahía de Banderas, in the present state of Nayarit, Mexico. San Blas was specifically established by Inspector General Gálvez in 1768 to supply the Californias, and to serve as customs port for all legally traded goods between Mexico and California. The port was in turn supplied by a land route to Mexico City via Guadalajara. When it was in danger of being abandoned in 1773, Serra fought for its retention as indispensable to the maintenance of the California mission system. He argued that the alternative land supply-route would be more expensive due to maintenance of a fleet of mules, more dangerous due to threat of Indian attack, and would not

> mean any progress. . . . The proposal to transport by land provisions and equipment to Monterey and its missions . . . would be a great setback. And this without any reference whatever to such inevitable accidents as the fall of many mules, the destruction of their loads, the breaking of vessels, the spillage of liquids, and many other sources of damage, as has been my own experience in the journeys I have made by land. [Tibesar, *Writings of Junípero Serra*, 1:343]

The port remained open, but waned in importance as the missions achieved near self-sufficieny by the late eighteenth century. San Blas was reduced to a naval defensive base in 1790, and was still in operation as late as 1808, when its existence was attributed to "the zeal of Junípero Serra" (Geiger, *Palóu's Life of Fray Junípero Serra*, p. 359). Today San Blas is a small coastal village, its bay filled with sand, it customs house abandoned, its hilltop stone church in ruins.

SANCHO DE LA TORRE, O.F.M., REVEREND JUAN (1722—c.1794): Born in Mallorca; entered Franciscan Order (1746); arrrived at San Fernando College (1761); served at Mission Nuestra Señora de Guadalupe, Lower California, during Serra's presidency of the the Lower California missions (1768-69), and offered Serra supplies, hospitality, and "a little page . . . a smart Indian lad" when he passed through on his way to San Diego (9 April 1769). Serra wrote:

> During that time, Father Preacher Fray Juan Sancho, Master of Arts, and successively Professor of Philosophy and Theology in his native country, and now minister of this mission, did all he could to find ways and means to help me on my trip. . . . Circumstances

have so contrived that I have known this Father since his student days in the world. May God Bless him. [Tibesar, *Writings of Junípero Serra*, 1:47-49]

Sancho remained at Mission Guadalupe until the missions were turned over to the Dominicans (April 1772); returned to Mexico City and held a number of minor offices within San Fernando College; was elected college guardian (1783) with eighteen votes (the absent Serra and Palóu also received votes—fifteen for Serra, fourteen for Palóu); and was the receipient of Serra's last recorded letter (written 8 August 1784). At Palóu's request (in a letter of 13 September 1784), Sancho arranged for the commission of a memorial painting, *Serra's Viaticum*, and was the first to announce the news of Serra's death to Mallorca's Franciscans (letter of 25 November 1784). His term of office as guardian ended in 1786 (he was succeeded by Palóu), and little is known of his later life.

SANCTUARY: The section of a church reserved for the altar, and clearly distinct from the nave (main body of the church). From the Latin *sanctuarium* (holy place). The Gospel side of the altar is on the left side of the santuary (with one's perspective from the nave). The Epistle side is on the right.

SALTIRE: A heraldic design in the form of a diagonal or X-shaped cross, sometimes called a St. Andrew's Cross or "cross decussata" (from the Latin for the numeral ten [X]).

SALVE REGINA: *Hail, Holy Queen*. One of the oldest Latin antiphons (devotional compositions sung responsively as part of a liturgy), probably written in the eleventh century, and part of the Divine Office.

SECULARIZATION: The transfer of an ecclesiastical institution's permanent endowment to civil or lay use/ownership. Every mission in the Spanish empire was theoretically temporary, the plan being that within ten to twenty years each mission would be "secularized," i.e. the mission church would be turned over to "secular" parish priests, and the land and fields parceled out among the Indians. In practice, the schedule was never met, and in California the mission system remained intact until forcibly secularized after Mexico's independence from Spain (1821). The new liberal and anti-clerical government sought to dismantle its colonial dependence on the Catholic Church. The first California decree of secularization was issued by Governor José Echeandía (1826), allowing married Indians to leave the missions, but few took advantage of the policy. The Mexican Congress adopted an immediate general secularization law (1833), which was enacted in California pursuant to Governor José Figueroa's *Reglamento Provisional* (*Provisional Regulation*) of 9 August 1834, which signaled the end of the "mission period." The *Reglamento* ordered ten missions to be secularized that year (including Mission Carmel), six in 1835, and the last five in 1836. Governor Manuel Micheltorena disposed of all remaining mission property (1834), and Governor Pío Pico planned to sell all the mission buildings at public auction (1845), but was prevented from doing so by the Mexican Congress. In theory, half of each mission's former land was to have been handled by lay administrators, and half given to the Indians. However, the Indians were not experienced at land ownership/maintenance, and the vast majority of acreage eventually passed through the administrators to *rancheros* and other private individuals.

SERRA, CAUSE OF DEATH: Serra's chest trouble and "shortness of breath" (Bolton, *Historical Memoirs of New California*, 4:349) began in the late 1750s', after his term in the damp Sierra Gorda mountain region. He never mentioned any ailments in family correspondence, generally shunned medical treatment, and instead left such matters in the "hands of the Divine Physician" (Geiger, *The Life and Times of Junípero Serra, O.F.M.*, 2:213). Palóu wrote:

> This illness, the pain in his chest, he . . . suffered . . . for many years, from the time he was at the college (San Fernando], although he never complained about it or made the least effort to obtain treatment, for he paid as little attention to that as to the wound and swelling of his foot and leg. When we spoke to him about using some remedy, he would reply: "Let us forget about that; we might make it worse. We will get along all right." He added the saying of St. Agatha: *Medicinam carnalem corpori meo nunquam exhibui* [I have never used carnal medicine for my body]. Although he never stated whether this pain and congestion of the chest really hurt him or not, I thought it actually did. [Geiger, *Palóu's Life of Fray Junípero Serra*, p. 235]

Contemporary historians and physicians have labeled the condition asthma or tuberculosis, but no one is certain of the exact cause of Serra's death. However, his age, strenuous lifestyle, chest ailment, and ulcerated leg certainly add up to Palóu's simple prognosis of a "worn-out body" (Geiger, *Palóu's Life of Fray Junípero Serra*, p. 244). Due to the canonical prohibition against pathological testing during Serra's 1943 exhumation, the McCown Report was unable to conclusively determine his cause of death, or if his skeleton showed any sign of disease.

SERRA, CONFIRMATION CONTROVERSY: Since Serra was not a bishop, he had to apply for the right to confirm. Pope Clement XIV granted him a ten year faculty effective 16 July 1774, but still requiring Spain's *Pase Regio* (*Royal Permit* of governmental approval) of the papal brief, and San Fernando College's issuance of an evidential patent (only after receiving the viceroy's additional *pase* of the same Papal brief). This hindered Serra's receipt of the patent until 20 June 1778. He received the patent devoid of proof of *pase* (only the original brief, stored in the viceregal archives, was stamped with the *pase*) This technicality led Governor Neve to question Serra's authority to confirm. Bolstered by a 1777 *Cedula Real* (*Royal Decree*), a document interpreted to give the government even more control over Papal decrees, Neve subsequently withheld his local *pase*, claiming that he needed to see the royal and viceregal *pases* before he could affix his own. For the next three years, the ensuing "Confirmation controversy" embroiled Serra, Neve, San Fernando College, and Teodoro de Croix (nephew of former Viceroy Carlos de Croix, and first commandant general of the *Provincias Internas*, which removed Upper California from Viceroy Bucareli's viceroyalty after August 1777). Under duress, Serra finally ceased solemnly confirming for more than a year (except to the dying). After Croix was finally satisfied that all the *pases* were in order, he instructed Neve that Serra could "legally" confirm, and Serra received the good news on 16 August 1781.

SERRA, MODE OF TRAVEL: Contrary to legend, Serra did not walk from California mission to mission, except once in 1779, from Mission Carmel to Mission Santa Clara (a distance of about 80 miles). He normally rode a mule, occasionally a horse, and was accompanied by a military guard. As Palóu said: "New California is two hundred and five leagues in length. It is impossible to traverse the distance on foot. The distances from one mission to another are immense" (Tibesar, *Writings of Junípero Serra*, 4:414). How did the legend start? Franciscans in Serra's day traveled mainly on foot, in imitation of the Apostles, and as prescribed in the Franciscan Rule. Serra did walk from Vera Cruz to Mexico City in 1749 (275 miles); from Mexico City to Jalpan in 1750 (175 miles); and from Mexico City to Oaxaca and back in 1762-63 (675 miles). But beyond this, there is no proof that Serra walked on other occasions. In the opinion of historian Maynard Geiger:

> Have translators read into several generic expressions of travel the phrase "walked on foot" where Palóu did not use the expression [in the *Vida*, his biography of Serra]? Did the fact of Serra's walking from Vera Cruz to Mexico on his intitial American journey create their belief that he did the same on subsequent trips? Did the fact of Palóu's occasional mention of the pain and inflamed condition of Serra's foot and leg, and his virtual inability to stand on it, coupled with such generic terms as *andar* [to walk] and *caminar* [to travel], falsely lead them to conclude that Serra nevertheless walked? . . . Going through the entire *Vida*, the writer found at least ninety-five references to Serra's land travels. . . . Only on four distinct occasions did he say that Serra went *a pie* [on foot]. . . . The rest merely express motion, movement, travel, arrival and departure, . . . [and] are colorless, indifferent, and indeterminate with regard to Serra's mode of travel. . . . We cannot conclusively prove that Serra walked, although in some or many instances he may have done so. [Geiger, "Junípero Serra, O.F.M., in the Light of Chronology and Geography, 1713-1784," *The Americas* 6:328-29]

Serra even rode in a coach on one occasion, when he was "in such poor health that he was almost unable to stand" (Geiger, *Palóu's Life of Fray Junípero Serra*, p. 143):

> Realizing Serra's weakened condition, advancing age, his need to be spared for the California missions, Verger [San Fernando College guardian] simply used his authority and put Serra under obedience to go a little more comfortably to Guadalajara [the first leg of his journey back to California in 1773]—and, of all things, in a coach! Serra's zeal was indeed restrained and, what is more, he willingly obeyed. [Ibid., p. 331]

SERRA, RELIGIOUS NAME: As a Franciscan novice at the Convento de Santa María de los Angeles de Jesús just outside Palma, young Miguel José Serra was faced with the option of retaining his baptismal name or choosing a new one when he made his profession into the Franciscan Order. He chose the name Junípero (Juniper) when he made the following profession to Very Rev. Antonio Perelló Moragues, Franciscan Provincial of Mallorca, on 15 September 1731:

> I, Fray Junípero Serra, vow and promise to Almighty God, to the ever blessed Virgin Mary, to Blessed Father Francis, to all the saints, and to you, Father, to observe for the whole span of my life the rule of the Friars Minor confirmed by His Holiness Pope Honorius III [in 1223], by living in obedience, without property, and in chastity. [Geiger, *The Life and Times of Fray Junípero Serra, O.F.M.*, 1:21-22]

Serra took the name Junípero from a companion of Saint Francis of Assisi as described in *I Fioretti di San Francesco* (*The Little Flowers of Saint Francis*), an anonymous fourteenth-century Italian translation of the Latin *Actus Beati Francisci et sociorum ejus* (*The Deeds of Saint Francis and his Companions*) written c. 1325 by Fra Ugolino Boniscambi of Montegiorgio in the Marches. Written only a century after Francis' death, the author's intention was to cure the Order of internal conflict by stimulating a return to the founder's original simplicity and spirituality. With Brother James of Massa as his principal source, who had known several of the saint's companions, he gathered together a score of vivid, often humorous vignettes about the "Povorello" (Little Poor Man of Assisi) and his companions. Although the *Fioretti's* historicity has often been questioned, its provides a fundamentally authentic spiritual profile of Saint Francis. "The Life of Brother Juniper," a record of the life and sayings of one of Saint Francis' closest companions, is actually an anonymous fifteenth-century addition to the *Fioretti*. Few facts are known about Juniper. He joined the Order c. 1210, accompanied Francis on journeys to Rome and Naples, and founded friaries in Gualdo Tadino and Viterbo. He died in Rome on 4 January 1258. Juniper was called the "Jester of God" because of his "foolish" simplicity and outrageous antics, but was also known for his charity, patience, and an intense desire to imitate the life of Jesus. The following excerpt from "The Life of Brother Juniper" characterizes the essence of Juniper's nature:

> Brother Juniper was by name, one of the most special first followers of St. Francis. He was humble and patient . . . and in spite of temptation and troubles he never wavered, in spite of great sufferings no one ever saw him upset. He had such contempt of self that those who did not know this thought he was stupid or a fool. St. Francis had this to say about Brother Juniper: "My brothers, my brothers, I wish I had a forest of such junipers. . . . Brother Juniper had such love for the poor that if he found someone dressed more poorly, he would immediately cut off a sleeve, his cowl, or some piece of his habit and give it to the poor person. Therefore his guardian ordered him not to give his tunic or any part of it to anyone. Once when he met a pauper who asked for alms, he said: "My dear friend, I do not have anything to give except this tunic and I cannot give it because of my vow of obedience. But if you take it from me, I will not stop you." So the beggar took it off, and left Brother Juniper standing naked. When Brother Juniper returned to the friars, he said that someone had robbed him. As his virtue of compassion grew, he not only gave away to the poor his own tunic, but also books, altar linens and capes belonging to the other friars. When the poor came for alms to Brother Juniper, the friars would take and hide what they wanted so Brother Juniper would not find it. [Bodo, *Juniper: Friend of Francis, Fool of God*, pp. 1, 28]

Palóu mentioned Serra's choice of religious name in his Serra biography:

> He took the name Junípero out of devotion to that holy companion of Our Seraphic Father St. Francis, whose deeds of holy simplicity and supernatural charm he commemorated and recounted with devout tenderness. (Geiger, *Palóu's Life of Fray Junípero Serra*, p. 5]

Historian Maynard Geiger also offered his insight:

> Serra himself sheds a little light on the matter and this, somewhat surprisingly, in his philosophical lectures. It was Serra's custom when a tract of philosophy was finished to dedicate his efforts to the honor of the Holy Trinity, to the Blessed Virgin, and to certain saints of the Order. At the end of the list he always mentioned Blessed Junípero, "the greatest exemplar of holy simplicity." Did . . . [he] see in St. Francis' companion a kindred spirit in the matter of simplicity and did he determine to plan his life in the direct and open way unhampered by politics or deviousness of any sort? There are abundant examples in Serra's later life showing how he took the direct path, the simple way. But Serra became nobody's fool. When he encountered sagacity in later life, he met the situation with a corresponding shrewdness. [Geiger, *The Life and Times of Fray Junípero Serra, O.F.M.*, 1:21]

S.J.: Society of Jesus, designating a member of the Jesuit Order.

SNUFF: A preparation of finely pulverized tobacco that can be chewed or drawn up into the nostrils by inhaling. This was a common eighteenth-century European practice.

SOLANO (SOLANUS), SAINT FRANCIS (2 March 1549—14 July 1610); Born in Montilla, Andalusia, Spain; solemn profession into the Observant Franciscan Order (1570); ordained (1576); served as teacher, novice master, eloquent preacher among the poor/sick, and assisted the plague-stricken of Granada with such compassion and medical expertise that he developed an early reputation for holiness; sailed for the New World at age forty to become an apostolic missionary (1589), and encountered severe coastal storm en route from Panama to Peru that prompted the crew to abandon ship, but according to tradition Francis insisted on staying aboard with black slaves left to their fate, and with his help the wreck and survivors washed ashore on a barren island, where he miraculously provided food for the group until rescued; arrived in Lima, Peru (1590); journeyed overland to Mission Santiago del Esteros, in the Río de la Plata region of Argentina, and served among the Socotonio and La Magdalena Indians (1590-91); served as guardian of the Tucumán region of Argentina and Paraguay (1591-98), where he gained many converts by learning the local dialects (which gave rise to the belief that he had a supernatural gift of tongues) and especially by using music to interest the Indians (he was a gifted violinist, and composed many religious songs and dances); recalled to Lima (1599), and spent the remainder of his life as guardian of Lima's Franciscan friary and ministering to the city's populace. Knowledgeable in medical lore, he was an early advocate of plague-victim quarantine, and burning the clothes of survivors. Tradition relates that in December 1604 Francis preached so powerfully in the city's marketplace against corruption that the crowd was literally panic-stricken. Lima's viceroy called on Archbishop Toribio de Mogrovejo to restore order, and with Francis' assistance they explained that the vivid portrayal of impending doom was not a prophecy, but merely an admonition for the wicked (Toribio is also a canonized saint. Remarkably, there were five future saints alive at this time in Lima: Saint Toribio (1538-1606); Saint Francis; Saint Martín de Porres (1579-1639); Saint Rose of Lima (1586-1617); and Blessed John Massias (1585-1645). Francis modeled his life after Saint Francis of Assisi, and was known in Lima as *Franciscus redivivus* (Revived Francis). His passion was to make Jesus Christ known and loved by all, and to this end he never spared himself. When novices asked him how they could become saints, he told them "by accepting the disappointments of everyday life." He was a lifelong student, especially of the writings of Saint Bonaventure. Unfortunately, Francis' writings and songs were lost after being sent to Rome as part of his canonization process. He was beatified in 1675, canonized in 1726, and is known as the "Apostle of South America" and the *Thaumaturgus* (Greek for "Wonder Worker") of the New World. His feast day is 24 July. Saint Francis was canonized when Serra was thirteen, a student at Petra's local Franciscan elementary school, and four years before becoming a novice. He developed a special "devotion to my Saint Francis Solano" (Tibesar, *Writings of Junípero Serra*, 1:9), and chose him as "his favorite saint" (Ibid., p. 17). When contemplating service as an apostolic missionary, he chose Saint Francis as one of his spiritual intercessors:

> Junípero was not deaf to this interior voice of the Lord, Who enkindled in his heart the living fire of charity toward his fellow beings. Consequently there arose within him the lively desire to shed his blood, if necessary, to obtain the salvation of the poor pagans. He re-enkindled in his heart those desires which had stirred him as a novice but which had become deadened because of his preoccupation with study. On feeling his reawakened vocation, he had recourse to God in prayer, choosing as his intercessors God's Most Pure Mother and St. Francis Solanus, Apostle of the Indies. [Geiger, *Palóu's Life of Fray Junípero Serra*, p. 8]

When journeying from Loreto to San Diego in 1769, Serra named a potential Lower California mission site after Saint Francis:

> To this place we gave the name of San Francisco Solano, feeling confident that, thanks to the patronage of the Holy Apostle of the Spanish Indies, all that multitude of gentile Indians who came to meet us here will come to the bosom of the Church. [Tibesar, *Writings of Junípero Serra*, 1:111]

A mission was not established there, so Serra tried again in 1771, when Palóu was president of the Lower California missions. Names for future missions were being discussed, and Serra wrote him: "In case he [Viceroy Croix] did not specify them, [the names], and they are left to the free choice of Your Reverence, I hope that our San Francisco Solano will not be forgotten" (Ibid., 1:239). Serra would not live to see his "favorite saint" receive his own mission. Mission San Francisco Solano, the last of the Upper California missions, was founded in 1823.

SOLDADO DE CUERA: "Leather soldier," a mounted soldier named for his distinctive arrowproof buckskin vest/coat. Miguel Costansó, member of the 1769 Portolá expedition and military engineer, described their uniform:

> [They] use two sorts of arms, offensive and defensive. The defensive are the leather jacket and the shield. The first, whose make is like that of a coat without sleeves, is composed of six or seven thicknesses of white skins of deer, tanned, impenetrable to the arrows of the Indians since they are not discharged from a close range. The shield is of two thicknesses of raw bullhide. It is held with the left arm, and with it lances or arrows are deflected, the trooper defending himself and his horse. They use, beside the aforesaid, a kind of apron of leather, fastened to the pommel of the saddle and which lays over each side, which they call *armas* or protection, which cover their thighs and legs so as not to be hurt when running in the thickets. Their offensive weapons are the lance, which they manage dexterously on horseback; the broadsword, and a short flintlock musket which they carry thrust into and made fast in its sheath. They are men of much endurance and long-suffering under fatigue. They are obedient, resolute, agile, and we do not hesitate to say that they are the best troopers in the world. [Brandes, *The Costansó Narrative of the Portolá Expedition*, p. 90]

SOLEMNITIES: Catholic feast days of the highest rank in the ecclesiastical calendar. The following are mentioned in the text:
1) Saint Joseph: 19 March—honored as the husband of Mary, protector/patron of the universal Catholic Church, and of all workmen.
2) Saint Peter and Saint Paul: 29 June—joint commemoration of the chief apostles and their martyrdom (Peter by crucifixion and Paul by beheading during the Neronian persecutions).
3) Lent: This is a Church season, and not a feast as such. The season begins on Ash Wednesday, and lasts until the Mass of the Lord's Supper (Holy Thursday). The last Sunday in Lent is Passion (formerly Palm) Sunday, and marks the beginning of Holy Week. Lent commemorates Jesus' forty-day fast in the desert before he began his public life.
4) Good Friday: The Friday before Easter, commemorating the Passion of Jesus.
5) Pentecost Sunday: Fifty days after Easter, the last day of the Easter season, commemorating the descent of the Holy Spirit upon the Apostles and the beginning of their apostolic ministries. Regarded as the birthday of the Roman Catholic Church.
6) Holy Trinity: The Sunday after Pentecost, commemorating the mystery of the Three Divine Persons—Father, Son, and Holy Spirit—in one God.
7) Corpus Christi: The Thursday after Holy Trinity (the Sunday after Holy Trinity in the U.S.). Commemorates the institution of the Holy Eucharist, and includes a ceremony of carrying the consecrated Host in procession.

STATIONS OF THE CROSS: A devotion consisting of meditation before each of fourteen crosses set up in a church or along a path commemorating fourteen events in the Passion of Jesus. First popularized by the Franciscan Saint Leonard of Port Maurice (1676-1751).

S.T.D.: Doctor of Sacred Theology.

TABERNACLE: A case or box on a church altar containing the consecrated Host and wine of the Eucharist.

TANTUM ERGO: *Tantum ergo, Sacramentum, veneremur cernui* (Down in adoration falling, Lo the sacred host we hail). Opening line of the last two verses of the Latin hymn *Pange lingua gloriosi Corporis* (*Sing, My Tongue, the Savior's Glory*), attributed to St. Thomas Aquinas (c. 1225-74). Although sung primarily during Benediction of the Blessed Sacrament, Serra sang the *Tantum ergo* when he received his last Holy Communion on 27 August 1784.

TE DEUM LAUDÁMUS: *We praise thee, O God.* A Latin hymn, probably written in the early fifth century A.D, sung as part of the Mass, especially on feast days/occasions of great joy, etc. Serra sang this at the conclusion of Mass on the 3 June 1770 founding of Presidio-Mission San Carlos Borromeo.

TEMPERA: A painting medium in which pigment is mixed with water-soluble glutinous materials such as egg yolk or size.

TITULAR PATRON: A saint in whose honor and under whose name a church, other building, or institution is dedicated.

VENI, CREATOR SPIRITUS: *Come, Holy Spirit.* A Latin hymn of invocation to the Holy Spirit. Serra sang this during the 3 June 1770 founding ceremony of Presidio-Mission San Carlos Boromeo.

VIATICUM: The Eucharist, as given to a dying person or one in danger of death, from the Latin *viāticum* (traveling provisions).

VIZCAÍNO-SERRA OAK TREE: Historian Hubert Bancroft begged to differ with the identity of the tree that we today accept as the California's "Plymouth Rock," the Vizcaíno-Serra oak tree. He wrote:

> As the . . . tree is at some distance from the tide-water the identity may be questioned. David Spence, an old and well known citizen of Monterey, said that Junípero's tree was shown him in 1824 by Mariano Estrada, and that it fell in 1837 or 1838, the water having washed away the earth from its roots. Spence thought there was no doubt of its identity. [Bancroft, *History of California*, 1:169-70]

Bancroft's *History* was published in 1886, so he wrote his appraisal sometime *before* the cove next to the tree was filled in for a railroad embankment in 1889, which placed the tree even further from the shore. His opinion is therefore based on the original geographical juxtaposition of tree to shore, from which he concluded that the tree was already too far away from the shore to be the original Vizcaíno-Serra oak. When combined with Palóu's statement that the tree was so close to the water that its "branches bathe in the waters of the sea at high tide," a strong case is presented that the original oak may have indeed fallen. How credible are his witnesses? José Mariano Estrada arrived in Montery in 1806, a twenty-two year old ensign and protege of Governor José Arrillaga. David Spence was a Scottish businessman who arrived in 1824, and married Estrada's daughter Adelaide in 1827. Neither was present at Monterey's 1770 founding, but Estrada could have discussed the tree with an "old-timer." Whether or not we are dealing with the true Vizcaíno-Serra oak, late-nineteenth-century tradition assumed it was the genuine article, and that it had been severely damaged by lightning sometime in the 1840s,' but managed to survive. Also, local Indians were known to reverentially gather the tree's acorns because of its association with Serra, and several Monterey oaks were claimed as descendents, most notably the Stokes adobe oak on Hartnell Street, still growing today. According to pioneer Mariano Guadalupe Vallejo's unpublished "Historia de California:" "The tree under which Ascensión [Vizcaíno-expedition chaplain] said mass in 1602, and Serra in 1770, is still standing, being that under which a new [wooden] cross was set up on the 100th anniversary of June 3, 1870" (Bancroft, *History of California*, 1:169). Vallejo was born in Monterey in 1808. His father Ignacio had arrived in Monterey as a Mexican soldier in 1781. Serra and many of the original 1770 settlers were still alive, and he certainly could have pointed out the correct tree to his son. Further uncertainty surrounds the tree's relocation after it had died in 1905. Local legend says it traveled a rather circuitous route to the rear of Monterey's Royal Presidio Chapel. At its original location, the dead trunk was allegedly dug up and thrown into Monterey Bay by unsuspecting road or electrical workmen. Father Mestres learned of this after it had "floated halfway" to Santa Cruz, and sent Portuguese fishermen to harpoon it and bring it back. Whether fact, fiction, or both, by 1917 the story had already appeared in print:

> A few years ago, while workmen were constructing a culvert near it [the oak], its roots were greatly injured, and shortly following, it was torn up and without ceremony or farewell, thrown into the bay. Monterey's most public spirited citizen, the Hon H. A. Greene, and the zealous pastor of San Carlos Church, the Rev. R. M. Mestres, feeling the pathos of it, and the value of this venerable tree as an object lesson and historical relic, rescued it from the bay, and had it placed in the rear of the church. [Anna Geil Andreson, *Historical Landmarks of Monterey, California*, p. 14]

In August 1905, the California Historical Landmarks League (formed by U.S. Congressman Joseph R. Knowland, and with William Randolph Hearst acting as treasurer and publicist), purchased the original landing site with $13,000 in private donations (along with Mission Sonoma and Fort Ross), and deeded it to the state of California for a park. On 3 June 1949, the California Centennial Commission placed a bronze plaque nearby, honoring Gaspar de Portolá for his role in the founding of Monterey. The site is registered California Historical Landmark number 128.

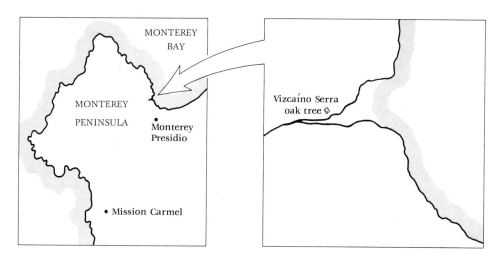

Monterey Peninsula.

Vizcaíno-Serra landing site, c. 1770.

Father Serra's Landing Place. *Agatha Hilby Few. Oil on canvas, c. 1875. This early view looking north shows: 1) Vizcaíno-Serra oak tree; 2) commemorative cross; 3) redwood bridge (predecessor to Pacific Street/Lighthouse Avenue; 4) Vizcaíno-Serra landing cove; 5) American-period Fort Mervine, built 1847, abandoned 1866; 6) ruins of Spanish/Mexican-period El Castillo fortification.*

Vizcaíno-Serra landing cove, c.1878. Looking south, this view shows the cove, the upper branches of the Vizcaíno-Serra oak tree in the ravine (arrow), and the wooden commemorative cross. Note Monterey cityscape in background.

Aerial view of Monterey's Vizcaíno-Serra landing site, 1984. Photograph shows: 1) Monterey Harbor; 2) Pacific Street/Lighthouse Avenue built on site of former landing cove; 3) original location of Vizcaíno-Serra oak tree, now marked by Celtic Cross monument at corner of Pacific and Artillery Streets; 4) course of ravine and stream that still empties into Monterey Harbor via drainage under Pacific Street/Lighthouse Avenue; 5) location of El Castillo foundation and Stanford Serra monument; 6) location of Fort Mervine foundation.

Vizcaíno-Serra landing site, 1987.

Vizcaíno-Serra oak tree stump, 1987. Located directly behind San Carlos Cathedral, 550 Church Street, Monterey.

WEIGHTS AND MEASURES, SPANISH:

Weight:

1 *marco* = 230 grams

1 *arroba* = 25.4 pounds

1 *quintal* = 101.5 pounds

Linear Measure:

1 *vara* = 33 inches

1 musket/rifle/gunshot = approximately 1/3rd of a statute mile

1 *legua* (league) = 2.6 statute miles

1 cannon-shot = approximately 1 *legua*

Dry Measure:

1 *almud* = 1/12th of a *fanega*

1 *fanega* = 2.6 bushels

1 *tercio* = A colonial measure for grain/seed/sand that was never standardized

Sources

BOOKS

Academy of Pacific Coast History. *Publications: Volume 1.* Berkeley: University of California, 1910.

Acceptance and Unveiling of the Statues of Junipero Serra and Thomas Starr King. Washington, D.C.: United States Government Printing Office, 1932.

Anderson, Lawrence. *The Art of the Silversmith in Mexico, 1519-1936.* 2 vols. New York: Hacker Art Books, 1975.

Andreson, Anna Geil. *Historic Landmarks of Monterey, California.* Salinas: California History Committee, 1917.

Archibald, Robert. *The Economic Aspects of the California Missions.* Washington, D.C.: Academy of American Franciscan History, 1978.

Bancroft, Hubert Howe. *History of California.* 7 vols. San Francisco: The History Company, Publishers, 1886.

Bannon, John Francis. *The Spanish Borderlands Frontier, 1513-1821.* Albuquerque: University of New Mexico Press, 1963.

Beechey, F.W. *An Account of a Visit to California, 1826-27.* San Francisco: Grabhorn Press, 1941.

Bobb, Bernard E. *The Viceregency of Antonio María Bucareli in New Spain, 1771-79.* Austin: Univeristy of Texas Press, 1962.

Bodo, Murray. *Juniper: Friend of Francis, Fool of God.* Cincinnati: St. Anthony Messenger Press, 1983.

Bolton, Herbert Eugene.

   Anza's California Expeditions. 5 vols. Berkeley: University of California Press, 1930.

   Font's Complete Diary. Berkeley: University of California Press, 1933.

   Fray Juan Crespi: Missionary Explorer on the Pacific Coast, 1769-1774. Berkeley: University of California Press, 1927.

   Historical Memoirs of New California. 4 vols. Berkeley: University of California Press, 1926.

   Spanish Exploration in the Southwest, 1542-1706. New York: Charles Scribner's Sons, 1916.

Brandes, Ray. *The Costansó Narrative of the Portolá Expedition.* Newhall: Hogarth Press, 1970.

Chapman, Charles E. *A History of California: The Spanish Period.* New York: The MacMillan Company, 1921.

Charlot, Jean. *Mexican Art and the Academy of San Carlos, 1785-1915.* Austin: University of Texas Press, 1962.

Chauvet, Fidel de Jesús. *La Iglesia de San Fernando de México y su Extinto Colegio Apostólico*. Mexico City: Centro de Estudios Bernardino de Sahagún, A.C., 1980.

Cook, Sherburne F.

    The Conflict Between the California Indian and White Civilization. Berkeley: University of California Press, 1976.

    The Population of the California Indians, 1769-1970. Berkeley: University of California Press, 1976.

Dana, Richard Henry, Jr. *Two Years Before the Mast*. New York: New American Library, 1964.

De Nevi, Don, and Moholy, Noel F. *Junipero Serra*. New York: Harper & Row, 1985.

Earnest, Aileen Ryan. *Mission Vestments*. San Gabriel: The Claretian Fathers, 1975.

Engelhardt, Zephyrin.

    Mission San Carlos Borromeo. Santa Barbara: Mission Santa Barbara, 1934.

    Mission San Juan Capistrano. Santa Barbara: Mission Santa Barbara, 1934.

Exercises Commemorating and Honoring the Memory of Father Junipero Serra, O.F.M. Washington, D.C.: United States Government Printing Office, 1960.

Farnham, Thomas Jefferson. *Travels in California*. Oakland: Biobooks, 1947.

Farquhar, Francis P., ed. *Up and Down California in 1860-1864: The Journal of William H. Brewer*. New Haven: Yale University Press, 1930.

Felder, Hilarin. *The Ideals of St. Francis of Assisi*. Chicago: Franciscan Herald Press, 1982.

Fernández, Jacinto, comp. *Summarium Beatificationis et Canonizationis Servi Dei Juniperi Serra Sacerdotis Professi, O.F.M.* Vatican City: Vatican Polyglot Press, 1981.

Forbes, A.S.C. *California Missions and Landmarks*. Los Angeles: A.S.C. Forbes, 1925.

Fortescue, Adrian. *The Ceremonies of the Roman Rite Described*. London: Burns, Oates and Washbourne, Ltd., 1943.

Garner, William Robert. *Letters from California, 1846-1847*. Berkeley: University of California Press, 1970.

Geiger, Maynard J.

    Franciscan Missionaries in Hispanic California, 1769-1848. San Marino: The Huntington Library, 1969.

    Junipero Serra's Enduring Fame in Spain, Mexico and California. Santa Barbara: The Franciscan Fathers, 1960.

    trans. and ed. *Palóu's Life of Fray Junípero Serra*. Washington, D.C.: Academy of American Franciscan History, 1955.

    The Life and Times of Fray Juniípero Serra, O.F.M. 2 vols. Washington, D.C.: Academy of American Franciscan History, 1959.

    The Long Road: Padre Serra's March to Saintly Honors. Santa Barbara: The Cause of Padre Serra, 1957.

    Representations of Father Junipero Serra in Painting and Woodcut: Their History and Evaluation. Santa Barbara: The Franciscan Fathers, 1958.

Gemelli, Agostino. *The Franciscan Message to the World*. London: Burns, Oates and Washbourne, Ltd., 1934.

Guest, Francis F. *Fermin Francisco de Lasuen*. Washington, D.C.: Academy of American Franciscan History, 1973.

Hall, James. *Dictionary of Subjects and Symbols in Art*. New York: Harper and Row, 1974.

Hart, James D. *A Companion to California*. New York: Oxford University Press, 1978.

Herbermann, Charles G., ed. *The Catholic Encyclopedia*. 15 vols. New York: Robert Appleton Company, 1902.

Kenneally, Finbar, trans. and ed. *Writings of Fermín Francisco de Lasuén*. 2 vols. Washington, D.C.: Academy of American Franciscan History, 1965.

Knox, Ronald A. *The Missal in Latin and English*. Westminster: The Newman Press, 1958.

The New American Bible. New York: Thomas Nelson Publishers, 1971.

New Catholic Encyclopedia. 16 vols. Washington, D.C.: Catholic University of America, 1967.

Ord, Angustias de la Guerra. *Hispanic Occurences in Hispanic California*. Washington, D.C.: Academy of American Franciscan History, 1956.

Personal Glimpses of Padre Junipero Serra. Santa Barbara: The Serra Shop, 1949.

Rawls, James J. *Indians of California: The Changing Image*. Norman: University of Oklahoma Press, 1984.

Rudkin, Charles, ed. *The First French Expedition to California: Lapérouse in 1786*. Los Angeles: Glen Dawson, 1959.

Smith, Frances Rand. *The Architectural History of Mission San Carlos Borromeo*. Berkeley: California Historical Survey Commission, 1921.

Spearman, Arthur Dunning. *The Five Mission Churches of Mission Santa Clara: 1777-1825*. Palo Alto: The National Press, 1963.

Starr, Kevin. *Americans and the California Dream, 1850-1915*. New York: Oxford University Press, 1973.

Stevenson, Robert Louis. *The Travels and Essays of Robert Louis Stevenson*. New York: Charles Scribner's Sons, 1895.

Sturtevant, William C., gen. ed. *Handbook of North American Indians*. 20 vols. Washington, D.C.: Smithsonian Institution, 1978. Vol. 8: *California*, Robert F. Heizer, ed.

Taylor, Bayard. *Eldorado, or, Adventures in the Path of Empire*. London: George Routledge and Co., 1850.

Temple, Sydney. *The Carmel Mission*. Fresno: Valley Publishers, 1980.

Thurston, Herbert, and Attwater, Donald, eds. *Butler's Lives of the Saints*. 4 vols. Westminster: Christian Classics, Inc., 1956.

Tibesar, Antonine, ed. *Writings of Junípero Serra*. 4 vols. Washington, D.C.: Academy of American Franciscan History, 1955-66.

Toussaint, Manuel. *Colonial Art in Mexico*. Austin: University of Texas Press, 1967.

Van Nostrand, Jeanne.

The First Hundred Years of Painting in California, 1775-1875. San Francisco: John Howell Books, 1980.

Monterey: Adobe Capital of California, 1770-1847. San Francisco: California Historical Society, 1968.

Vizcaíno, Sebastián. *The Voyage of Sebastián Vízcaino*. San Francisco: The Book Club of California, 1933.

Wagner, Henry R. *Spanish Voyages to the Northwest Coast of America in the Sixteenth Century*. San Francisco: California Historical Society, 1929.

Walsh, Marie T. *The Mission Bells of California*. San Francisco: Harr Wagner Publishing Company, 1934.

Webber, F.R. *Church Symbolism*. Cleveland: J. H. Jansen, 1938.

Weber, Francis J.

> comp. and ed. *Father of the Missions: A Documentary History of San Carlos Borromeo*. Hong Kong: Libra Press Limited, 1984.

> *The Missions & Missionaries of Baja California*. Los Angeles: Dawson's Book Shop, 1968.

> comp and ed. *Some "Fugitive" Glimpses at Fray Junípero Serra*. Hong Kong: Libra Press Limited, 1983.

> ed. *Some Reminiscences about Fray Junípero Serra*. Santa Barbara: California Catholic Conference, 1985.

Weber, Francis J., and Nunis, Doyce B. *Maynard J. Geiger, O.F.M.: Franciscan and Historian*. Santa Barbara: Friends of the Santa Barbara Mission Archive-Library, 1971.

White, R. E. *Padre Junipero Serra and The Mission Church of San Carlos del Carmelo*. San Francisco: R. E. White, 1884.

Wilbur, Marguerite Eyer.

> ed. *Duflot de Mofras: Travels on the Pacific Coast*. 2 vols. Santa Ana: The Fine Arts Press, 1937.

> ed. *Vancouver in California, 1792-1794*. Los Angeles: Glen Dawson, 1954.

JOURNALS

Bowman, J. N. "The Names of the California Missions." *The Americas* 21 (April 1965):363-374.

Donahue, William H. "Mary of Agreda and the Southwest United States." *The Americas* 9 (January 1953):291-314.

"Father Serra's Grave." *Academy Scrapbook* 1 (October 1950):97-108.

Geiger, Maynard J.

> "Fray Junípero Serra: Organizer and Administrator of the Upper California Missions, 1769-1784." *The California Historical Society Quarterly* 42 (September 1963):195-220.

> "Junípero Serra, O.F.M., in the Light of Chronology and Geography." *The Americas* 6 (January 1950):291-333.

> "The Scholastic Career and Preaching Apostolate of Fray Junipero Serra, O.F.M., S.T.D. (1730-1749)." *The Americas* 4 (July 1947):65-82.

> "The Story of California's First Libraries." *Southern California Quarterly* 46 (June 1964):109-24.

> "Where is Serra Buried?" *Provincial Annals* 23 (October 1960):79-84; 23 (October 1960):363-368; 24 (January 1962):58-62; 24 (April 1962):123-28; 24 (July 1962):177-181; 24 (October 1962):231-37; 25 (January 1963):57-62; 25 (April 1963):120-23; 25 (July 1963):186-91; 25 (October 1963):250-55; 26 (January 1964):76-80; 26 (April 1964):142-46.

Guest, Francis F. "Junípero Serra and His Approach to the Indians." *Southern California Quarterly* 67 (Fall 1985):223-261.

McCarty, Kieran. "Anniversary of Birth of Fray Junípero Serra." *The Americas* 20 (October 1963):204-07.

Smith, Frances Rand. "The Spanish Missions of California: The Burial Place of Father Junípero Serra." *Hispania* 7 (November 1924):285-98.

Stampa, Manuel Carrera. "The Evolution of Weights and Measures in New Spain." *The Hispanic American Historical Review* 29 (February 1949):2-24.

Treutlein, Theodore E. "The Portolá Expedition of 1769-1770." *The California Historical Society Quarterly* 47 (December 1968):291-313.

Wagner, Henry R. "The Last Mass of Father Junipero Serra." *Westways* 26 (September 1934):9, 41.

NEWSPAPERS

"A Pioneer Padre. The 100th Anniversary of Junipero Serra's Death." *Daily Alta California*, 29 August 1884, p. 1.

"At San Carlos. Padre Serra's Life Work Commemorated." *San Francisco Chronicle*, 29 August 1884, p.1.

"Carmel Mission Bible to be Used by Reagan." *Monterey Peninsula Herald*, 28 December 1966, p. 1.

"Four Thousand Attend Carmel Mission Marian Rites." *Monterey Peninsula Herald*, 10 May 1954, p. 1.

"Harry Downey [sic] Finds Rare Copy of Serra Portrait in Mexico." *Monterey Peninsula Herald,* 11 February 1954, p. 3.

"Historic Cross is Erected in Carmel." *Monterey Peninsula Herald*, 30 November 1944, p. 1.

"Historic Oak to be Preserved." *Monterey New Era,* 4 October 1905, p. 1.

"Historic Oak Tree is Dead." *Monterey New Era*, 6 July 1904, p. 3.

"Junipero Serra Celebration at Carmel by the Sea." *Monterey Daily Cypress*, 25 November 1913, p. 1.

"Kennedy Denies Charges by Morse." *Monterey Peninsula Herald*, 30 May 1960, p. 1.

"Monterey News Items." *Pacific Grove Daily Review*, 16 November 1906, p.1.

"Monterey News Items." *Pacific Grove Daily Review*, 21 November 1906.

"Monument for Serra's Landing Place." *Monterey New Era*, 30 August 1905, p. 1.

"Monument Has Arrived." *Monterey Daily Cypress*, 24 March 1908, p. 1.

"News Comments: A Day That Will Be Remembered." *Monterey Peninsula Herald*, 27 August 1956, p. 1.

"Old Statue Comes Home on Christmas Eve." *Monterey Peninsula Herald*, 18 December 1945, p. 4.

"Portola Cross at Carmel River to be Dedicated this Sunday." *Monterey Peninsula Herald*, 8 December 1944, p. 1.

"President Visits Carmel Mission." *Monterey Peninsula Herald*, 27 August 1956, p. 1.

"Serra Stamp to be Issued in San Diego." *The Tidings*, 16 August 1985, p. 3.

"Serra's Death Remembered Here Sunday." *Monterey Peninsula Herald*, 26 August 1937, p. 9.

"Site of First Mission Cross is Located." *Monterey Peninsula Herald*, 19 December 1939, p. 7.

"Statuary Plebiscite at End." *San Francisco Bulletin*, 1 January 1921, p. 2.

"The Junipero Monument." *Pacific Grove Review*, 6 June 1891, p. 2.

"Two Clerics Chosen for Fame." *San Francisco Chronicle*, 30 March 1927, p. 1.

"Will Fray Junípero Serra be Declared a Saint?" *Monterey Peninsula Herald Weekend Magazine,* 10 February 1973, p. 11.

PUBLIC DOCUMENTS

Public Law 88-143—October 16, 1963. *United States Statutes at Large.* vol. 77 (1963):251.

U.S. Congress, House. "Harry Downie: Bringing History to Life." 96th Cong., 2nd sess., 1 July 1980. *Congressional Record,* vol. 126, part 14, pp. 18040-41.

U.S. Congress, House. "Padre Junipero Serra 250th Anniversary Medals." 88th Cong., 1st sess., 25 September 1963. *House Reports: Miscellaneous Reports on Public Bills,* vol. 4, report no. 768, pp. 1-3.

U.S. Congress, Senate. "Padre Junipero Serra 250th Anniversary Medals." 88th Cong., 1st sess., 24 June 1963. *Senate Reports: Miscellaneous Reports on Public Bills,* vol. 2, report no. 291, pp. 1-5.

UNPUBLISHED MATERIALS

Archivo General de la Nación, Mexico City:

"*Memoria.*" *Legajo* 383-61. Californias Section.

Santa Barbara Historical Society, Santa Barbara:

Perret, Ferdinand. "La Perret-enciclopedia de arte Hispano-Americano de la época colonial." 1958.

Mission Carmel Archives, Carmel:

Geiger, Maynard J. "History of the Development of the Buildings of Mission San Carlos, Carmel, California, 1771-1797."

"General Inventory of Existing Things in the Church, Sacristy, Chapel, Baptistry, and House of the Father Ministers of the Mission of San Carlos of Monterey, June 22, 1842."

Harry Downie to Vice-Postulator Eric O'Brien, O.F.M, letter, 1 March 1945.

"Inventory and Evaluation of the Chattel of the *Pueblo* of San Carlos, 10 December 1834."

Manning, Timothy Cardinal. Homily, video-tape transcript, 28 August 1984.

Pagliarulo, Marie C. "The Restoration of Mission San Carlos Borromeo, Carmel, California, 1931-1967." Master's Thesis, University of San Francisco, 1968.

Panetta, Rep. Leon E. "For Immediate Release—March 20, 1984: Panetta Leads Effort for Commemorative Stamp to Honor Father Serra."

President Ronald Reagan to Most Rev. Thaddeus Shubsda, telegram, 19 August 1985.

"Report of the State of this Mission of San Carlos of Monterey. Annual Reports 1786-1825."

"San Carlos Book of Baptisms, volume 1, 1770-1820."

"San Carlos Book of Confirmations, 1778-1896."

"San Carlos Book of Deaths, volume 1, 1770-1829."

Scott, Harry L. "Mission San Carlos Borromeo del Rio Carmelo Silver Collection Appraisal, 28 July 1982."

U.S. Army Museum, Presidio of Monterey, Monterey:

Jane Stanford to Secretary of War Reofield Proctor, letter, 17 May 1890.

"Document 12, Headquarters of the Army, Washington, July 9, 1890."

Index

stump. *Illus.*, 222

Serra's final resting place, Basilica Mission San Carlos Borromeo del Río Carmelo.

2-05-13